ODIE
HENDERSON

BLACK CAESARS AND FOXY CLEOPATRAS

A HISTORY OF BLAXPLOITATION CINEMA

Abrams Press, New York

Library of Congress Control Number: 2023933930

ISBN: 978-1-4197-5841-6
eISBN: 978-1-64700-506-1

Printed and bound in the United States
10 9 8 7 6 5 4 3 2 1

Abrams books are available at special discounts when purchased in quantity for premiums and
promotions as well as fundraising or educational use. Special editions can also be created to
specification. For details, contact specialsales@abramsbooks.com or the address below.

Abrams Press® is a registered trademark of Harry N. Abrams, Inc.

ABRAMS The Art of Books
195 Broadway, New York, NY 10007
abramsbooks.com

For Dr. Michał Oleszczyk and Steven C. Boone, Hnic.

CONTENTS

Prologue

When I was a college student back in the late 1980s, I worked in a video store. Actually, I just hung around the video store all day. Since I was a fixture, the proprietor eventually gave me something to do. I stood behind the counter writing out the cards that indicated a VHS tape had been taken out by a member. Sometimes I held videos for people who asked me to put aside the hottest releases when they were returned to the store. As if predicting my future life as a film critic, I was always yelling at people who picked up movies I thought were godawful.

The best part of my job was keeping the teenagers from sneaking into the porn section in the rear of the store. This back room was made even more enticing by a pair of swinging saloon doors, a fitting accoutrement for a place that held copies of *RoboHo* and *Wet Dream on Elm Street*. Porn was one of the categories that set our store apart from the big chains like Blockbuster; in fact, we stayed in business because we carried several specialties that were all but ignored by Big Video: in addition to dirty movies, we offered kung fu flicks, shorts featuring the Mexican comedian Cantínflas, and Blaxploitation classics.

Blaxploitation movies were quite popular among our Black and brown clientele. Perhaps it was because, like me, they'd grown up seeing these movies on Forty-Second Street (aka "The Deuce") or in our local grindhouse theaters in Jersey City, New Jersey. The younger folks had seen only the butchered TV prints that occasionally ran on New York City's independent television channels, and they were looking forward to finally figuring out what the hell was missing from all those choppily edited reruns of movies like *Three the Hard Way*.

One day, a movie called *Street Fight* appeared in the latest delivery of new releases. It was listed in our order as a Blaxploitation film, but the cover art made it look as if it were more recent. It was also a cartoon, one that starred Philip Michael Thomas; Scatman Crothers; Charles Gordone, the first Black winner of the Pulitzer Prize for Drama; and singer Barry White. They appeared in live-action human form when not portraying their animated roles. *Street Fight* was directed by Ralph Bakshi, the director notorious for making X-rated animated features like *Fritz the Cat* and *Heavy Traffic*. The box said it had been made in 1974, smack-dab in the middle of the Blaxploitation era.

Had IMDb existed back then, I would have easily discovered *Street Fight* was originally called *Coonskin*, a far more offensive title that seemed quaint when one considered its era had given us slur-filled titles like *The Legend of Nigger Charley* and *Freebie and the Bean*. A parody of Disney's controversial post–Civil War musical, *Song of the South*, *Coonskin* really leaned into everything the Disney film had been accused of being. It was intentionally racist, though Bakshi's penchant for equal-opportunity racial mockery was evident. It also courted trouble with Black civil rights organizations. While *Song* incurred the wrath of the National Association for the Advancement of Colored People (NAACP) back in 1946, *Coonskin* drew the ire of the Congress of Racial Equality (CORE), which attended a screening at the Museum of Modern Art in New York City and caused all manner of havoc. The controversy was so intense that Paramount Pictures, the film's original distributor, dropped it after their offices were picketed by CORE.

So *Street Fight* was perfect for our store. It was provocative, controversial, outrageous, and downright nasty and perverted. It was also funny as hell, imbued with the type of gallows humor that only the truly downtrodden can appreciate. One of the characters is a psychopathic, scantily clad White woman named Miss America, who appears every so often to nonchalantly kill minorities. People brought it back with a mixture of shock, awe, and surprise. They told their friends to rent it, and they asked those of us behind the counter if we had seen it.

We had a top rental on our hands, for sure. There was just one problem. One of our co-workers was a twentysomething guy I'll call Tee. Tee was the most militant Black man I'd ever met. I was fascinated by the things he said, and I learned many things about myself and my people from him. Tee didn't condemn the Blaxploitation films we rented—like us, he'd grown up with them and had some affection for them. But there was a line with Tee, and certain movies crossed it with their depiction of Black people. *Coonskin* didn't just cross the line—it drove two or three miles past it.

"We cannot let Tee watch this movie," another co-worker told me. "He will burn down the store." In hindsight, this was an exaggeration; at the moment, however, it was plausible. So we designed a system of keeping *Street Fight* out of Tee's hands. At first, it was easy—the movie had an extensive waiting list. But the more people came in the store, asking Tee, "Have you seen this shit?!" the harder it became to maintain our plan. Whenever Tee jumped the queue and reserved a copy for himself, a perk we all utilized, we'd somehow "accidentally" rent out his copy.

But we couldn't keep it up forever, and my own weakness was to blame. One night I was playing keep-away with the VHS cassette and Tee grew tired of my shenanigans. He physically overpowered me, wrestled me to the floor, and snatched the movie. It was more a slapstick routine than a violent insurrection, but I acquiesced without much struggle because Tee could have broken me in half with his pinky toe.

"Please don't watch that," I begged him. "It's gonna make you so mad."

"Go home, Odie," he told me. "Get your ass outta here."

I was certain I was going to return the next day to find a gaping, scorched hole where the video store used to be, a giant, blackened void located between the quack doctor's office and the overpriced dry cleaners. Instead, I found the building intact and Tee inside, loading a tape into the VCR that played on the one television we had in the store. "How was the movie?" I asked him as I walked toward the counter.

Tee looked at me with the bemused smirk he reserved for whenever I said something he deemed stupid. Then he laughed. "Man, this was racist as shit!" he said. "But we win at the end, so I can forgive it."

But we win at the end. Those words carry a lot of weight whenever I think of Blaxploitation movies. These films of my childhood were double-edged swords in terms of the stereotypes they often presented. Today, I can parse the contradictions inherent in Tee's statement. As a child of the 1970s, however, all I saw were the coolest of heroes and the most recognizable of characters. These were people I knew from my 'hood, God-fearing types, outright criminals, badass little brats, and colorful hustlers. As Melle Mel said in "The Message," seeing all these "big moneymakers . . . *you wanna grow up to be just like them.*"

Blaxploitation was in my blood. I wanted to grow up to be John Shaft, the bad mother shut-yo-mouth played by Richard Roundtree in three films, seven TV episodes, and two remakes. When I was three, I had a coat and hat inspired by the threads worn by *Super Fly*'s protagonist, Youngblood Priest. I knew *Black Caesar* before I discovered he was derived from *Little Caesar*. My first crushes were Foxy Brown and Cleopatra Jones. The only cops I trusted were Coffin Ed and Grave Digger Jones, Chester Himes's creations as brought to life in *Cotton Comes to Harlem*. And I loved kung fu superstar Jim Kelly with the same intensity I loved his *Enter the Dragon* co-star Bruce Lee. I knew why all these characters mattered so much to me: *Because they win at the end.*

For better and for worse, Black people were front and center in Blaxploitation, playing the heroes and starring in their own tales. It beat the hell out of cameoing as "Thug #3" on an episode of TV's *Baretta* or potentially getting one's face blown off by Clint Eastwood's Dirty Harry because he had forgotten how many bullets he fired from his .44 Magnum. At far too young an age, I watched with rapt attention, absorbing everything I could whenever a cousin or an aunt would take me to these movies. The theaters of the New York City area provided an escape for a shy, introverted, constantly beaten-up, asthmatic kid like me. I developed a love for these films that persists to this day. It's the reason I wanted to write this book.

When I started writing about the films of my youth at my blog, *Big Media Vandalism*, the definitive book I turned to was Josiah Howard's *Blaxploitation Cinema: The Essential Reference Guide*. Published in 2008, Howard's paperback guide contains interviews with some of the big (and not-so-big) names who have directed films in this genre, from Arthur Marks to Larry Cohen to Jonathan Kaplan. Howard's primary goal was to provide a comprehensive list of films that fit neatly into the category as well as the films hovering around the margins that define Blaxploitation. Howard does critique some of the films while giving pertinent information, such as studio, year, and (this is quite important) whether one or more of the filmmakers was Black. It is a very good book, an indispensable resource I have turned to many times in the years I've written about Blaxploitation. Howard's book is an encyclopedic reference; this will be a deeper dive into specific films and the history surrounding them.

Since there are so many films that fall within the genre, this isn't going to be as macro as a comprehensive reference guide. Instead, I will break down the elements of Blaxploitation—that is, what begat them and what they eventually begat in turn. And I'll tell the story of an influential series of films while invoking a historical and contextual perspective to trace this cinematic discipline's rise and fall. It is also important to talk about what came before, because everything in Hollywood is cyclical. Parallels can be drawn from the race movies of the 1920s to the Black-themed films of the 1970s.

But what exactly is Blaxploitation? Is it a genre, like comedy or Western, or something more fluid and harder to define? I like to describe it the way I'd describe the equally slippery term "film noir": Blaxploitation is an era, a period of time when certain films are definitive examples and others are up for discussion and debate. I'm going to set the timeframe from roughly 1970 to 1978. My birth year, 1970, was when *Cotton Comes to Harlem* premiered, making enough money for Hollywood to notice that, yes, Black people do go to the movies. In 1977, there was a glut of films featuring Black protagonists, after which they practically disappeared from the screen until Spike Lee and the Black New Wave emerged in Hollywood. Again, everything in Hollywood is cyclical.

There's much to discuss, from the classic soundtracks to the stars of the era and the folks behind the camera who got their start (or ended their careers) in Blaxploitation. I've no plans to sugarcoat, so expect profanities and some very disrespectful words you shouldn't say in polite company, if at all. As an added bonus, by virtue of being old, I can offer testimonials on what it was like to see some of these films during their first run at the forgotten movie palaces in my hometown of Jersey City and the seedier ones on the Deuce.

But first, let's start with the original independent moviemakers, the Black folks who did it for themselves when Hollywood wouldn't let them work in the old studio system. They set the groundwork as the originators of proving that there was a market for Black movies. As we'll see, Hollywood wasn't listening yet. But these filmmakers knew the power of Black characters surmounting the odds to win at the end.

CHAPTER 1

WHAT HAPPENED BEFORE COTTON CAME TO HARLEM?

Since the silent era, African-Americans have been depicted onscreen in American cinema the way Hollywood assumed White audiences wanted to see them. Film historian Donald Bogle explored the depictions of Black characters on film in his book *Toms, Coons, Mulattoes, Mammies, & Bucks*. The title categorized five offensive stereotypes that stretched the cinematic landscape for decades. "All were character types used for the same effect," Bogle wrote, "to entertain by stressing Negro inferiority." Originally played by White actors in blackface, these types were soon played by Black actors like Stepin Fetchit, Willie Best, and Hattie McDaniel, the latter of whom made history by winning—deservedly—an Oscar for playing the quintessential iteration of a mammy in *Gone with the Wind*.

Later, Hollywood added concepts like "Magical Negroes," "Sidekick Negroes," and "Noble Negroes," folks who, respectively, helped out, accompanied, or died for the White hero. There were also the overly religious Black characters who repeatedly fell to their knees for a bout of over-the-top prayin', as well as those whose sole job was to sing a stand-alone musical number that could easily be edited out of the film when it played in the Jim Crow South. Perhaps those musical numbers were a form of showing Negro superiority because, oddly enough, the cooning comedy sequences that humiliated Blackness were never removed.

Whenever Hollywood wanted to capitalize on the Black talent that sold records or club tickets, they resorted to the "all-cullud musical," films where the all-Black cast put on a show. King Vidor's 1929 film, *Hallelujah*, for MGM, was an early example. Seven years later, Marc Connelly adapted his Pulitzer

Prize–winning play, *The Green Pastures*, for Warner Bros. As offensive as that film is, with its scenes of cee-lo and fried chicken in Heaven, it remains a point of fascination simply because it depicted God and many Old Testament biblical figures as African-Americans, yet only generated complaints from Black critics. In interrogating that divide, historian Curtis J. Evans wrote that "the play had widespread appeal for whites in part because it reinstated 'rural values' that many of them had lost in their move to an urban environment."

In 1943, the legendary director (and Liza's papa) Vincente Minnelli made his directorial debut with his own "all-cullud musical" for MGM, *Cabin in the Sky*. Then 20th Century–Fox went meta by framing 1943's *Stormy Weather* as a tribute to Shirley Temple's tap-dancing-down-the-staircase co-star, Bill "Bojangles" Robinson. "Celebrating the magnificent contributions of the colored race to the entertainment of the world during the past twenty-five years," reads a hilariously ironic magazine cover in *Stormy Weather*'s opening scene. It makes up for that by ending with the greatest tap dance number ever, an acrobatic tour de force by Harold and Fayard Nicholas that still earns gasps at screenings and on social media eight decades later.

Though these films have memorable moments featuring Lena Horne, Ethel Waters, Rex Ingram, and the aforementioned incomparable Nicholas brothers, they did more for the White folks behind the camera than the talent in front of it. Dorothy Dandridge did receive a well-earned Best Actress Oscar nomination (the first for an African-American) for her fiery work in 1954's *Carmen Jones*, but it did little to help her career. In *That's Entertainment III*, a documentary released in 1994 for the studio's seventieth anniversary, Horne speaks with shocking frankness about how she got only bit parts that could be left on the cutting room floor for some audiences. At least in *Stormy* and *Cabin*, the studios couldn't edit her out. She's the lead in the former and the main plot device in the latter. MGM did, however, edit out one of the numbers Minnelli shot because Horne appeared in a bubble bath, an absolute no-no, as it might scandalize the audience.

Running parallel to Hollywood's output was an independent thread of African-American moviemakers who were employing a "for us, by us" approach and making what were classified as "race films." Race films had "all-Negro casts" and were made outside of the studio system between 1915, when D. W. Griffith's *The Birth of a Nation* became the most well-known depiction of Black characters, and 1950, when Sidney Poitier made his fiery debut in Joe Mankiewicz's

No Way Out. Race films provided a steady stream of content to segregated Black theaters. This should have proven to Hollywood early on that there was a profitable market for content, but the studios weren't financially strapped enough to consider this option yet.

Oscar Micheaux is widely considered to be the first major Black director/producer. He was born in 1884 in Metropolis, Illinois, and his restlessness and desire to see the world put him at odds with his father, who eventually sent him to Chicago to find a marketing job. Working there as a Pullman porter, Micheaux observed many aspects of human nature and used many of the characteristics and situations he saw once he began writing novels.

Micheaux made over forty "race films," both in the silent and sound eras, starting with an adaptation of his book *The Conquest* in 1918. He followed that with his most famous film, *Within Our Gates*, a pseudo-response to *The Birth of a Nation* that was banned in some areas for being too controversial. Micheaux also made *The House Behind the Cedars*, which, like many of his films, dealt with a Black woman passing for White—the tragic mulatto, in Donald Bogle's description. This film was also so controversial that the state of Virginia forced him to cut parts of it.

Micheaux may be the best-known auteur from this era, but Spencer Williams's work had a more widely reaching effect. His religious treatises are a precursor to the films and gospel plays of Tyler Perry. Like the man who would be Madea, Williams wrote, directed, and starred in films, including his most famous work, *The Blood of Jesus*. He also created the first all-Black talkie in 1929, *The Melancholy Dame*. Like John Cassavetes would do decades later, Williams made bit appearances in Hollywood pictures to finance his own independent films.

Race movies were the only places in the film business Blacks could get non-acting jobs like writing, directing, and scoring. That didn't start to change until Duke Ellington and Billy Strayhorn composed the score for Otto Preminger's 1959 court drama, *Anatomy of a Murder*. Ellington followed that score with one for Marty Ritt's 1961 film, *Paris Blues*, which made him the first Black person nominated for the Academy Award for Best Original Score (he lost to *West Side Story*). This feat paved the way for nominations in this category for Calvin Jackson, Quincy Jones, and *Shaft*'s composer, Isaac Hayes. Of course, Hayes would win a different Oscar for that Blaxploitation classic, but that's getting ahead of the story.

Speaking of Oscars, Hollywood's premier Black actor of this era, Sidney Poitier, became the first to be nominated for the Academy Award for Best Actor alongside his co-star Tony Curtis for 1958's *The Defiant Ones*. The same year *Paris Blues* was making Oscar history, another Poitier film was making Hollywood history by featuring the first screenplay written by an African-American woman, Lorraine Hansberry, who adapted her play *A Raisin in the Sun* for director Daniel Petrie. Though he should have won the Oscar for playing Hansberry's Walter Lee Younger, Poitier instead won for the *Sister Act* of 1963, *Lilies of the Field*.

This was the first *competitive* Oscar received by a Black actor for a leading performance; James Baskett received an honorary Oscar in 1948 that, due to segregation, he couldn't pick up at the Oscar ceremony. Though Hattie McDaniel had received her Supporting Actress Oscar in person eight years earlier, her ceremony was held in Hollywood. Baskett's was held in Atlanta. According to the Academy, Baskett received the award for "his able and heart-warming characterization of Uncle Remus, friend and story teller to the children of the world, in Walt Disney's *Song of the South*."

Sidney Poitier and *Lilies of the Field* made history in 1964, but the real game-changer in Hollywood happened in 1967. That year, Poitier was the top box office draw in America. It had taken him seventeen years to accomplish this feat, a first for a Black actor. The three-picture achievement began in June with James Clavell's *To Sir, with Love*, followed in August by director Norman Jewison's Oscar-winning Best Picture *In the Heat of the Night*, and ending in December with Stanley Kramer's *Guess Who's Coming to Dinner*. Respectively, Poitier played a Guyanese high school teacher in England, a Philadelphia homicide cop named Mr. Virgil Tibbs, and a son-in-law candidate so perfect that even the Grand Duke Wizard of the Ku Klux Klan would have let him marry his daughter. Three big hits for the man who was, at more than one point during his career, the only Black actor getting leading roles in large Hollywood films. In total, his cinematic output sold 102,927,317 tickets and grossed $123,512,781 in 1967 dollars. Adjusted for inflation, that's over a billion dollars.

The cinematic hat trick showed the actor's versatility, even if, for the most part, he was playing some form of the familiar Poitier persona in each. Those box office numbers forced a reevaluation of Poitier, and the fledgling studios started to ask what type of people were going to these movies and why. Columbia did surveys asking why viewers went to see *To Sir, with Love*, and the number one answer was Sidney Poitier. As an added bonus, the actor did the film for a modest $30,000 fee, but also 10 percent of its gross. His reward for that shrewd deal was $4,246,280.30, a tremendous amount of money in 1967.

As an entry in the much-maligned "beloved teacher" genre, *To Sir, with Love* ranks near the top of the list. (Full disclosure: it is the author's favorite Poitier movie.) Seeing Poitier command—and get—the respect for his authority was quite satisfying when one remembers the types of roles he was often cast to play, and 1967 was all about the reimagining of the near-perfect Negroes in Poitier's oeuvre. At least until December.

Sir was a bigger hit, but *In the Heat of the Night* is the movie that put a major crack in the White audience's comfort with a Sidney Poitier character. The plot involves a murder investigation conducted by Virgil Tibbs (Poitier), a Black Philadelphia homicide detective, and Sergeant Gillespie (Rod Steiger), the White police chief of the racist town of Sparta, Mississippi. Tibbs gets involved after White police officers arrest him on suspicion of the murder of a wealthy Chicago man. When they discover Tibbs is loaded with cash, the cops assume he's their man.

After Gillespie confirms Tibbs is a cop, he has no reason to hold him. However, after seeing just how good Tibbs is at homicide investigations, Gillespie realizes he needs someone of Tibbs's talent to help him, color be damned.

Two scenes in *In the Heat of the Night* take a sledgehammer to Poitier's old personae. In the first, Gillespie mocks his name. "Virgil?" he asks. "That's a funny name for a nigger boy to come from Philadelphia. What do they call you up there?"

"They call me *Mister* Tibbs," he forcefully replies.

The second scene all but obliterates the image of that polite Negro who helped those nuns and won an Oscar for it. This unexpected moment is so well-known that it has a nickname: "The Slap Heard 'Round the World."

Gillespie takes Tibbs to see Endicott, the wealthiest man in town—and the dead man's enemy. Endicott's thoughts on race relations are represented by the racist lawn jockey that greets the two men before they join him in his greenhouse. Feigning ignorance, Tibbs asks about the orchids. Endicott takes him to some more admirable examples of the plant. Using an overly polite tone of voice, the rich man compares these orchids to Black people. "You should prefer the epiphytics," he says. "Like the nigra, they need care, and feedin', and cultivatin', and that takes time. That's something you can't make some people understand."

Endicott abandons his Southern Gentleman act when he realizes that Gillespie and Tibbs are there to question him about their case. *How dare the police chief bring this uppity Negro in here to disrespect him?* When Tibbs asks him his whereabouts on the night of the murder, Endicott hauls off and slaps him in the face. Immediately, Tibbs returns the favor. It's so spontaneous that it feels improvised on the spot. But Poitier would not have made the movie if that reaction wasn't in the script.

"In my life, whether I'm a detective or not, and I don't care where I am, if such a thing happened to me, the likelihood is I would respond," he told AFI. "And my response would certainly not be to absorb it."

"This was the first time in an American movie that a black man had slapped a white man back," director Norman Jewison wrote in his book, *This Terrible Business Has Been Good to Me*. "And that fact added to the shock of the scene." Poitier wasn't just hitting some random White man; he was slapping the piss out of an entire way of life. Black audiences went *batshit*. They had been waiting forever to see this new side of Sidney.

Unfortunately, the release of Stanley Kramer's *Guess Who's Coming to Dinner* in December 1967 brought back the old Sidney. Poitier co-starred alongside Spencer Tracy, Katharine Hepburn, his *In the Heat of the Night* co-star Beah Richards, and Weezy Jefferson herself, Isabel Sanford. Hepburn's niece, Katharine Houghton, plays her daughter, Joey, the White woman who brings him home to her parents and tells them she's going to marry him.

What is supposed to be a thoughtful investigation of interracial love instead turns out to be Poitier's worst movie. He and Houghton have zero chemistry. Poitier's John Prentice is as practically perfect as Mary Poppins and willing to spout the ridiculous words of William Rose's unbelievably clueless Oscar-winning screenplay. The insulting, unrealistic scene where Prentice tells his father, "You see yourself as a Black man, I see myself as a man," would have, in reality, resulted in Papa Prentice stomping a mud hole in his son's ass.

Of course, *Guess Who's Coming to Dinner* made the most money of Poitier's three 1967 films, because it had the version of him White audiences loved the most. But with several cities hosting race uprisings in the summer of 1967, Black audiences were tired of seeing the old studio-system iteration of Hollywood's biggest Black star, even if he were doing more action-oriented roles.

As a result, Poitier's next films were not successful, and he moved back to the Bahamas for a few years.

One of those Black folks who was definitely sick of seeing Sidney Poitier movies was future filmmaker Melvin Van Peebles. When asked what movies featuring Blacks he disliked, he replied, "Every damn last one of them." Van Peebles had been in France for eight years before he made his full-length feature debut with *The Story of a Three-Day Pass*, which he adapted from his own French-language novel. Like *Guess Who's Coming to Dinner*, this story features an interracial romance between a Black soldier on the titular leave in France and a White woman. Except here, the leads, Harry Baird and Nicole Berger, have endless chemistry and the movie isn't afraid to let us know they're going to have sex.

Though early in his career, Van Peebles's trickster tendencies are in full effect. He plays jungle noises in a romantic scene at one point, allows his characters to have fantasy sequences, and scores the film with his own avant-garde musical compositions. He also executes a double dolly shot two decades before Spike Lee made it his trademark. Van Peebles's biggest feat, however, is learning a language he didn't know, writing a book in that language, and then adapting it as a movie.

In 1957, Van Peebles had been thrown out of San Francisco, where he worked as a cable car gripman, over a discrimination suit. His desire to make movies sent him to Paris, where authors could be given a director's card so they could direct their own adaptations. On October 21, 1967, Van Peebles obtained a bit of sweet revenge: the city that wouldn't allow him to make movies showed one of them as part of the New Directors sidebar of the San Francisco Film Festival.

Thinking he was French (and therefore White), the festival handlers and employees were stunned when he disembarked from the plane. He was offered a limo and taken to the Mark Hopkins, a hotel he wouldn't have been able to stay at back in the 1950s. On the day *The Story of a Three-Day Pass* was shown at the Masonic Auditorium, more than one person mistook the director for a maintenance man. Everybody knew who he was once the end credits rolled. The screening went very well, and suddenly, Melvin Van Peebles was all over the newspapers.

"Festival Honor for Ex-Gripman," read the headline in the *San Francisco Examiner*. In the article, Jeanne Miller wrote, "There are certain minor flaws in the film—an artless simplicity and certain unpolished quality. But curiously enough, they serve to point up Van Peebles' distinctive style and the raw vigor of his concept." In the same periodical on October 29, the director was interviewed by Stanley Eichelbaum. He called *The Story of a Three-Day Pass* "an engaging comedy about a Negro, written and directed, for once, by a Negro."

Eichelbaum had some unusual observations about the filmmaker, writing that "at 35, he seems to have overcome the bitterness that a ghetto upbringing inevitably instills in a Negro." He also mentioned that he was surprised by Van Peebles's "confident and exuberant sense of success." The article ends with the journalist asking if the expatriate director would consider returning to America. "Of course I would," Van Peebles responded. "And I'd do a picture here if I were offered one." In 1970, he'd be offered a three-picture deal.

Meanwhile, future NFL Hall of Fame running back Jim Brown was at MGM–British Studios playing a role Sidney Poitier would never have been considered for, let alone offered to play. As one of the twelve criminals turned antiheroes in Robert Aldrich's *The Dirty Dozen*, Brown showed off his athletic skills as Robert Jefferson, a man sentenced to death by hanging for killing a White man in a racial brawl. The plot dropped Jefferson and eleven other condemned criminals into Project Amnesty, a World War II suicide mission involving a German stronghold and the assassination of numerous Nazi officers. If the mission succeeds, the surviving members will have their criminal records expunged. Aldrich directed a murderers' row of soon-to-be famous actors and vets including Robert Ryan, Ernie Borgnine, Telly Savalas, and Charles Bronson. One would think Brown stood out like a sore thumb among these White "World War II soldiers," but audiences had already grown used to seeing the equally Black Ivan Dixon on TV's *Hogan's Heroes*.

MGM opened *Dozen* on the same day as *To Sir, with Love*, pitting America's first Black star against America's first Black *action* star. Brown was also one of the first actors to play Donald E. Westlake's Parker character, doing so in the first movie to receive the R rating by the newly formed Motion Picture Association of America (MPAA), *The Split*. He would also be the first of several NFL players to graduate from the gridiron to the big screen in this era, a feat first done by Woody Strode, one of the two men who reintegrated football in 1948.

Defensive back Fred Williamson and occasional halfback Bernie Casey would join Brown in Blaxploitation movies, where they'd co-star multiple times.

Brown's *Dozen* co-star John Cassavetes would be instrumental in breaking the directorial color barrier in Hollywood. Gordon Parks, the famed *Life* photographer, had written a semi-autobiographical novel about his adolescence in his hometown of Fort Scott, Kansas. Published in 1963, *The Learning Tree* had a fan in Cassavetes, and the independent filmmaker thought its author should bring it to the screen. Parks had directed two documentary features but had not done any fiction films, because there was no such thing as an African-American director in White Hollywood.

Cassavetes suggested he set up a meeting between Parks and Kenny Hyman, the head of Warner Bros.–Seven Arts. This was in 1968. In 1967, however, Parks unexpectedly ran into his old pal Melvin Van Peebles on the Champs-Élysées in Paris. "I was with an ex-nun," Parks revealed to Warrington Hudlin in the 2005 Starz documentary *Unstoppable*. Van Peebles invited the ex-nun and his friend to a screening room so he could show them *The Story of a Three-Day Pass*. "It cost me a million dollars," Parks joked, mocking Van Peebles's penchant for demanding payment for anything he did. Seeing a Black auteur write and direct a film got Parks thinking about adapting his own material. "You gave me hope," he told Van Peebles.

So, Gordon Parks took up John Cassavetes on his offer. Hyman told him he loved the book, then asked who should write the screenplay. When Parks had no suggestions, Hyman offered him the job. He accepted. Then, Hyman offered Parks the scoring job, which he also accepted. When the directing and producing jobs were thrown in, two historic positions, Parks automatically said yes because "I wasn't buying a word he uttered." But the studio head wasn't kidding. With this deal, Gordon Parks became the first debut director since Orson Welles to have this much power. And he was about to become the first Black director and producer on a Hollywood film.

Hyman introduced Parks to some potential line producers who would help him learn the business. One of the candidates, Bill Conrad, wanted no part of this process. "The silent one, a large, heavyset man, avoided me as though I had lice," Parks remembered in his memoir *A Hungry Heart*. Despite being warned of how difficult Conrad could be, Parks hired him anyway. "Don't ask me why I made that decision," Parks wrote. "Perhaps I just wanted to be his boss."

Conrad lived up to his reputation, at one point challenging his superior's authority (and losing the battle). But in the end, it was a productive partnership. Conrad even helped with the casting, suggesting Dana Elcar for a role. Elcar's "audition" was him bursting into Parks's office, pleading, "I'm him! I'm Kirky! Can't you see it? I'm the one for the part! I'm your ornery killer sheriff!" Kirky was a nasty piece of work, a racist officer who shoots several Black men in the back. At one point, he makes Newt, the film's young stand-in for its director, dredge one of those dead bodies from the bottom of a lake. It's a juicy role, and as Elcar predicted, he is perfectly cast.

The Learning Tree had one of still photography's greatest legends behind the camera, and he was aided and abetted by one of the great cinematographers of the era, Burnett Guffey. Guffey was a master of black-and-white cinematography, with five Academy Award nominations and one win for Best Cinematography, Black-and-White. He shot film noirs like Don Siegel's *Private Hell 36*, Nicholas Ray's *In a Lonely Place*, and Joseph H. Lewis's *So Dark the Night*. He won the Oscar in 1954 for Fred Zinnemann's *From Here to Eternity*. One would think that a color film like *The Learning Tree* wouldn't be his speed, but Guffey had proven himself equally adept at that type of picture, winning the Oscar for 1967's extremely vivid *Bonnie and Clyde*. As an added bonus, Guffey started his cinematography career in the same decade *The Learning Tree* takes place, giving him a firsthand knowledge of what the era looked like.

Parks shot *The Learning Tree* on location in his former hometown of Fort Scott, Kansas, the basis for the novel's fictional town of Cherokee Flats. The townspeople at first were hostile toward these interlopers dredging up the past. They eventually came around after the mayor gave them a talking-to regarding how much money the town would make from the film being shot there. Some of the most vociferous townspeople even became extras.

"Entering Fort Scott was like driving into my past," Parks wrote. "The childhood I had spent there had dissolved into a blur of memories—some good, some bad." That feeling is reflected in the finished product, a film where the dignity of the African-American characters is powerfully felt and their dreams, fears, and wishes are thoroughly inspected. Hollywood had rarely given such rich interior lives and complex backgrounds to Black characters, even those played by Sidney Poitier.

On the first day of shooting, Parks went to Nichelle "*Star Trek*'s Lieutenant Uhura" Nichols's son, Kyle Johnson, the actor who would be playing fourteen-year-old Newt, and told him, "Well, Kyle, I lived it and wrote about it. Now I'm turning it over to you. Good luck." Johnson did a very good job experiencing the pangs of first love, the death of a family member, rampant racism, young friendship, and learning a lesson in doing the right thing despite the odds. In a scene that coincidentally links this film with a similar, far more explicit and controversial scene in Melvin Van Peebles's 1971 masterwork, *Sweet Sweetback's Baadasssss Song*, Newt is deflowered by a much older sex worker.

The Learning Tree opened in New York City on August 6, 1969. The *New York Times* gave it a mixed review, complaining about its clichéd sentimentality but enjoying its images, saying the film "is rich, distanced, cool and sophisticated in its appreciation of formal visual properties." Peter Davis Dibble of *Women's Wear Daily* called it "great, baby, great," a play on the film's original, discarded title, *Learn, Baby, Learn*. Ann Guarino in the New York *Daily News* gave it three stars out of four, calling the film "a welcome change of pace from the exaggerated violence concocted lately for screen consumption."

Surprisingly, *Ebony* and *Jet*, two of the biggest Black magazines in America, had nothing to say about *The Learning Tree*. They completely ignored the film, upsetting Parks greatly.

The Learning Tree kicked open the door for African-American writers and directors in Hollywood. Before Gordon Parks made his next film in 1971, three more directors would sit behind the camera to helm features in 1970.

1970
1970

WHAT WILL IT BE IN '70?

1970
1970

A great event occurred in 1970, one that shook up the computer world. No, it's not my birth, although that happened this year. Unix time reached its epoch on January 1, 1970. This is a rather useless detail for anyone reading this book who isn't, like its author, a techie. However, we've got to start somewhere, and the Unix epoch, or the time from which all Unix computer timekeeping is measured, is a symbolic beginning. It started at 00:00:00 on New Year's Day, and the Blaxploitation era's "epoch" occurred on May 27, 1970, with the opening of two films. One of those would make enough money to convince Hollywood that Black folks would come out to see a film about themselves. But I'm getting ahead of the story.

These introductory chapters at the beginning of each year's section are intended to give a lay of the land, a sort of primer on what else was going on in the world while Blaxploitation films unspooled for their audiences. They also give me a chance to ramble on outside of the more rigid constraints of the more formal chapters. So let's set the stage by first describing what happened seventeen days before the "epoch" of Blaxploitation.

On May 10, 1970, the last film by legendary Hollywood director William Wyler was playing at the Hudson Mall Cinemas in Jersey City. Wyler hadn't technically directed a Blaxploitation movie, but his film did have several components that might allow it to be grandfathered in. *The Liberation of L.B. Jones* starred Roscoe Lee Browne, Yaphet Kotto, and Lola Falana, three names that will pop up more than once later in this book. Wyler's swan song was a nasty piece of work, filled with interracial sex and racial violence, including a castration. Columbia Pictures, the distributor of this junk, passed on Robert Altman's *M*A*S*H* (which featured future Blaxploitation legend Fred Williamson) because, according to the studio, "people don't say the word 'fuck' in Columbia Pictures!" Maybe not, but their torch lady logo apparently didn't mind genital mutilation.

For some ungodly reason, my mother went to see *The Liberation of L.B. Jones* on the day she went into labor with me. At least, that's the story I've been told, and if that part of it isn't true, I'm going to print the legend. This part is indisputable, however: I was born two weeks earlier than Mom's due date. To be exact, I was supposed to be born on May 27, the same day as the film widely considered to be "the first Blaxploitation movie" was released.

See, the story *did* have a point.

This year marked the end of the turbulent 1960s, a decade populated with violent uprisings, civil rights struggles, and numerous assassinations. President John F. Kennedy and his brother, Robert, were shot and killed, as were Malcolm X, Dr. Martin Luther King Jr., and Medgar Evers. The first year of the new decade had its own infamous shooting, this one at Kent State, where four people were killed by the Ohio National Guard.

Huey P. Newton, co-founder of the Black Panther Party, was still incarcerated after being charged with the voluntary manslaughter of Oakland police officer John Frey in 1967. "Free Huey" was still a rallying cry, at least until his release in August. Members of the Black Panthers went to China and North Korea in 1970. They also visited North Vietnam that year, while the Vietnam War was still raging.

Newton's fellow Black Panther and deputy chairman, Fred Hampton, had been murdered by the Chicago Police Department on December 4, 1969, shot up while he slept during an illicit raid facilitated by double agent William O'Neal, who provided the layout of Hampton's apartment. In 1970, survivors of that massacre and relatives of Hampton sued Cook County, Illinois, and the federal government for $48 million over civil rights violations. The case wouldn't be settled for another twelve years.

The top dog in the White House in 1970 was a Republican, a feature that would be consistent during Blaxploitation's heyday. The GOPer in question was Richard Milhous Nixon, the former two-time vice president whose ascendancy to the Oval Office was temporarily derailed by JFK in 1960. If ever a caricature of frequent Blaxploitation enemy "The Man" could be personified, it would have been Nixon. Along with future president Ronald Reagan, who combatted the Panthers' blatant use of open carry by creating the anti-gun legislation Mulford Act, he was no friend of Black people. Curtis Mayfield and Stevie Wonder would write songs about how unpopular he was.

Cinematically, Nixon would make an appearance, in effigy, as a mask worn by Black robbers in a 1971 Sidney Poitier movie. Reagan's face would do the same in Kathryn Bigelow's 1991 heist film, *Point Break*. Nixon also showed up in 1974 as a visual punchline in the office of a Republican politician played by, of all people, Roscoe Lee Browne.

In September, comedian (and native of my hometown of Jersey City) Flip Wilson became the first Black person to host a successful variety program. His eponymous TV series ran on CBS for four years and, for a time, was the second-most popular show on television.

Wilson's crossover appeal was huge, earning him two Emmys and immortalizing his most famous character, the sassy Black woman Geraldine. Like Tyler Perry's Madea, Geraldine was quite popular, and her catchphrase "The Devil made me do it" was everywhere. Geraldine would also help Wilson win the Best Comedy Recording Grammy in 1970 for the album *The Devil Made Me Buy This Dress.*

Though primarily on television, Wilson would make a Blaxploitation appearance in that same movie where Roscoe Lee Browne was caping for Nixon. In that film, *Uptown Saturday Night,* he emulated another of his famous TV show characters, a preacher with questionable tactics and comments.

Ron Howard got a hit movie out of the event that occurred on April 11, 1970. The *Apollo 13* lunar mission began on that day. James Lovell, John Swigert, and Fred Haise didn't make it to the moon like their predecessors on *Apollos 11* and *12.* Astronauts did succeed in 1970, however, when Gil Scott-Heron's classic Afrofuturism poetry slam, "Whitey on the Moon," was released.

Also in April, *Midnight Cowboy* became the first and only X-rated film to win Best Picture at the Academy Awards. Its editor, Hugh A. Robertson, was the first Black person nominated in that category. Robertson didn't win, but by chance, that same month, his next project was set in motion: Ernest Tidyman published a book about a Black detective named John Shaft. *Shaft* would be optioned by one of the numerous Hollywood studios in dire straits in 1970, Metro-Goldwyn-Mayer.

For now, however, there were two other literary detectives who would kick off Blaxploitation: Chester Himes's Coffin Ed and Grave Digger Jones. Director Ossie Davis was about to prove to Hollywood that Black characters could captivate Black audiences without necessarily leaning on crossover appeal.

And I thought I was writing realism. It never occurred to me that I was writing absurdity. Realism and absurdity are so similar in the lives of American blacks one cannot tell the difference.

—CHESTER HIMES

CHAPTER 2
Ain't Now, But It's Gonna Be

Born in Jefferson City, Missouri, in 1909, Chester B. Himes grew up in a middle-class family. His father was a college professor and his mother a teacher; their focus on education led to Himes attending Ohio State when his parents relocated to Cleveland, Ohio, in 1925. After being expelled for some kind of fraternity prank, Himes turned to a life of crime that would land him a twenty-year bid in jail, of which he'd serve six years.

While incarcerated, Himes started writing fiction. He saw it as a way to stay out of trouble. His published articles impressed the guards at Ohio Penitentiary, and the novels he wrote once he got out of jail ranged from autobiographical stories about racism to a candid take on homosexuality. A wide streak of pitch-black humor runs through his work, often existing side by side with harsh, brutal violence. Characters in Chester Himes's novels knew the streets and often used that knowledge to execute all manner of side hustles and schemes, many of them with fatal results.

Himes is best known for his Harlem Detective series, seven novels (and one unfinished work) that feature Harlem-based police detectives Coffin Ed Johnson and Grave Digger "Digger" Jones. Three books from that series were adapted for the screen: *For Love of Imabelle* (which became Bill Duke's spectacular 1991 film, *A Rage in Harlem*); *Come Back, Charleston Blue*; and *Cotton Comes to Harlem*. There was also a *very* loose adaptation of Himes's debut novel, *If He Hollers Let Him Go*, adapted in 1968, thereby making it the first of his works to hit the screen. It counts despite so many deviations that the source material is unrecognizable outside of the title and having starred the actor who would also play Coffin Ed, Raymond St. Jacques.

In March 1969, Ossie Davis was tapped to direct the aforementioned adaptation of *Cotton Comes to Harlem* for famed producer Sam Goldwyn Jr. This made Davis the second African-American to helm a Hollywood film. He also did the screenplay adaptation with Arnold Perl and cast Godfrey Cambridge as Digger and Raymond St. Jacques as Coffin Ed. United Artists gave him a $2 million ($16 million in 2023) budget. "This is something I've been dreaming about doing for some time, and at last, we're doing it," said the man whose dad, Sam Sr., put the "Goldwyn" in Metro-Goldwyn-Mayer.

Unlike Kenneth Hyman, Goldwyn didn't ask Davis to score the picture—that went to Galt MacDermot, whose musical *Hair* was in its second year of introducing blue-haired Broadway theatergoers to the Age of Aquarius. Davis did, however, contribute the lyrics to the film's opening credits song, "Ain't Now, but It's Gonna Be," sung by the loudest soul singer this side of Patti LaBelle, Melba Moore. Her opening line is "Ain't now, but it's gonna be Black enough for me." Throughout the film, characters ask one another, "Was that Black enough for ya?"

"I came into the business as a writer," said Davis, referring to his career as a playwright. He was more widely known as an actor in Hollywood, appearing in Sidney Poitier's 1950 debut, *No Way Out*, alongside his wife, Ruby Dee. Like screenwriters Charles Brackett and Billy Wilder, or "brackettandwilder," as they were colloquially known, Davis and Dee were inextricably linked professionally and in the hearts of fans. They were always referred to as "OssieDavisandRubyDee" by Black folks, as if it were one word, one powerful entity of talent.

Dee encouraged Davis to accept the directing job, knowing that he would be a great fit for the material's broad comedy and its intimate knowledge of the hustles, joys, and dangers that populate a Black neighborhood. Davis's biting 1961 satire, *Purlie Victorious*, proves she was right. It's a kindred spirit to *Cotton Comes to Harlem*, sharing numerous plot elements even though it takes place in the boondocks of the South. There's a preacher involved in a monetary scam, a motley crew of memorable characters surrounding him in the neighborhood, and a fearless level of Black humor (with a capital *B*, that is) that knowingly sticks one toe over the line of respectability. And they both have Helen Martin and Godfrey Cambridge; the latter received a Tony nomination for his performance as Gitlow Judson, the resident trickster who plays dumb just to get one over on the White man.

Davis assembled his Broadway cast (minus Martin) and wrote the screenplay for director Nicholas Webster's little-seen 1963 film adaptation, alternately titled *Gone Are the Days!* This marked the movie debut of Alan Alda, re-creating his role as Charley Cotchipee, son of the wealthiest (and most racist) man in the county, Stonewall Jackson Cotchipee (Sorrell Booke), aka "Ol' Cap'n." When the movie begins, the elder Cotchipee is dead, resulting in "the first integrated funeral in the sovereign segregated state of Georgia." His funeral is presided over by Charley's childhood friend, Reverend Purlie Victorious Judson (Davis).

Judson states that Ol' Cap'n Cotchipee was "brave enough to die standing for what he believes in, and it is the wish of his family, and of his friends, that he be buried likewise." His coffin is indeed wheeled into the once all-Black Big Bethel Church standing up, the same position in which its inhabitant met his maker. The coffin is adorned by his hat, the Confederate flag, and the bullwhip that Ol' Cap'n used on several members of Big Bethel Church's congregation, all of whom are happy to sing him off to his rightful place in hell. Adding to the absurdity, there's a medal pinned to the coffin.

From there, *Gone Are the Days!* flashes back to show what led to this joyous event. The story takes place in the Jim Crow South, where numerous Blacks work on the Cotchipee plantation to settle debts with Ol' Cap'n they will never be able to repay. To this plantation returns Reverend Purlie. His mission is to underhandedly obtain an inheritance that is rightfully his. The plan is to use his country bumpkin sweetheart, Lutibelle (Ruby Dee), to impersonate a cousin whose mother, by virtue of working for Cap'n Cotchipee, is entitled to a $500 inheritance. Since those relatives are deceased, Purlie is next in line for the money. The Big Bethel Church is up for sale, and he wants to buy it. Ol' Cap'n, however, wants to buy the building and burn it down. As expected, everyone's plans go comically awry.

Davis and his company are playing stereotypes. But Purlie and his cohorts are putting on an act in order to keep those in power oblivious to just how smart they really are. As Cap'n Cotchipee's self-proclaimed "favorite darkie," Cambridge's Gitlow has the most incendiary lines to say, many of which would have been played as straight cooning in a Hollywood production. But Cambridge's delivery lets the audience know that this is all a ruse to deceive a White character who would never consider that he was being played. "Some of the best pretendin' in the world is done in front of White folks," Purlie says.

Gone Are the Days! was rare in that it was a comedy featuring African-American performers whose characters were the main focus of the material. Black characters were used as comedic relief in White films, and racist relief at that. Films featuring Black leads like Sidney Poitier or Harry Belafonte were most often dramas dealing with racial strife and issues. So it was notable that *Cotton Comes to Harlem* was a comedy made by, for, and featuring Black people. According to Cambridge, it was "the first major motion picture to be made within and about the black American life-style that is concerned mainly with entertaining and not with preaching equality."

The main antagonist of *Cotton Comes to Harlem* is also not preaching equality. Reverend Deke O'Malley (Calvin Lockhart) is evangelizing a "Back to Africa" movement that promises investors a guaranteed seat to the motherland on a boat named *Black Beauty*. The poor denizens of places like Detroit and Chicago have already lined O'Malley's pockets with money, and now he's extending the opportunity to the residents of Harlem, many of whom believe he's on the level. One such believer is Uncle Bud, a junkman played by stand-up comedian Redd Foxx in what is clearly the origin of his Fred Sanford character on the sitcom *Sanford and Son*. Uncle Bud gives every penny he has to the cause.

Perhaps the only people who see through Deke O'Malley are Coffin Ed and Digger. Coffin Ed, the bad cop in this good cop/bad cop pairing, wants to beat O'Malley senseless for scamming his own people. "You could have been the next Marcus Garvey," he says to the preacher at one point. Before the heroes can arrest O'Malley, a gunfight breaks out. It's the first of several sharp, abrupt veers from comedy to violence, faithfully keeping the same shifts in tone as Himes's novel. Several people are shot, cars explode, Coffin Ed and Digger have an unfortunate mishap with a watermelon truck, and a bale of cotton flies out of one truck and onto the streets of Harlem. Uncle Bud obtains it and sells it for $25, only to buy it back for $30 when he discovers what might be in it.

"What would a bale of cotton be doing in Harlem?" is a question asked by several characters in the film. Those who know why also know that there's $87,000 of the faux "Back to Africa" movement's money hidden in it. Deke O'Malley is aware of its presence—he staged the attempt on his life—but once the cotton goes missing, he's stuck in Harlem trying to find it. When his right-hand man is accidentally killed in the planned melee, O'Malley shacks up with his widow, Mabel, in order to evade Digger and Ed.

Assisting O'Malley, at least initially, is his girlfriend, Iris. Played by Judy Pace, Iris is one tough, smart, and very violent cookie. The spirit of Himes's turn-on-a-dime prose lives in Pace's performance: she's a real sweetheart until she's crossed and becomes vengeful. The film uses her in comedic fashion at first, in a scene where she pretends to seduce the goofy White cop assigned to keep watch over her. The officer winds up locked out of her apartment stark naked except for a paper bag on his head. But later, in a fit of jealousy, Iris ruthlessly smashes a model of *Black Beauty* over Mabel's head, nearly killing her. In a film full of machine-gun-toting baddies, the Mafia, and other assorted riffraff, Iris is the most unpredictable criminal—and the most dangerous.

Harlem would become the setting for many a Blaxploitation film, but in 1969, it was a new cinematic location. The days of when White audiences would go uptown for "all-cullud" entertainment were long gone. Like much of New York City, Harlem had fallen into a disrepair exacerbated by poverty and redlining. Davis pointed this out in an interview. "An entertainment about Harlem at this time is revolutionary," he told *Newsday*. "Harlem has been an example of oppression, a symbol of what remains to be done. It has also been an example of the exotic, the quaint, the different—how Black people live."

The characters and situations in *Cotton Comes to Harlem* bear out that latter example. From the old woman who keeps her money under her dress to the stripper whose batshit musical number at the Apollo Theater features a mammy caricature dancing atop that newfound bale of cotton, Davis's Harlem is filled with weird, funky people heretofore unseen in mainstream movies. They're hustling, having fun, and not as gullible as they appear. When O'Malley fails to deliver, his wronged constituency seek him out. His ultimate, violent fate is a pointed commentary on prosperity preachers and the congregations they fleece, as well as the level of police brutality allowed in service to catching the bad guys. Coffin Ed and Digger's methods are at times as brutal as those of Dirty Harry or *The French Connection*'s Popeye Doyle.

Speaking about the toughness of his cop protagonists and their snarky sense of humor, Davis said, "We are creating a totally new stereotype to replace one that has become obsolete." He was referring to the prior history of the shuffling coons and toms Hollywood turned out for decades. Black audiences welcomed the change, coming out in droves. As a result, *Cotton Comes to Harlem* became the twenty-second-highest grossing film of 1970. Hollywood finally took notice that Black folks did indeed go to the movies. As a result, *Cotton Comes to Harlem* is widely considered the first Blaxploitation movie.

Cotton Comes to Harlem wasn't the only comedy featuring Black characters to appear in 1970. Jumping on the Black director bandwagon, Columbia Pictures signed Melvin Van Peebles to direct *Watermelon Man*, the only film he'd make in the studio system. It was based on a script called *The Night the Sun Came Out in Happy Hollow Lane*, written by a White writer, Herman Raucher, one year before he struck gold with his novel *Summer of '42*. The studio was afraid that the subject matter would cause controversy if a White director tackled its racially incendiary story.

The plot fit Van Peebles's penchant for sly satire and daring provocation. Raucher's script tells the story of Jeff Gerber, a White bigot who inexplicably wakes up Black one morning. The resulting color change wreaks all manner of havoc on his daily life. At the end, he wakes up from this nightmare and triumphantly returns to Whiteness, fully aware of the Black man's plight and bursting with empathy for his compatriots of color. Finally, he would understand "The Negro Problem" his liberal wife kept nagging him about!

Despite their timidity at having a White director shoot this material, Columbia wanted an established White actor in the lead. They floated Jack Lemmon and Alan Arkin as potential choices. Since Jeff Gerber was Black for 75 percent of the movie, any White actor would have to play the majority of the role in blackface. Either the studio was fine with this, completely oblivious to the optics, or, considering that they gave Van Peebles twenty-four days to shoot the film instead of the usual sixty, priming the film for failure. Regardless, their director was not onboard with this idea.

Instead, Van Peebles suggested that a Black actor could perform the first part of the role in whiteface. This had never been done before. Surprisingly, the studio acquiesced. As if hoping to provoke makeup man Ben Lane's nervous breakdown, Van Peebles cast the dark-skinned star of *Cotton Comes to Harlem*, Godfrey Cambridge, as Jeff Gerber. As White Gerber, Cambridge appears completely naked at one point, lying facedown in the tanning bed that might be the cause of his unexpected Blackness. His bare ass is prominently displayed, and not for the last time. As makeup jobs go, it's a far cry from Eddie Murphy's more convincing appearance in his *Saturday Night Live* skit "White Like Me" thirteen years later.

But it was enough to intrigue a few beachgoers during a publicity stunt held on a Los Angeles beach just before filming began. Cambridge walked around in makeup from the neck up, chatting with people while a camera crew followed him around. Looking at this hybrid of White face/Black body, one person thought he was an albino. Another thought he was a White man covered in black makeup. "My problem isn't looking White," Cambridge said, "but in thinking White!"

Cambridge was fresh from shooting *Cotton Comes to Harlem* when filming began in Hollywood in September 1969. Oscar-winner Estelle Parsons was cast as his wife, Althea, and his daughter was played by Erin Moran, later known to TV fans as *Happy Days'* Joanie Cunningham. Oscar-winning singer-songwriter Paul Williams had a bit part. Actor-director D'Urville Martin, a staple of Blaxploitation films, played a bus driver fed up by Gerber's racist microaggressions. Van Peebles gave himself a cameo as an office door stencil artist.

Considering how much disdain he had for the studio system's stereotypical Black roles, the most surprising person Van Peebles cast was Mantan Moreland, the chauffeur from the 1940s Charlie Chan movies and a known purveyor of the bug-eyed, open-mouthed coon stylings Van Peebles despised. Moreland plays the counterman at the diner where Gerber eats his breakfast every morning. He delivers his lines to White Jeff Gerber using his well-known facial expressions, but there's a moment when he briefly drops the facade to show the viewer that this is a put-on for his customer. The audience catches it; Gerber does not. In exposing this okey-doke, *Watermelon Man* takes a page from Reverend Purlie's playbook: *Some of the best pretendin' in the world is done in front of White folks.*

Or, to quote Van Peebles directly, "Take the stereotypes and kick ass with the motherfuckers. That's how you do it."

No amount of pretending is going to help Jeff Gerber when he sees a Black man staring back at him in the mirror. *Watermelon Man*'s staging of this scene hints at the avant-garde visuals Van Peebles would employ in his next film, *Sweet Sweetback's Baadasssss Song.* The screen turns a variety of colors as Gerber walks to the bathroom to take a middle-of-the-night piss, his journey edited in a ragged fashion while odd noises blare on the soundtrack. It culminates in a tight close-up of Godfrey Cambridge's posterior; his Black ass fills the entire screen and gives the film its biggest laugh. Not even the TV print edited out this moment, censors be damned!

Once Jeff Gerber becomes colorized, *Watermelon Man* becomes a sitcom version of journalist John Howard Griffin's 1961 nonfiction book, *Black Like Me*. In that book, Griffin darkened his skin so that he could experience racism and segregationist attitudes firsthand. He accomplished this by taking drugs and spending fifteen hours in a tanning bed. Gerber's twice-a-day tanning routine becomes a running joke for this reason. When he complains to the tanning bed company, they offer to send him another tanning bed.

Unlike Griffin's, Gerber's color doesn't wear off. Medical tests (and text superimposed on the screen in a garish font) inform him that he is now, genetically, "a Negro." Upon introspection, Althea realizes that some of her husband's family members *did* kinda look Black. She even points out that Gerber's full name, Jefferson Washington Gerber, might have been his folks' subtle way of telling him he was merely passing for White. Parsons and Cambridge handle the consistently offensive one-liners with hilarious aplomb. When Althea looks under Jeff's towel, he snaps, "That's a myth!"

Being Black has unintended side effects for a bigot. Gerber is no longer allowed inside the yacht club where he usually conducted business. His insurance agency prefers he sell to Black customers only. His buxom blond co-worker is ogling him to a fetishistic degree. And whenever he's on the street, the cops show up and he's accused of theft. The neighbors call at all hours of the day and night, demanding he move out. And Althea, once so concerned with the Negro Problem, doesn't know how to deal with the problem Negro in her house.

Oddly enough, the Black bus driver and diner worker don't seem at all surprised their tormentor is as dark-skinned as they are. They're the only people who treat him with any decency, which finally helps Gerber ease into acceptance of his fate. *Watermelon Man* ends with him joining a Black revolution group.

Now, here's where Melvin Van Peebles got into trouble. Raucher's original ending was unacceptable to him because "being Black is not a disease from which to be cured." Columbia wanted the original ending, so the director offered to shoot that ending as well as the one he preferred. The studio could watch both and decide which was better.

Except Van Peebles never shot the original ending.

Columbia released the movie anyway. Raucher was livid about this and wrote a novelization of the film to retain his original vision. "I hope he's forgiven me," Van Peebles said in the introduction to the Criterion Collection edition of *Watermelon Man*.

Raucher had an unexpected partner in outrage—Godfrey Cambridge! Not only was he pissed off about a plot development that had Gerber taking a job as a garbageman, he hated the film's title and refused to promote it. On *The Merv Griffin Show*, he called *Watermelon Man* "a racist title" and claimed the studio was only screening it for bougie Black folks with money. "They'll sneak preview the film this week on Manhattan's East Side," he told Merv. "Has there been a sudden influx of Black people on the East Side?" One can only imagine his reaction to the film's tagline, "The Uppity Movie."

Since both of the films Cambridge made in 1970 opened on May 27, viewers could choose between cotton or watermelon. *Watermelon Man* made only 15 percent of *Cotton*'s gross and received more negative reviews, but it did earn Melvin Van Peebles a three-picture deal at Columbia, a first for an African-American director. The soundtrack album also charted. Written and sung (if that's the proper word) by Melvin Van Peebles, its lead single, "Love, That's America," had a resurgence forty-one years later when it was adopted by the Occupy Wall Street movement. Not bad for a composer who couldn't read music and wrote all his songs on a kazoo and whose singing voice made alley cats sound like Stevie Wonder by comparison. Van Peebles would eventually get two Tony Award–nominated musicals and several successful albums out of that kazoo.

African-American talent continued to make strides behind the camera in 1970. Writer-director-actor Bill Gunn adapted two films for United Artists, *The Landlord* and *The Angel Levine*, from a novel by African-American writer Kristin Hunter and a Bernard Malamud short story, respectively. Both films showed Gunn's versatility while highlighting that Blacks could write about subject matter that was not explicitly Black. There are Black characters in both films, but the lead character is not. Also, like Van Peebles, Gunn had a penchant for the surreal that would greatly influence a later Blaxploitation-era masterpiece, 1973's *Ganja & Hess*.

Regarding his two adaptations: *Levine* is the stranger film, the tale of Morris, a faithless Jewish man (Zero Mostel) whose wife (Polish theater legend Ida Kamińska) suffers from severe heart problems. When Morris calls attention to a Black thief stealing a fur coat, the escaping thief gets killed by a car. Soon after, that same man appears in Morris's house, claiming to be a Jewish angel-in-training who must perform a miracle in order to earn his wings. He is the titular angel, played by the film's producer, Harry Belafonte. Belafonte had actually preceded Gordon Parks as the first Black producer when he made 1959's *Odds Against Tomorrow*, but his name did not appear on the producing credit. Though Malamud had no issues with the adaptation, *The Angel Levine* was poorly received and faded into obscurity.

Gunn had much better luck with *The Landlord*, a satire on race and class that was well-suited for its debuting director, Hal Ashby. It's funky and quirky and possesses a darkly bitter world-weariness that seeps through its bright satirical facade like bubbles rising up from a tar pit. It's also wildly different than the novel, which drew praise for its sympathetic portrayal of a White character in a book penned by a Black author. Gunn's changes to the protagonist are much more ruthless.

Taking place in Park Slope, this is perhaps the first movie about how gentrification affects poor minority neighborhoods. Beau Bridges plays Elgar, the rich, bored son of socialite Mrs. Enders (Lee Grant). He buys a building in the 'hood, one that's populated by a number of quirky Black characters, including Copee, played by an ax-wielding Louis Gossett Jr., and Marge, a sassy blues singer played by Pearl Bailey. The scene where Grant (Oscar-nominated for this role) and Pearlie Mae, as Bailey was known familiarly, bond over booze and pot liquor is a master class of writing, directing, and acting.

Diana Sands was the real standout in the cast. An eclectic actress who played opposite Gossett in *A Raisin in the Sun* and Alan Alda in the stage production of *The Owl and the Pussycat*, she tragically died at thirty-nine on September 21, 1973. Her résumé included playing strong, complicated characters in works by African-American women like Lorraine Hansberry, Maya Angelou (who wrote Sands's underseen disaster, 1972's *Georgia, Georgia*), and Hunter. Her last role was Cora, a self-proclaimed "Ralph Nader for Hookers" in Gilbert Moses's massively entertaining 1974 Blaxploitation pimp epic, *Willie Dynamite*.

In *The Landlord*, Sands plays Francine Johnson, who initially appears to be the stereotypical sexual chocolate fantasy. But there's something off about that characterization. First, she's bold and terrifying. She openly flirts with the landlord, sizing him up immediately and calibrating her hustle. Second, she's married to Copee, who is clearly crazy but controllable in her presence. Third, she was "Miss Sepia 1957" (the way she says this is wonderful) and could definitely do better in both her situation and her romantic choices. The film does give Francine and Elgar a sex scene, but afterward, she makes it clear that she's uninterested in further trysts. And when she becomes pregnant with Elgar's baby, she has no aspirations for support. Putting the child up for adoption, she tells Elgar, "I want him to be adopted White, so he can grow up casual. Like his daddy."

Satires on race like *The Landlord* and *Watermelon Man* would become few and far between once the Blaxploitation era ushered in characters more interested in kicking ass and taking names. But this shift could be seen not only in *Cotton Comes to Harlem*'s potent hybrid of violence and comedy, but in a familiar character's return to the screen.

In the Heat of the Night's Virgil Tibbs was back in 1970, making him the first Black character to have a sequel. Sidney Poitier reprised his role as the Philly homicide detective, and once again Quincy Jones supplied the score. But the Mr. Tibbs of *They Call Me MISTER Tibbs!* was no longer from Philly; he was now a twelve-year veteran of the San Francisco Police Department. And the formerly childless and single character now had a wife and two kids. A lot can happen in three years, apparently including amnesia about the first movie whose most famous line is quoted in the title.

This time, Tibbs has to solve the brutal murder of a sex worker whose head is caved in by an impotent man during the first five minutes of the movie. It's a rather vicious murder, though not enough to justify the MPAA rerating the GP-rated *They Call Me MISTER Tibbs!* R in 1996. Perhaps they objected to the nudity, a new feature for a Sidney Poitier movie. Also new was the amount of action scenes. Poitier had done these scenes before, but not with this much frequency. Lieutenant Tibbs has an extended foot chase, beats up several people, shoots a few more, and even whups his son's ass for being a disrespectful little brat.

They Call Me MISTER Tibbs! was released in July 1970 and made $5 million, enough for the producers, the Mirisch Corporation, to bring back Virgil Tibbs for an unheard of third film. With *The Organization*, Tibbs became the first Black character to earn a trilogy and the first police officer character to do so as well. Interestingly enough, in 1971, John Shaft would begin his path to repeat that first achievement while Clint Eastwood's "Dirty" Harry Callahan would start working toward repeating the second.

Before Poitier reported to San Francisco, he was in Mexico with his best buddy, Harry Belafonte, making a Western called *Buck and the Preacher* for director Joseph Sargent. On February 24, 1971, twenty days after filming started, the *San Francisco Examiner* reported that Sargent "stalked off [the picture] due to differences with the stars." Columbia replaced him with the film's star, Sidney Poitier, marking the beginning of his second career as a film director. After Gordon Parks, Ossie Davis, Melvin Van Peebles, and Bill Gunn, Mr. Tibbs was finally on his way to taking control of his career from behind the camera.

Poitier would, nine years later, give Columbia one of its biggest hits when he directed *Stir Crazy*; for now, he was happy to let his pal, whom he playfully called "that old, decrepit folk singer, what's-his-name Belafonte," go stir-crazy in his scenes. The "Jump in the Line" singer even gets a comic nude scene, which surely made those appreciative of the male form very happy. Filming concluded in late April. Belafonte went to do club dates and Poitier went to his next movie set while working on postproduction on *Buck and the Preacher*.

While shooting *The Organization* in May 1971, director Don Medford and his crew found themselves sharing Washington Square in San Francisco with *Dirty Harry* director Don Siegel and his team. "Loads of fraternizing" occurred, according to the *San Francisco Chronicle*. Imagine if the filmmakers had decided, right then and there, to do a Tibbs–Dirty Harry collaboration!

Tibbs's third case involves the mysterious organization in the title. The film opens with a virtuoso eight-minute scene without dialogue, setting up what appears to be a heist. The meticulous attention to detail adds to the suspense, as viewers have no idea why all this effort is being taken to break into what looks like a furniture factory closed for the night. Turns out there's $4 million in heroin in an office safe. The criminals make the factory manager open the safe by dangling him out the window. They make off with the drugs but leave the manager alive. However, he's dead when the cops investigate.

Tibbs discovers that the culprits (who turn themselves in so they can solicit his help) are a vigilante group out to squash "the organization" that's pushing heroin into San Francisco. Each member has lost someone to the drug. The vigilante crew features an unbelievably sexy, young Raul Julia as one of its leaders and a shockingly old and balding Ron O'Neal as its tragic sacrificial lamb. Considering the gorgeous mane of hair and the unshakable swagger O'Neal had a year later in *Super Fly*, it's jarring to see him look, dare it be said, like a normal, rundown human being. No matter how twisty and violent *The*

Organization gets, O'Neal's and Julia's performances keep the viewer riveted. The film's "you can't beat the system" downer ending is also par for the course in the decade known for its downer movie endings.

Current San Francisco residents and fans of nostalgia will dig a late reel chase scene through the then-unfinished Montgomery BART station. In this and other scenes of carnage, Poitier proved that the action hero he'd become in the prior Tibbs feature wasn't a fluke. Like that film, the MPAA also took a more puritanical swipe at *The Organization*, changing its rating from GP to PG-13 two decades after its initial release. After this film, there would be no more cases for Mr. Tibbs, at least not the one portrayed by Sidney Poitier. (Howard Rollins would play him in a 1980s TV series opposite Carroll O'Connor.) He was about to shake off Old Hollywood's perception of him for good.

Buck and the Preacher, the film that allowed this transition, was supposed to have its world premiere on October 24, 1971, at Virginia Union University, a historically Black university in Richmond of which Poitier was a trustee. But, as the *Tri-City Herald* reported, "The only thing missing from the world premiere of 'Buck and the Preacher' . . . will be the film 'Buck and the Preacher.'" The film simply wasn't finished in post. So, *The Organization*, which had opened the week before, took its place. Audiences would have to wait six more months to see Harry Belafonte's bare ass, as big as day, on the silver screen.

CHAPTER 3

STOP! OR MY DIRECTOR WILL SHOOT!: A HOLLYWOOD MYSTERY

Ossie Davis and Melvin Van Peebles weren't the only African-American directors to shoot a Hollywood studio movie on location in 1969. In addition to adapting *The Landlord* and co-writing *The Angel Levine*, Bill Gunn had also written an original screenplay for Warner Bros. called *Stop!* The studio financed the film for $400,000 and, as they did for Gordon Parks, allowed the screenwriter to direct his own film. Officially, the timing of the deal made Gunn the second African-American director, but Davis and Van Peebles already had their films in the can when Gunn started shooting in Puerto Rico on December 1, 1969.

More importantly, Davis and Van Peebles got their films released. *Stop!* was shelved by its studio with no explanation, despite numerous articles announcing and promoting its upcoming 1970 release. Outside of a few museum screenings several decades later and a raggedy bootleg burn available online, Gunn's film has never been screened for a general, wide audience. As a result, it's very difficult to see the debut of five-time Oscar-nominated cinematographer Owen Roizman, not to mention impossible to watch *Stop!* in the pristine way he and Gunn intended it to be seen.

Why did Warner Bros. put a stop to *Stop!?* Did they believe it would be a box office failure? Unlike *Cotton Comes to Harlem* and *Watermelon Man*, Gunn's film was not specifically about the Black experience—it concerned itself with a White couple's marital problems, and a Black character doesn't factor in the plot until two-thirds of the way through its run time. This in itself was not a surprise for anyone familiar with Gunn's 1959 play, *Marcus in the High Grass*, referred to by Steve Ryfle in *Cineaste* magazine as "the first play about white people by a Negro writer." Considering that *Stop!* was green-lit before Hollywood started pitching films exclusively to Black audiences, its potential appeal to White moviegoers would have been a major selling point.

Was it the rating that scared Warners? *Stop!* was given an X rating by the MPAA, but *Midnight Cowboy* had just been crowned Best Picture by the Academy Awards, bringing a legitimacy to the X rating that would soon be negated by the porn industry's parodic use of it. Gunn's star, former Maine resident Edward Bell, told the *Bangor Daily News* that he anticipated it would be X-rated, eliminating any surprise when it was. And two of the studio's most controversial 1971 releases, Stanley Kubrick's *A Clockwork Orange* and Ken Russell's *The Devils*, would originally be slapped with X ratings, proving a lack of MPAA skittishness on WB's part. Those films have far more incendiary material than *Stop!* and would both be pulled by the studio later on, but at least they were released.

One theory that's been floated is that *Stop!* was shelved due to its gay subject matter. Like *Midnight Cowboy*, the film's homoerotic content earned its MPAA rating. However, *Stop!* is more explicit in depicting sex between men. Gunn's camera is as fixated on the nude male form as it is on the female (the director was a gay man who occasionally slept with women). The plot gives him reason to depict both. His protagonists, Michael (Bell) and Lee (Linda Marsh), are in a loveless marriage that is crumbling while they're visiting Puerto Rico. Lee catches Michael having sex with a prostitute in an explicit scene. Later, when the couple decides to try swinging with interracial couple Richard (Richard Dow) and Marlene (Marlene Clark), a drug-fueled sex scene between Richard and Michael skirts the line of the latter's consent. There is also a lesbian sex scene between the two women.

By 1970, American moviegoers had borne witness to those Swedish "art films" like *I Am Curious Yellow*, movies that offered a bucket of pretentiousness to go with a soupçon of explicit nudity and sex. But that sex was almost always heterosexual. *Stop!* is certainly as avant-garde and arty as the European films of its time (Gunn was a fan of Antonioni and Fellini). Like Antonioni's famous films of the 1960s, *Stop!* is a boring slog through the ennui of its privileged White characters.

As strange, slow, and weird as *Stop!* is, that's no excuse for shelving it. The studio had obviously read the script and enjoyed it enough to offer $1.2 million for Gunn and his cast to make another film should this one make back its money. Additionally, in October 1970, Warners donated Gunn's outtakes to

New York University for its students to use as guides on how to edit features. *Stop!* was already finished but had yet to be released. Then, suddenly, it disappeared, supposedly after the studio refused the director's cut and butchered the film on their own.

There may never be a definitive explanation for Warners' decision, at least not from their side. Gunn's 1981 roman à clef novel, *Rhinestone Sharecropping*, is a take on the making of *Stop!* and may provide a thinly veiled interpretation of Gunn's opinion. In 2018, the film's producer, Paul Heller, told *Cineaste* magazine, "I just don't think they ever felt it would find an audience. The eroticism just overwhelmed what could have been a tight character study. It was too heavy-handed, too intense for its own sake. I was totally supportive of [Gunn] and did everything I could to help the picture get made and also get a release for it. But when it was finished, they just didn't want it."

That's as good an explanation as history is going to get. Still, one wonders what types of stories African-American filmmakers would have been allowed to tell in the Blaxploitation era had *Stop!* been a hit.

1971
1971

HOW It GOt DONe iN '71

1971
1971

ho's the Black private dick that's a sex machine to all the chicks? American moviegoers found out in 1971. They also learned about a "Baadasssss nigger" comin' back to collect some dues, courtesy of Melvin Van Peebles. And on television in Chicago, you could bet your last money that a new music show was about to take Black America by storm.

In 1971, Warner Bros., Paramount, and United Artists were all owned by enormous non-movie companies (Kinney, Gulf + Western, and Transamerica, respectively). They were all in financial trouble, as were 20th Century–Fox and MGM. Though 20th Century–Fox had scandalous X-rated hits like 1970's *Myra Breckinridge* and *Beyond the Valley of the Dolls*, their box office wasn't robust enough to keep them from a potential merger with the latter. Warners was still afloat with its own X-rated hit in 1971, however, Stanley Kubrick's *A Clockwork Orange*.

George Lucas, one of the architects of the box office blockbuster, made his debut in March with the strange sci-fi film *THX 1138*. The first IMAX movies were shown in May. And Sean Connery returned to the role that made him famous; his James Bond walked through *Diamonds Are Forever* before Connery resigned a second time from the role. Clint Eastwood, once considered to play 007, was instead appearing as a corrupt San Francisco cop in the movie San Francisco native Pauline Kael called "a right-wing fantasy," *Dirty Harry*. There was also *Fiddler on the Roof*, which would fiddle its way to the number one box office spot when 1971 ended.

On the idiot box, Norman Lear made history in January by introducing audiences to Carroll O'Connor's famous bigot, Archie Bunker, on the CBS sitcom *All in the Family*. The show was such a success that Archie's trademark chair is currently in the Smithsonian.

The Bunkers' neighbor on their street in Queens were the Jeffersons, a Black family who would later make a bit of history of their own when they got their own show four years later.

Over in Chicago, a DJ named Don Cornelius was putting together a scrappy little dance and music show, a Black answer to Dick Clark's *American Bandstand*. In a few months, the show's hometown success would allow it to expand to over eighteen urban markets. It had a regular series of dancers, performances by soul and R&B singers like Joe Tex, and a game called the Scramble Board that future employee Rosie Perez once told me was fixed for its contestants. Of course, I'm talking about *Soul Train*.

In sports, Satchel Paige, who would be paid tribute in a Blaxploitation-era film a few years later, became the first Negro League player to be inducted into the Baseball Hall of Fame in August. A far more fraught event occurred in March, when undefeated boxers Joe Frazier and Muhammad Ali met in the "Fight of the Century," the first of their three grueling boxing matches. It had been three and a half years since Ali was stripped of his titles for being a conscientious objector to the Vietnam War. Pro-war fans were in Frazier's camp, making him a variation of the people's champion. Though the two boxers were very evenly matched, Frazier kept his title after going the distance and winning by decision.

The Vietnam War was still raging and still unpopular in 1971. Two hundred thousand people marched on Washington to protest it in May. A Harris Poll had opposition to the war at 60 percent. Making matters worse, the *New York Times*' publication of the Pentagon Papers let the public know that Lyndon B. Johnson's reasons for going to war were different than what the public had been led to believe.

Like many a Blaxploitation hero, President Nixon started his "War on Drugs." Unlike a Blaxploitation hero, his actions wouldn't get drugs off the street. They did, however, set the stage for decades of disproportionate prosecutions of Black and brown people.

The Black Panthers endorsed Sweet Sweetback. They also suffered a split in leadership, with Eldridge Cleaver exiting the party. Huey P. Newton went to China in 1971, a year before his nemesis Nixon did. Panthers co-founder Bobby Seale was acquitted of murder charges.

While Seale returned to Oakland, Whitey returned to the moon via the *Apollo 14* mission. Black people like Gil Scott-Heron's "sister Nell" were still broke and living in many of the neighborhoods we were about to see on movie screens everywhere.

While Stevie Wonder released an album of songs written by him and his then wife Syreeta Wright, his fellow Motown alum Marvin Gaye released perhaps the most important social statement the label would produce. *What's Going On*, which Berry Gordy didn't want to release, was Gaye's magnum opus, a concept album of songs whose lyrics laid bare the Black experience in America. References to poverty, church, love, friendship, Vietnam, joy, the environment, drugs, and the general struggle of being Black in America were sprinkled throughout the lyrics. Its success gave Motown artists the freedom to write and sing about social issues, something Stevie Wonder would excel at during the 1970s.

Gaye's masterpiece "Inner City Blues" closes the album, and listening to it, one can hear its influence in several Blaxploitation songs, including the one Gaye would compose a year later. Motown would become the primary label of Blaxploitation soundtracks, with songs by Martha Reeves and Willie Hutch underscoring the era's biggest stars.

CHAPTER 4

"SOULSVILLE," *SHAFT,* AND LONG-TIME WOMEN

On January 11, 1971, *Shaft* began shooting on location in New York City. It was a ten-week shoot, with Richard Roundtree and company appearing in Hell's Kitchen, Greenwich Village, Harlem, and Times Square. Director Gordon Parks's second fiction feature was adapted by White writer Ernest Tidyman, the source novel's author, with some additional screenplay work by a credited John D. F. Black. Tidyman would ultimately write seven Shaft novels and would reteam with Parks for the film version of *Shaft's Big Score!* in 1972. The screenwriter's other adaptation, *The French Connection*, was also filming in New York City at the time, continuing a shoot that began in November 1970.

Meanwhile, a different drama was brewing in Hollywood. MGM, the studio that put up *Shaft*'s retainer fee, was in talks to merge with the equally floundering 20th Century–Fox. Bloated budgets, movie musical flops like *Hello, Dolly!*, and corporate raiders were contributing to the potential bankruptcy of several studios. To paraphrase Mae West, insolvency worked at Paramount by day and at Fox all night. The year before, it seemed like Mae's old studio would go down in flames under the auspices of barely thirty-year-old Stanley Jaffe. But Paramount scored a major hit with 1970's *Love Story* and did very well in the TV market. Such successes ensured it would survive to give the world one of the trashiest Blaxploitation movies, 1975's *Mandingo*.

On the same day the *Los Angeles Times* ran a piece extoling the virtues of Jaffe's financial brilliance at Paramount (complete with very catty commentary from its subject), it ran a one-column article about MGM selling off seventy acres of its Culver City lot for $10 million. Thanks to Kirk Kerkorian and MGM president James T. Aubrey Jr.'s brutal dismantling of the studio's fabled lot, there wasn't much more MGM to sell. It had already been shorn of sixty-eight acres back in October 1970, a few months after the rights for *Shaft* had been obtained. "It has been learned by the [*Los Angeles*] *Times* that the Kerkorian Group is quite resolute in its quest to take over Fox," wrote Robert E. Dallos. A meeting with Aubrey and the world-renowned creator of Fox, Darryl F. Zanuck, sent so many tongues wagging in Hollywood that Zanuck had to deny he'd been bought out.

Two weeks later, the MGM-Fox deal was dead. On January 27, 1971, Aubrey abruptly issued a statement saying, "The decision to withdraw from further discussion at present is the result of the failure of Fox management to respond favorably to our initial proposals. Although we were given to understand that the board of directors of Fox was to consider our suggestion, they have to date remained silent." Perhaps that seventy-acre sale had staved off the vultures hoping to pick at Leo the Lion's carcass.

Despite his earlier acknowledgment of a meeting with Aubrey, Zanuck denied any notion of a merger after this news came out: "Let me categorically state for what I hope will be the last time: there have not been, are not now and are not scheduled for the future any discussions concerning a merger or any other type of combination between our two companies." Soon after, Zanuck fired his own kid, Richard, who was the president of Fox during this debacle.

MGM and Fox were connected in one way, however: Ernest Tidyman's screenplays were about to bring them two enormous, Oscar-winning hits.

Not every studio was in dire financial straits. American International Pictures, or AIP as it was affectionately known, announced a thirty-film lineup for 1971. The studio's strange, stylized "Ai" logo, trapped in a circle in the sky, would appear on many Blaxploitation and Blaxploitation-adjacent films later, an appropriate place for the studio created by James Nicholson and Samuel Z. Arkoff on April 2, 1954. AIP was known for movies that catered to the youth market; Arkoff was responsible for creating the beach party and biker films genres in the 1960s and produced numerous horror movies, including Michael Landon's *I Was a Teenage Werewolf.* AIP was also the home of Roger Corman, whose Edgar Allan Poe movies with Vincent Price were major successes.

Arkoff had the greatest surname of any studio head (sorry, Mssrs. Selznick and Zanuck,) and he put it to good use. The "ARKOFF formula," he explained, was what guided the movies they produced. It stood for:

Action (exciting, entertaining drama)
Revolution (novel or controversial themes and ideas)
Killing (a modicum of violence)
Oratory (notable dialogue and speeches)
Fantasy (acted-out fantasies common to the audience)
Fornication (sex appeal for young adults)

One wonders which of those corresponded to their 1970 version of *Wuthering Heights* starring a future James Bond, Timothy Dalton. Certainly not fornication; it's rated G.

AIP was responsible for the Pam Grier tetralogy of *Coffy*, *Foxy Brown*, *Friday Foster*, and *Sheba, Baby*. She was also their receptionist before her career kicked off, and even in between films! Grier was an air force brat, born on May 26, 1949, in Winston-Salem, North Carolina, to Clarence Grier, a biracial mechanic and technical sergeant who could pass for White, and Gwendolyn Sylvia, a nurse. Her grandfather Raymundo "Daddy Ray" Parrilla was of Filipino descent. Due to her father's military service, Grier relocated frequently during her childhood, from Columbus, Ohio, to England. She also spent time on farms riding (and falling off) horses. These experiences gave her a love for visiting exotic places and for animals.

It was Daddy Ray who inadvertently kick-started her love for movies; when she was seven, he gave her a dime to go see *Godzilla*. Grier's desire to go to film school and be an actress stemmed from the movies she saw. Money was an issue in terms of attending a prestigious East Coast university. So, in 1967, when she was eighteen, Grier enrolled in Denver's Metropolitan State College. To earn money, she worked in a record store and as a receptionist for KHOW, a local radio station.

One day, her boss invited her to participate in the Miss KHOW beauty pageant. In her book, *Foxy*, Grier acknowledged that she had not thought of herself as a great beauty, but she entered because "this is what women did." She was a very inexperienced pageant entrant—for the swimsuit competition, she put her one-piece bathing suit on *backward*—but she won the first prize and $100.

"Maybe I won because I was the only participant," she wrote, "but that's beside the point."

It was another beauty pageant that got Grier to Hollywood. The Miss Colorado Universe Pageant, to be exact. She wanted to be "Miss Africa," but that was taken. So she entered as Miss India (nobody knew the difference) and managed to win the swimsuit competition ("This time, I'd managed to get my suit on frontward!" she wrote) and the evening gown competition. She also won the formal gown competition. However, when it came time to crown Miss Colorado Universe, she lost to a White woman and came in second place. It almost caused a riot, but it got Grier $1,000 and the notice of agents David Baumgarten and Marty Klein.

"There's a movement in Hollywood right now," Klein told her. He represented a young fashion model named Richard Roundtree, whom he'd just signed up to do *Shaft*. "This would be the perfect time for you to come to Hollywood and become an actress."

So Grier and her aunt Mignonne drove west to Hollywood. There, she got gigs singing backup for Bobby Womack and Stevie Wonder. She also got that receptionist job at AIP, as well as another reception gig at a talent agency called APA. That was where agent Hal Gefsky asked her if she'd ever considered acting. She'd briefly appeared in a cameo in Russ Meyer and Roger Ebert's *Beyond the Valley of the Dolls*, but that was hardly acting.

"Me, an actress?" Grier asked incredulously.

Roger Corman, former kingmaker at AIP, was seeking pretty girls to star in productions for his newly formed outlet, New World Pictures. Gefsky thought she could do it. When asked what the film was about, Gefsky replied, "It's about women in a prison in the jungle. Bondage, torture, attempted escape, punishment, drug addiction, machine guns, sex. The usual," he told her.

The job paid $500 a week for six weeks. Grier went to meet with Corman and director Jack Hill, who hired her on the spot. Even so, she refused to give up her receptionist gigs, opting to return to them afterward so she could keep a steady job. Unbeknownst to her, acting was about to replace reception work as her means of employment.

In 1971, Grier went to the Philippines to make *The Big Doll House*. "Say hello to your relatives there!" she was told by her aunt. When that film was done, the studio asked her to stay and do another film. Eventually, Grier shot a trio of "chicks in chains" (women's prison) movies for New World Pictures before returning to the States.

Grier made her speaking-role debut in Hill's *The Big Doll House* (1971) alongside Sid Haig, with whom she'd make five more movies, and Kathryn

Loder, who'd later play her psychopathic nemesis in *Foxy Brown*. As Lucian, Loder's an incredibly entertaining sicko here, too. Usually, it's the warden who's into all the sadistic things that go down in this type of picture. Here, it's also Warden Dietrich's right-hand woman. Lucian tortures prisoners to death with a terrifying series of methods ranging from electroshock to live cobra. Before inmates graduate to Lucian's lethal punishments, they're strung up in cages outside the prison so the sun can roast their skin.

Miss Grier plays Grear, a rough-and-tumble lesbian whose latest prison side piece is smack addict Harrad (Brooke Mills), an unpredictable wild card imprisoned for infanticide. They're in the same cell as Alcott (Roberta Collins), political prisoner Bodine (Pat Woodell), Ferina (Gina Stuart) and Ferina's very vocal pet cat. Scrawled on the wall behind Ferina's bunk, in big letters, is graffiti reading, "A dead bee makes no honey."

Into this den of iniquity comes the newly widowed Collier (Judy Brown). She caught her rich, eye-patch-wearing husband screwing the house boy. When she opted to see if the house boy was worth it, her husband decided to kill her. "To hell with that!" Collier tells her cellmates. "So I went to get his gun, which he keeps under his pillow. And I put one right through his patch!"

"Good for you!" yells Grear. "That son of a bitch!"

The same tropes that have existed in chicks-in-chains movies since 1955's *Women's Prison* are present. There's the wicked warden, there are outbursts of torture and violence, catfights, and, in the climax, the women band together against a common enemy to attempt a prison break. These Philippines-set flicks added the nudity, sex, and graphic violence they couldn't show in 1955, as well as the revolution plotlines. There's always a revolution of some type going on outside the prison walls.

One thing remained constant: no matter how decrepit the prison is supposed to be, the women always look like they just came out of the salon. It's as if every prisoner had been issued appointments with Vidal Sassoon along with their uniforms. Everyone is tall, lanky, and sexy. The junkie even gets to do a ballet number—Hill added it because Mills was a professional dancer. And everyone gets to shine in the action scenes, even the cat.

As for Sid Haig, he plays Harry, a horny guy who brings produce to the prisoners and moonshine to the guards. He's joined by Fred (Jerry Franks), his equally horny accomplice. They both want to score, but they're quite inept and stupid. Grear tempts Harry by crushing his hand with a body part that's kept salaciously hidden below the screen, and Alcott corners Fred after catching him watching her in the shower. "Get it up or I'll cut it off," she tells a terrified Fred when he realizes he's going to be the submissive one in this encounter.

Grier showed enough promise here for her to be cast in two other prison films while in the Philippines, *Women in Cages* (1971), which retains many of the actors from *The Big Doll House*, but in vastly different roles; and Jack Hill's 1972 film, *The Big Bird Cage*, a semi-sequel of sorts that's more a parody than a straight-on prison movie. These films had a major effect on Quentin Tarantino. He named Patricia Arquette's character in *True Romance* after Grier's character in *Women in Cages*, and in *Jackie Brown*, QT reunited Grier with Haig but reversed the dynamic. In their pairings, Grier usually got the best of Haig; in *Jackie Brown*, he plays the judge sentencing the titular character to jail. As he does, Grier can be heard singing "Long Time Woman," the theme song of *The Big Doll House*, on the soundtrack.

In Gene Siskel's very short pan of *The Big Doll House*, he references one of Grier's song lyrics about her character's prison sentence: "In the first two minutes of this sextravaganza about a South American jail full of Naughty Mariettas, one of the brighter inmates says, 'Ninety-nine years is a long time.' So were those two minutes." Siskel may not have liked it, but audiences did. *The Big Doll House* made $3 million at the box office. Pam Grier was off to a promising start on the silver screen.

When he was cast as John Shaft, Richard Roundtree was twenty-nine years old and had been in numerous stage performances for the Negro Ensemble Company, a prestigious group based in New York City. Since 1967, they provided a stage for writers such as August Wilson and actors from Denzel Washington to Roscoe Lee Browne. Roundtree had just finished appearing in a production of *The Great White Hope*, in the role that would earn James Earl Jones a Tony Award and an Oscar nomination.

Born in New Rochelle on July 9, 1942, Roundtree had his first brush with success playing football for the town high school's famous team. After a brief stint at Southern Illinois University, he dropped out. In 1963, he became a model for the renowned and Black-owned Ebony Fashion Fair. In 1967, he began working for the Negro Ensemble, where he stayed until Marty Klein got him his debut movie role.

As a former model, he cast a very striking figure, a gorgeous specimen of brother whose face was crowned with a short, impeccable Afro, bracketed by killer sideburns, and underlined by a mustache that meant business. A Black man with a mustache onscreen wasn't common at the time. Even Jim Brown, whose muscular 'stache became one of his trademarks in Blaxploitation films, was usually clean-shaven in movies like 1969's *100 Rifles*. Roundtree also knew how to maximize the attire he paraded around in (and got out of) onscreen. The complete package arrived fully assembled (even if the mustache was fake) on the frigid January morning he stepped on location.

The Deuce, or Forty-Second Street, is where viewers are first introduced to John Shaft. After Leo the Lion roars his approval from inside the MGM logo, Gordon Parks's camera strolls leisurely down the block. His protagonist emerges from the subway on Forty-Second and Broadway in perfect time with the opening wah-wah guitar of Isaac Hayes's theme song. Dialogue heard later in the film clocks Shaft's arrival on the scene at around 8:00 a.m. He's wearing his iconic attire: a three-quarter-length leather coat ("the Shaft coat," as it would come to be known), his blazer, and his turtleneck. He moves with the quick stride of the typical New Yorker, fast and confident, with no time for bullshit. The preternatural sync between man, attitude, and movie score makes this one of the greatest entrances in film history.

Shaft takes the long way to his office, as if he knew his theme needed to be heard in full. A montage of people and places populate the screen. A picket line marches by, and one's eye is drawn to a sign that echoes one of the Gray Lady's slogans: "I got my job through the *New York Times*." Times Square unfolds before us, but this isn't the Disneyfied Times Square of today; it's a hellscape full of porn theaters, hustlers who sell hot merchandise, hookers, drug pushers, the downtrodden, and tourists just ripe for mugging. It was a different time, to be sure.

A time when the Deuce was a cool place to be.

By using real locations like Caffè Reggio, Café Borgia, Arthur's Tavern, and No Name Bar in the Village, and exteriors on Forty-Second and 125th Streets, Shaft plays like a time capsule for a city that, like the Hollywood studios, was slipping into financial insolvency. It's four years from the famous New York *Daily News* headline "Ford to City: Drop Dead," but in some scenes one can see New York City's on life support. Times Square is no exception.

En route to his office, Shaft is almost run over by one of New York's finest hacks. Like Dustin Hoffman's immortal "I'm walkin' here" near-miss with a cab in *Midnight Cowboy* (a film with Oscar-nominated editing by *Shaft*'s editor, Hugh A. Robertson), this was not scripted. Parks told Roundtree to jaywalk with impunity because his character was too cool to look both ways before crossing the street. Having his lead actor get run over as the first scene was being filmed would have changed the trajectory of both Roundtree's and Parks's careers. Thankfully, Shaft is a professional jaywalker.

The first person Shaft converses with on his early-morning route is Marty the newspaper man (Lee Steele). Marty is blind, but he "sees" everything going on around here. He has a stutter, and tufts of gray hair flow with purpose from under his hat. His sunglasses are as dark as his sense of humor. "Shaft, two guys were lookin' for you, like ten minutes ago," he says. Robertson cuts to a wonderful close-up of the two men, framed as if intimate secrets were about to be revealed.

"Harlem cats?" Shaft inquires of the guys looking for him.

"How in the hell should I know?" replies Marty. "Everybody looks the same to me!" The close-up sells the punch line.

The scene ends with Shaft emerging from behind Parks's directing credit, a not-so-subtle nod to the well-established notion that the director had modeled Roundtree's image on his own. "Shaft was Gordon," said culture critic and filmmaker Nelson George in *Unstoppable*, a 2005 Starz cable documentary that profiled Parks, Melvin Van Peebles, and Ossie Davis, pointing out how well Parks was able to navigate between Black and White spaces. "Shaft had that mobility to move from the Village to midtown to uptown, when Black people were just beginning to have that mobility."

Shaft's morning walk continues with a visit to his regular shoeshine man. "Coupla dudes from uptown looking for you," he says, echoing Marty's information and adding the visual details that will allow Shaft to get the jump on the men. "One was wearing a funky plaid coat. The other was sharp. Fifty-dollar shoes." (Those shoes would be worth $347 now.) "Now you'll be able to go out and make something of yourself," the shine man tells Shaft upon finishing. Shaft pays him handsomely for the lowdown.

The next character Shaft meets is Lieutenant Vic (Charles Cioffi), the police officer type who keeps tabs on the hero in detective fiction. Vic makes the third mention of those cats who've been looking for Shaft while setting up the dynamics of their relationship: there's a begrudging, no-bullshit admiration that's mutual. When an attempt to lean on Shaft for information yields nothing, he's warned that the possible mob war between Blacks and Italians in Harlem may find its way across 110th Street and well into downtown Manhattan.

After Shaft overpowers the two goons who've been looking for him (the funky plaid coat guy takes an impressively rendered dive through a fourth-floor office window), he learns that they've been sent to take him to see Bumpy Jonas (Moses Gunn). If the name sounds familiar, it's because Jonas is based on real-life Harlem gangster Bumpy Johnson. Johnson, and fellow Harlem gangster Frank Lucas, would provide inspiration for several Blaxploitation mobsters, and would also be portrayed decades later by Laurence Fishburne and Denzel Washington, respectively.

Shaft has a basic detective novel plot: a private eye has a case he needs to solve, one that will put him in danger and in touch with several strange supporting characters. Here, Bumpy Jonas's daughter has been kidnapped and he wants Shaft to find her. Jonas believes that either the Italian Mafia or a crew of Black revolutionaries led by Ben Buford (Christopher St. John) may have taken her as retribution. So instead of a foxy femme fatale seeking help, as Sam Spade or Philip Marlowe normally would have received, Shaft gets a weepy gangster and a teenage girl to save.

But don't feel badly for John Shaft. As his theme song goes, he's a "sex machine to all the chicks." Shaft has two ladies, Ellie (Gwenn Mitchell), his main Black squeeze, and Linda (Margaret Warncke), a White hippie he meets in the No Name Bar. Sleeping with White women is par for the course in Blaxploitation films, but very few of these ladies get to be as hilariously mouthy as Linda. After being summarily dismissed by Shaft, she responds to his request to shut the apartment door by telling him to "close it yourself, shitty!" It's such a good line that it will return as the film's final words, uttered by Shaft in a different context as all hell breaks loose behind him.

Shaft provided the blueprint for many Blaxploitation movies to follow. There's the tough, macho hero and his sexy ladies, colorful side characters deeply rooted in their neighborhood, a Harlem location, scenes with cops both racist and cooperative, a subplot featuring a Black militant group, and, last but certainly not least, a score and theme song by a famous African-American soul/R&B artist. Stax legend Isaac Hayes provided those last two items. After being rejected for the role of John Shaft, Hayes cosplayed him on the best-selling soundtrack album, giving the character his theme song and his walking-around music.

Most of *Shaft*'s score features instrumentals used to evoke everything from a violent shoot-out to scenes inside Greenwich Village's cafés and bars, to a sexy, nude love scene in Shaft's apartment at 55 Jane Street. But when Hayes's baritone comes through the speakers, it means business. The songwriter's voice on his masterpiece, "Soulsville," mournfully underscores the visuals reminiscent of Parks's photography as Shaft goes "uptown" to Harlem. Hayes also tells us who Shaft is in that theme song and advises him to "do his thing" in a later scene. The music, editing, directing, and cinematography (the last of these by Urs Furrer) form a powerful behind-the-camera team, working together to ensure that there's very little fat on this lean thriller. Hayes's score would earn him two Grammy Awards with his arranger, Johnny Allen, and two Oscar nominations.

Shaft finished filming on March 12, 1971. It opened on July 2, 1971, at the DeMille Theater in Times Square, where it played for forty-eight straight hours. The DeMille gets a cameo in the film—Shaft tries to get a cab in front of it— which must have been quite meta for viewers to see. *New York Times* critic Vincent Canby, who liked the film, called it "a good Saturday night movie," and he would have known; he saw it at 10:50 p.m. on Saturday night during that aforementioned marathon at the DeMille.

Along with his fellow New York critics Judith Crist and Jeffrey Lyons, Canby was in the critical minority. Most reviews of *Shaft* were mixed to negative. The *Chicago Tribune*'s Gene Siskel gave it two stars out of four, and his rival across the street, Roger Ebert, gave it two and a half out of four. Ebert's words are worth quoting; they point out that, had all things been equal in Hollywood for African-American actors, Black private-eye films would have existed decades before *Shaft*. "Hell, a private-eye movie without clichés wouldn't be worth the price of admission," Ebert wrote in the *Chicago Sun-Times*. "We don't go to Westerns to see cowboys riding ostriches. The strength of Parks's movie is his willingness to let his hero fully inhabit the private-eye genre, with all of its obligatory violence, blood, obscenity, and plot gimmicks. The weakness of 'Shaft,' I suspect, is that Parks is not very eager to inhabit that world along with his hero."

Several Black writers didn't like it either, although Parks's former employer, *Essence* magazine, gave it a good review. Under a *New York Times* headline that announced "A Black Critic's View of Shaft," Clayton Riley called the film "A Black Movie for White Audiences." Though he expressed much admiration for Parks, he called his film "a disaster" and proceeded to describe it as some sort of minstrel show whose success would prevent more serious Black films from being made. "Sam Spade is all right for the field hands because the White folks don't want to carry that weight any more," he wrote. "But how seriously would 'Five Easy Pieces' have been taken with a Black pianist as the weary protagonist? I mean niggers get tired of playing the piano, too."

Parks took this article so personally that he wrote a rebuttal in the *Times'* Letters to the Editor section. It ran a month after the original piece. "I share Riley's desire to see black actors playing roles now assumed by actors such as Jack Nicholson or Dustin Hoffman," he wrote, "but I don't think the choice for black people is limited to either 'Five Easy Pieces' or Stepin Fetchit." Further, he accused the critic of ulterior motives: "Perhaps he just believes that a black writer attacking a black movie has got to be more provocative than a black writer praising a black movie. This saddens me."

And then Parks got real salty, ending the letter thusly: "I will hold Riley in higher esteem when he gains more experience as a reviewer of all filmmakers— not as a self-appointed, executioner of blacks who have survived the purgatorial haunts of Hollywood to become directors and producers."

Also throwing shade at the production, though not in as public a forum, was Ernest Tidyman. He hated Hayes's score, mocking it at parties. He hated what he called the "fake Black slang" dialogue that had been added by White screenwriter John D. F. Black. He felt they'd made Shaft too smooth, distancing him from the novel's far meaner and more brutal incarnation. Tidyman wasn't so offended that he turned down accolades from the NAACP, nor did it stop him from reteaming with Parks and Roundtree for an adaptation of another of his novels, *Shaft's Big Score!*

MGM didn't give a shit about any of this infighting between Black intellectuals nor complaints from its ungrateful White screenwriter. A lot of people came out to see *Shaft*, turning a $1.5 million investment into the twelfth-highest grossing film of 1971. It practically saved the studio, buying it a few more years before the next financial disaster befell it. And their *Shaft* luck was about to get even better.

Hayes's work on the film earned Oscar nominations for song and score at the 1972 Academy Awards. His performance of "Theme from *Shaft*" on the show remains the Blackest and most spectacular musical number to ever grace the Oscars. Decked out in the full bare-chested and gold-chained regalia of his

Black Moses character, Hayes glided across the stage as enough smoke to flavor a Texas barbecue enveloped him and his dancers. Hayes told those polite White folks in the audience about the "bad mother-shut-yo-mouth" who was John Shaft. For his troubles, Hayes was awarded the Best Song Oscar, making him the third African-American to win an Academy Award and the first to win for a non-acting category.

"Theme from *Shaft*" would have a life of its own, remaining in the cultural zeitgeist long enough to be covered by everyone from Bart Simpson two decades later to a disco-era parody by Cookie Monster from *Sesame Street*, decked out in Ike Hayes's outrageous attire and a fake beard. Roundtree would appear as John Shaft a total of twelve times, including in a TV series, two sequels, and two remakes, the latest of which, 2019's *Shaft*, has all the homophobia and misogyny that was missing from the 1971 original.

As successful as John Shaft was as a character, he was preceded in movie theaters two months earlier by a vastly different Black character, one Clayton Riley championed in his *New York Times* takedown. That character's name was Sweet Sweetback, owner of one baadasssss song.

CHAPTER 5
COMING BACK TO COLLECT SOME DUES

In her 1976 *CLA Journal* article, "Sweetback: The Black Hero and Universal Myth," Norma R. Jones asks, "Does the Black artist have the freedom of 'art for art's sake' as long as Blacks are the victims of oppression?" It's a question that often gets raised, along with several others, when evaluating a controversial work made by a Black person. Does it harm the culture? What does it say to non-Black consumers of the art? Should there solely be positive images and depictions of Black people in films, plays, and literature?

When Melvin Van Peebles made *Sweet Sweetback's Baadasssss Song*, he did not consider any potential restrictions from the powers that be prohibiting his art. He saw it as a response to years of studio system depictions of his people as toms, coons, mulattos, mammies, and bucks. When asked what movies upset him in this regard, he said, "Every damn last one of them." The roles that Sidney Poitier, Ossie Davis, Juano Hernandez, Paul Robeson, James Edwards, and other character actors of color played may have been dignified, but they were rarely afforded the kind of sexual prowess or desire that someone like Paul Newman got in his films. Unless, of course, they were being seen as a threat to White women.

The funny thing is that all the "bougie" Black writers who took swipes at Van Peebles for being a purveyor of lowbrow depictions of worthless Negroes never took into account that, according to Van Peebles, he'd had "a happily bourgeois childhood." Before he made the fateful trip to San Francisco to work on cable cars, he'd grown up on the South Side of Chicago. Van is actually his middle name, not part of his last name. "It's on the old birth certificate," he said of the document issued on August 21, 1932. "I think my mother just thought it sounded aristo."

Van Peebles graduated from Ohio Wesleyan University in 1953 with a degree in English lit, then joined the air force, where he served for three and a half years. That led him to San Francisco and his first attempts at filmmaking. By this time, he had two children and a wife. He held down three jobs and even took in a roomer to help cover the bills. One of Van Peebles's most famous anecdotes involves his wife asking, "What would you say if I told you I was sleeping with the roomer?"

"I'd raise his rent," Van Peebles replied. This fits in with his philosophy that one can't get something for nothing. Everything costs.

The way Van Peebles tells it, the origin of *Sweet Sweetback's Baadasssss Song* began with a trip to the Mojave Desert back in February 1970. This would have placed the timeframe a few months after *Watermelon Man* wrapped filming, and three months before its release. The desert trip was designed to get back to nature so that inspiration would strike. To hasten that inspiration, Van Peebles began to stroke his peter in the desert while squatting down behind his car—"semen shock," he called it—while the muses impatiently waited for the inevitable biological outcome.

"Anyway, what am I apologizing for?" Van Peebles wrote in a retelling of this story. "They have electro-shock, so why not semen-shock. I even saw this jive-ass movie where the doctor used racial-shock." Whatever methods, sordid or otherwise, Van Peebles employed, he wound up with a screenplay for *Sweetback*, turned in to his typist and finished on March 6, 1970, at 6:20 p.m. The only problem was Van Peebles was still under contract to Columbia, and they were not going to make this script. He submitted it anyway.

The executive at Columbia told Van Peebles that *Sweetback* wouldn't fly because they'd just made a movie about the cops and Black people. That movie was director William Wyler's swan song, *The Liberation of L.B. Jones.* Wyler's film was about a Black man, L.B. Jones (Roscoe Lee Browne), whose wife (Lola Falana) had an affair with a White cop named Worth (Anthony Zerbe) and is impregnated. Refusing to cancel his divorce papers, Jones was subsequently castrated, murdered, and hanged on a hook by Worth and his accomplice, Bumpas (Arch Johnson). The film ends with Bumpas being pushed into a thresher by a militant played by Yaphet Kotto. Worth gets away with the murder.

This "wasn't the same thing AT ALL as Sweetback!" wrote Van Peebles.

Anyway, Columbia wasn't going to agree to his terms of final cut or a mixed-race crew. The unions had all the below-the-line jobs wrapped up, and they were not a diverse bunch of individuals. However, they refused to work on pornographic features, so Van Peebles pretended he was making a dirty movie so he could choose the non-union crew he wanted. He then used his formidable marketing skills to come up with the $500,000 budget. Fifty thousand dollars of that money came from Bill Cosby, who had hired Van Peebles to direct episodes of his pre–*Cosby Show* sitcom. There were also funds from workman's comp, which Van Peebles earned after contracting an STI during an unsimulated sex scene.

The next problem was finding someone to play Sweet Sweetback, a man who figured in several sex scenes, would be full-frontal nude, say fewer than forty words in the entire picture, and, most importantly, had to run and *run* and RUN! After being unable to find a satisfactory (by his standards) actor, Van Peebles decided to do it himself. For those keeping count of his roles, he was now the writer, director, producer, score composer, and lead. He was also the primary editor, staring at the rushes so long that he temporarily lost vision in one eye.

"Rated X by an all white jury," scream the posters for *Sweet Sweetback's Baadasssss Song*. A whole lot of marketing gets embellished with a little bit of truth. One of the rules of Jack Valenti's barely three-year-old ratings board, the MPAA, was, if a filmmaker did not want to submit a film to be rated, it would automatically be rated X. The artist would have to self-apply the rating to their film. Which is what Melvin Van Peebles did on the poster, but not before suing the MPAA over this rule.

In his letter to Jack Valenti on March 22, 1971, Van Peebles wrote, "I charge that your film rating body has no right to tell the Black community what it may or may not see . . . White standards shall no longer be imposed on the Black community." This bought the film some free press. Truth be told, this was just clever marketing. *Sweet Sweetback's Baadasssss Song* would have easily gotten an X rating from the MPAA anyway. They gave *Midnight Cowboy* the X in 1969 for far less. In 1971, they also gave it to Stanley Kubrick's *A Clockwork Orange* and Ken Russell's *The Devils*, both of which are comrades in salaciousness with this film.

Continuing his marketing plan, Van Peebles put out a soundtrack album on Stax Records before the movie was released and a how-to manifesto afterward.

The soundtrack featured a then unknown band called Earth Wind & Fire, marking their first major musical contribution. The book, *Sweet Sweetback's Baadasssss Song: A Guerilla Filmmaking Manifesto*, was the definitive word on the film, part mythmaking, part instruction manual. The complete shooting script for the film was also included, giving the numerous detractors fuel for quotes in their articles. Words from Huey P. Newton, an early champion of the movie, open the book. In later editions, contemporary essays were added to provide a new perspective on the material.

Perhaps the key to why Van Peebles made Sweet Sweetback a super stud, the quintessential Black buck whose name is slang for a skilled cocksman, lay in his comment to Mantan Moreland on the set of *Watermelon Man*: "Don't make it too clear that we're saying 'Fuck you.'" Couple that with his line about taking "the stereotypes and kick ass with the motherfuckers," and the filmmaker's intent comes into sharper focus. "You want a big Black sex machine?" Van Peebles seems to ask. "Let me show you how it's done."

To make his point, Van Peebles opened *Sweet Sweetback's Baadasssss Song* with a still-controversial deflowering of the protagonist by a much older sex worker. He's found on the street, hungry and raggedy. After being fed and cleaned up, he gets a job replacing sheets and towels in the brothel. In the next scene, a woman invites the kid to her room and undresses him for sex. Ten-year-old Sweetback is played in this scene by Van Peebles's then fourteen-year-old son, Mario. It's not only the future actor-director's first acting role, it's also his first nude scene and his first sex scene. In a memorable edit, Melvin is seen rising from the same bed his younger incarnation laid down in, symbolically showing that his character "has become a man."

This is clearly a rape scene, with Sweet Sweetback being the victim. It's also a nasty bit of realism, as many of the Black men interviewed for a documentary on *Sweetback* mentioned that they, too, had been sexually initiated in their pre- or early adolescence. Any serious discussion on this very sensitive topic is well out of scope of this book. Regardless, the scene is extremely jarring and uncomfortable to watch. In the United Kingdom, the explicit (and simulated) scene is censored by a black screen for its duration due to the 1978 Protection of Children Act. On the American version of the 2022 Criterion Collection release, it remains uncensored.

Now grown, Sweetback becomes a performer in the brothel's sex show, playing a former lesbian who has been granted a penis by a gay man calling himself the "Good Dyke Fairy Godmother." After his latest show, the cops arrive seeking a man they can drive around so it looks like they have a suspect in an unsolved murder case. Brothel owner Beetle (Simon Chuckster) offers up Sweetback to play the part. Handcuffed in the back of the police cruiser, Sweetback is soon joined by a Black militant named Mu-Mu (Hubert Scales), whom the police pick up during a protest.

Initially, Mu-Mu is handcuffed to Sweetback, but the cops have trouble beating him in that configuration. After they remove the cuffs from Mu-Mu and resume beating him, Sweetback suddenly decides to fight back. Using the empty handcuff like brass knuckles, he beats the two cops unconscious. After he drags Mu-Mu to safety, the militant says, "Thanks, man! Where we goin'?"

"Where'd you get that 'we' shit?" asks Sweetback before taking off.

Sweet Sweetback is now on the run, but he will get help from "the Black community" (as they are credited in the opening titles). Kids set fire to a police car to help him escape, a stunt that was done without any prior approval or permit. A constant refrain of "Where's Sweetback?" is uttered by the cops, yet nobody has an answer, not even Beetle after he is brutally tortured. Several characters talk directly to the camera, either feigning ignorance or lashing out for being asked to rat out a hero. In the film's climax, Sweetback trades clothes with an old wino to throw the cops off his trail. This is "the Black community" according to the filmmaker.

Though he says very little and appears to care only about himself, Sweet Sweetback has several friends in low places. A preacher explains why the cops are after him—Mu-Mu's death was supposed to send a message to the militants. Saving him put a price on Sweetback's head. "I'm going to say a Black Ave Maria for you," the preacher tells him in his last line of dialogue. It's the perfect capper for a character whose first line is "Yes, Lord. Black misery."

Van Peebles's script throws several dilemmas at his character, then has him literally screw his way out of them. To get the lethal handcuffs removed from his wrist, Sweetback offers sexual favors to an old flame. When he and Mu-Mu find themselves at the mercy of a biker gang, Sweetback offers to challenge their White female leader, Big Sadie, to a duel where the battle weapon is "fucking." Big Sadie's earth-shattering orgasm earns Sweetback an escape to a pool hall, where he and Mu-Mu are ambushed and injured before being saved by one of Big Sadie's gang members.

"I can only take one of you," the motorcycle guy says. In a scene designed to show his growth from a narcissistic man to one concerned about the Black revolution, Sweetback gives the ride to Mu-Mu. "He's our future now, Brer," he says to the driver. Mu-Mu rides off into the sunset, and Sweetback runs the other way. And runs. And runs.

"Come on, feet! Do your thing!" goes a song on the *Sweetback* soundtrack, one of many times the film's avant-garde score is in conversation with its protagonist or its audience. As danger gets closer, a "Chorus of Colored Bourgeois Angels" (as they're credited in the script) sing a call-and-response with Sweetback on the soundtrack.

"They bled yo' pappa! They bled yo' mama!" the angels sing.

"But they won't bleed me!" replies Sweetback. "Nigger scared and pretend they don't see!"

The cops chase the injured Sweetback as he tries to make it to the border of Mexico. Van Peebles shoots himself running incredibly long distances in one camera shot, showing off his marathon training. When things look most dire, Sweetback butchers, then eats a lizard (for real—animals *were* harmed in the making of this picture!) and is set upon by bloodhounds sent by the cops as he's trying to cross the Rio Grande into Mexico.

The audience is primed to believe this is the end of the hero, until the camera pulls back to show a slew of dead dogs (also real, though they were already dead when Van Peebles got them) and Sweetback nowhere to be found. Suddenly, an onscreen message flies at the viewer, stating, "WATCH OUT: A BAADASSSSS NIGGER IS COMING BACK TO COLLECT SOME DUES!"

The shock of that statement matched the audience's shock at Sweetback staying alive at the end. Black characters *never* got away with sticking it to the Man in movies before. Of all the reasons Van Peebles gave for making the film, allowing the hero to escape punishment was the ultimate one. It's almost as if the movie was saying: "Finally, we win at the end!"

After a test screening, Van Peebles was approached by several women in the audience who (according to his account) commended him on the film and its sex scenes. "They loved that shot of Sweetback standing there with the hat on digging Beatle and the two detectives," he wrote in his manifesto. "They said at that moment, they would have done anything Sweetback asked." As a result, Sweetback and his ultra-cool hat became the poster's iconic image.

Despite the test audience's reaction, *Sweet Sweetback's Baadasssss Song* almost didn't get a theatrical release at all. To keep total control of his work,

Van Peebles did not even court the major studios who still had much control over theater bookings, opting to lease the film to Jerry Gross's Cinemation Industries. Couple that with the lack of an MPAA ratings certificate and there was no hope for wide release unless, miracle of miracles, it was a hit wherever it ended up playing. Hollywood has "an Achilles pocketbook," to use Van Peebles's phrase, and would jump on the release bandwagon if box office were good.

The best Cinemation could do was to open it at two theaters, Detroit's Grand Circus Theatre on March 31, 1971, and the Coronet Theatre in Atlanta on April 2. Before the weekend was over, lines were around the block. The Grand Circus alone pulled $70,000 in ticket sales in the first week alone. Suddenly, lots of theaters were eager to hear this baadasssss song. Three weeks later, on April 23, *Sweetback* opened in the three places Black people frequented in New York City: Times Square, Harlem, and Greenwich Village.

In Chicago, it opened in the Loop's Oriental Theatre on May 7, which is where Gene Siskel saw it. Five days later, Siskel's two-and-a-half-star review ran in the *Chicago Tribune*. The film was simply called *Sweet Sweetback* there "because of the *Tribune*'s policy of being a 'family paper' not allowing for uncensored obscenities to be printed in its pages." However, this family paper had no such problems printing the word "nigger." Siskel quotes Van Peebles saying, "I wanted [to make] a victorious film. A film where niggers could walk out standing tall instead of avoiding each other's eyes, looking once again like they'd had it."

Though he called it "frequently dreary in its development," Siskel acknowledged, as other White film critics, like *The New Yorker*'s Penelope Gilliatt, did, that this was a film about Black rage and the successful evocation of it. He also stated the obvious: "The artistic quality of *Sweetback* may be beside the point in terms of film history . . . it is doing big business. It has found an enthusiastic audience." That enthusiastic audience resulted in a $15 million box office gross against a $500,000 budget.

Not everybody was swinging and swaying with *Sweet Sweetback*. The biggest tug-of-war of the Blaxploitation era seemed to be between a certain type of "Black intellectual" who loathed the films and their seemingly "lowbrow" skinfolk who made those films a hit. In the *Chicago Tribune*, Black columnist Vernon Jarrett had very strong words for Van Peebles and his movie, calling the film a travesty, a fraud, and an insult to Blacks. His article generated several letters (mostly in support of his position) from readers and a mention in an editorial, though the editors were casting a wider net to include other controversial films, like *Carnal Knowledge*, Mike Nichols's 1971 exploration of sexuality.

"Jarrett finds the movie repellent in its distortion of the black characters and its obsession with weirdos, sex and gore," the editors wrote about *Sweetback*. "Indeed, [Jarrett's complaint] is one which can be made about too many films these days which advertise themselves as incisive commentaries on contemporary life."

Perhaps the most well-known and cited criticism of *Sweet Sweetback's Baadasssss Song* came from the September 1971 edition of *Ebony* magazine. The famous Black periodical featured the cartoon version of the Jackson 5 on the cover, promoting the Hanna-Barbera production that would become the first animated series featuring a predominantly Black cast. The Jackson 5's article followed Dr. Lerone Bennett Jr.'s takedown of *Sweetback*, entitled "The Emancipation Orgasm: Sweetback in Wonderland." Bennett's dismantling is thorough and well-researched, quoting everyone from Jean-Luc Godard to Flip Wilson's drag character, Geraldine (who, like Sweetback, did a disservice to the Black community, according to Bennett).

Interrupting the article are three ads for menthol cigarettes and one ad for "the poor man's champagne," Champale Malt Liquor. And yet, the movies are the more dangerous product being targeted to impressionable Negroes! Anyway, Bennett calls television and movies "two of the most powerful media developed by man." Then he correctly notes that none of the Black newspapers, radio stations, or magazines (*Ebony* included) has a resident film critic. Nobody's minding the ship, so all manner of havoc can be wreaked in terms of Black portrayals. The result is "the insidious reincarnation of the Sapphires and the Studs of yesteryear." According to this article, Black depictions were going back to the toms, coons, mulattos, mammies, and bucks Donald Bogle would later write about in his book of the same name.

Bennett takes the reader on a tour of these old stereotypes, from *Amos 'n' Andy* onward, stopping for analysis through the philosophies of Karl Marx, W. E. B. Du Bois, Ralph Ellison, and Jean-Paul Sartre. When he finally gets to *Sweetback*, he refers to it as "the most unremittingly bleak vision of the black experience ever filmed," but also praises some aspects of the film, like the cinematography and the concept of the colored angels. Unlike many other scholars, he also acknowledges why Black folks flocked to see *Sweet Sweetback's Baadasssss Song*: "First of all, and most importantly of all, the movie shows a black man thumbing his nose at society and getting away with it. If Sweetback does not, as Mr. Van Peebles claims, win, he at least escapes, and black America, the author included, said: 'It's about time.'"

Bennett repeatedly uses Van Peebles's own words from his manifesto and his interviews against him. The biggest problem appears to be with the politics of the film, specifically Van Peebles's comment that the film was Black and revolutionary. He vehemently disagrees with that, but he does say, "If . . . *Sweetback* is neither revolutionary nor black, it is by no means valueless. The film has, despite itself, a certain vulgar intensity" that he does not attribute to the titular sexual release of his title. The explanation for that is nothing short of brilliant. "It is disturbing to note Mr. Van Peebles' reliance on the emancipation orgasm. Sweetback saves himself three times by seduction . . . Now, with all due respect to the license of art, it is necessary to say that nobody ever f***ed his way to freedom. F***ing will not set you free. If f***ing freed, black people would have celebrated the millennium 400 years ago."

Throughout "The Emancipation Orgasm," Bennett asks if Van Peebles is "putting us on." In an interview, Van Peebles would neither confirm nor deny that he was. But Norma R. Jones's 1976 article "Sweetback: The Black Hero and Universal Myth" answers that question by suggesting Van Peebles may have been engaging in a kind of mythmaking. She writes, "The most striking thing about *Sweetback's Baadasssss Song* is the way in which it patently embodies so many aspects of the myth of the universal folk hero described in the scholarly tomes of Joseph Campbell . . . This hero is defined as 'the man of self-achieved submission.'"

Jones's article is in conversation with Bennett's; she agrees that the film is not revolutionary and certainly not a positive depiction of Blacks. Then she asks that question about whether Black art should always be positive. "More *Sounders* and *Miss Jane Pittmans* are needed," she says. However, myth has an equally important part to play:

"Our mythologies are the ways in which we express the truest things about our-selves. This is why the role of the artist as myth-maker is so important . . . For this writer, Sweetback-as-myth triumphantly speaks of Black resiliency and community and strength."

Of course, Melvin Van Peebles is on record numerous times saying all this criticism is out of touch with the common Black person. It's as bougie as his colored angels.

When Mario wanted to adapt *Sweet Sweetback's Baadasssss Song: A Guerilla Filmmaking Manifesto* into his superb 2004 film, *Baadasssss!* (which was originally called *How to Get the Man's Foot Outta Your Ass*), Melvin made him buy the rights. After that was settled, Melvin asked an important question: "Who are you gonna get to play me?" Mario answered that he would be taking the role, just as he had three decades prior when he played the young version of Sweet Sweetback. Once again, the son was becoming the father.

"Well, don't make me too nice," Melvin told him.

The younger Van Peebles made a better movie than his source material, but he didn't make a more influential one. For many years, *Sweet Sweetback's Baadasssss Song* was the most successful independent movie ever made. It remains an avant-garde provocation unmatched by any of the Blaxploitation films that would later try to emulate it. However, Van Peebles hated that it was later classified as a "Blaxploitation movie." The term "Blaxploitation" hadn't been coined yet, but a case could be made that *Sweetback* was the first definitive movie of that era.

A Side Hustle
The Case for *UpTight*

When did Blaxploitation "officially" begin? There are several possible answers to that question. As we'll soon see, the term itself was coined after *Super Fly* by Junius Griffin, the head of the NAACP in Los Angeles, but was used to describe the entire set of movies released by that point. This was well before many Blaxploitation staples had been released. The era had yet to produce the Pam Grier tetralogy or any of the films featuring the trio of machismo known as Brown-Williamson-Kelly. *Blacula* hadn't even bitten anybody yet. *The Mack* hadn't unleashed the power of the Players Ball, nor had *Dolemite* uttered one rhyme.

That leaves a few options. Does *Shaft* mark the entry point? What about *Sweet Sweetback's Baadasssss Song*? Melvin Van Peebles had a fit every time anyone referred to his film as "a Blaxploitation movie." Technically, he is correct, for if we were to operate solely on logistics, Blaxploitation did not exist until Junius Griffin coined it in 1972. That's far from a satisfactory—or definitive—answer. Arguments abound for the true heir of Blaxploitation's origin story.

I think the better question to ask is "What was the film that most influenced Blaxploitation?" *Shaft* and *Cotton Comes to Harlem* set the standards for cops/ detectives in the genre. *Coffy* and *Cleopatra Jones* ushered in the era of badass Black heroines. *Buck and the Preacher* expanded the market for the Black Westerns that would fall under the Blaxploitation banner. But many of the films that came in the latter half of the era tried to emulate the grit and salaciousness of *Sweet Sweetback's Baadasssss Song*. While I believe that Van Peebles's movie is the era's most influential film, I'd like to make the case that the blueprint of Blaxploitation was drawn three years earlier by *UpTight*, Jules Dassin and Ruby Dee's 1968 take on Liam O'Flaherty's novel *The Informer*.

In the Blaxploitation documentary *Is That Black Enough for You?!?*, director Elvis Mitchell makes a brief reference that ties *UpTight* to the Blaxploitation era, which made me even more confident in my own theorizing. This film features so many of the elements that are associated with Blaxploitation, and it does some of them better than the films that succeeded it. The script by Dassin, Dee, and her co-star Julian Mayfield handle the Black militant angle with a verisimilitude unmatched by any film before or since. Mayfield and future Blaxploitation legends Raymond St. Jacques and Max Julien play this plotline with such realism that the viewer can feel the tension, the anger, and the violence boiling over onscreen.

UpTight has other ingredients of the Blaxploitation canon. For starters, the score is by Booker T. Jones, who plays it with his band, the M.G.'s. Though it's not the first score by a Black composer—the work of Quincy Jones and Duke Ellington precede it—it's the first one to lean into the trappings of soul music. Booker T. and the M.G.'s were artists on Stax, the same label that employed *Shaft*'s composer, Isaac Hayes. The soundtrack's most well-known composition, "Time Is Tight," is a play on the film's titular adjective. In a rare vocal performance, Jones sings the film's hauntingly beautiful theme song, "Johnny, I Love You," over John and Faith Hubley's animated opening credits. Amid their images, the Hubleys pay homage to photos by Gordon Parks.

We've got a soul song over lively opening credits. Add to that the location of *UpTight*, Cleveland, Ohio, one of the northern cities to have a 'hood; in this case, it's called the Hough. As Harlem, Detroit, Chicago, and Oakland would be in Blaxploitation films, the Hough is another character in the film. It is the scene of police brutality and uprisings and serves as the final resting place for more than one of the film's protagonists. Dassin shot on location, just as Ossie Davis would do for *Cotton Comes to Harlem*.

In keeping with the source material, 1935's *The Informer* (which won director John Ford his first Oscar), *UpTight* has two characters who coincidentally mirror the types of heroes normally found in Blaxploitation. There's Tank (Mayfield), the conflicted man pulled into a situation he needs to overcome to get out of the game, and there's Johnny (Julien), his militant best friend (and the subject of "Johnny, I Love You"), a man of action willing to use violence to achieve his goals, yet who still has a soft spot for his mother. Julien would play a variation on both of these tropes in *The Mack*, and his mother in that film and this one is played by Juanita Moore.

There's even a White sidekick/ally in *UpTight*, though the film handles him quite differently than Blaxploitation films would do. Here, he's a lawyer and friend of B.G. (St. Jacques, in one of his best performances), the revolutionary group's leader. Once Johnny returns to town, and the group starts planning more acts of disobedience, B.G. dismisses the White guy, effectively kicking him out of the picture. "Thanks for your service," he basically says, "but it's Black folk business now."

Lest I forget, there's Laurie, a main squeeze for Tank, played by Dee. Unlike many Blaxploitation women before Pam Grier, her role is more than just a side piece. She and Johnny are the only characters Tank ever loved, and when he becomes an informer for the police against B.G.'s group, the fallout from his betrayal reverberates through their fates. There's also a scene, re-created more comically in 1974's *Claudine*, where Laurie is confronted by her welfare worker at home.

Roscoe Lee Browne, the soon-to-be Lord Byron Jones of *The Liberation of L.B. Jones*, plays Daisy, a self-proclaimed "nigger and faggot." Though the film throws those slurs around, Daisy is given more agency than most homosexual characters of this era. Browne's flamboyance is not overdone; it's quite convincing as a specific type of gay man. However, he's still villainous and ultimately weak-willed, something that would characterize several gay characters in Blaxploitation.

The one thing that *UpTight* truly has over the Blaxploitation films I believe it influenced was its sense of urgency and its unapologetic Black rage. Made just a few months after the assassination of Dr. Martin Luther King Jr., the film uses that event as the backdrop for its plot. Dassin opens the film with several minutes of newsreel footage of Dr. King's funeral and procession. His voice is heard in speeches as shots of the Hough appear. The character of Tank can't perform the tasks B.G. and Johnny want him to do because he's gotten drunk over MLK's death. With the Watts Uprising and other, more recent rebellions fresh in the minds of the audience and the filmmakers, *UpTight* is able to convey that time in history when the wounds were still fresh. Even *Sweet Sweetback's Baadasssss Song*, the film that comes closest to this level of rage, is working from more of a distance, which makes it feel less raw than it does in Dassin's film.

Regardless, it's worth contemplating whether *UpTight* is truly the first Blaxploitation film or merely the genre's first and most important architect.

1972
1972

WHAT DID THEY DO IN '72?

1972
1972

I n 1972, Blaxploitation got a name and a nemesis. Both were created by the same person. Before the term was coined, films like Jim Brown's *Slaughter* went by a slew of names in reviews, including "super nigger films." It'll always be jarring to read White critics of the day using that racial slur, but it was a different time and a different acceptance level. Also, that word was slapped on marquees for films like Fred Williamson's intriguing Western, *The Legend of Nigger Charley*.

Speaking of Westerns, it was the genre that brought Sidney Poitier behind the camera for the first time. *Buck and the Preacher* started what I like to refer to as the actor's "return to Black folks." That is, his work in the 1970s unshackled him from the White gaze and the noble Negritude that prevented him from the type of Black shorthand that someone like Ossie Davis could employ. Poitier's output in this period showed he could be funny, horny, petty, and even wrong. He didn't have to worry about being the sole representation of Blacks onscreen, and it liberated him.

Poitier's films were also counterprogramming to Blaxploitation itself, which was fast getting angry protests from the NAACP, CORE, and several Black intellectuals. They got together and formed a coalition that would be a thorn in the side of filmmakers and producers for several years. Their idea of wholesome family entertainment, which was all they wanted onscreen, was embodied by Marty Ritt's *Sounder*. Whether the coalition would be successful in contributing to the downfall of Blaxploitation was yet unknown in 1972. What was known was the straw that broke the camel's back and led to the formation of this coalition, a little film about a coke dealer scored to a Curtis Mayfield soundtrack.

The Republican incumbent Richard M. Nixon was on his way to a second term in 1972, but a historic event was happening on the Democratic side. Shirley Chisholm, the first Black woman elected to Congress in 1968, was running for president on a major party's ticket. This, too, was a first. Chisholm didn't win, but she stayed in office as the representative from New York's Twelfth District until 1983. Oddly enough, there was a 1972

James Earl Jones movie in which his character became the first Black president (it was called *The Man* and was scripted by Rod *"The Twilight Zone"* Serling), but nobody in this era dared to make a film about a Black woman president. In 1972 B.C. (Before *Coffy*), that absence made sense. Powerful Black women hadn't had their moment onscreen just yet.

Ralph Bakshi, who would have one of the more memorable run-ins with CORE over a Blaxploitation movie he made in 1974, first thumbed his nose at polite society this year with *Fritz the Cat*. *Fritz* was rated X, and the titular character was voiced by Skip Hinnant. Hopefully, no children saw *Fritz the Cat* (I didn't see it until I was thirty years old), because if they had, they would have heard the voice of *The Electric Company*'s Fargo North, Decoder emanating from a cat with its schlong hanging out. Kids like me would have to wait until 1974 for the opportunity to be confused by actors who switched between children's entertainment and smut. I'm sure more kids saw the R-rated *Willie Dynamite* starring an alumnus of *Sesame Street*.

The Godfather, a pulpy exploitation film based on the even pulpier exploitation novel by Mario Puzo, was so well made it convinced critics and the Academy Awards that it was a respectable motion picture. If you think my description isn't apt, just look at the movies producer Albert Ruddy made after *The Godfather*: *The Cannonball Run* movies, *The Longest Yard*, *Matilda* (a movie about a boxing kangaroo played by someone in a terrifying costume), the 3-D disaster *Megaforce*, and *Ladybugs*, where Rodney Dangerfield coaches a boy in drag on an all-girls soccer team. It's clear Ruddy knew—and loved to produce—trashy movies. His tie to Blaxploitation is his producer credit on the aforementioned Ralph Bakshi movie *Coonskin*.

In 1972, the Watergate office building complex earned its spot in infamy while ensuring that every scandal that followed it would have the suffix "-gate" attached to it. On June 17, five White House officials broke into the headquarters of the Democratic National Committee. The informant who'd eventually give information to journalists Bob Woodward and Carl Bernstein took his moniker from another infamous 1972 event, the pornographic movie *Deep Throat*.

US involvement in the war in Vietnam was still a year away from ending, but one wartime element that did end was conscription, aka the draft. This very unpopular war was made even less popular by Nick Ut's Pulitzer Prize–winning photograph *The Terror of War*.

Sanford and Son, the third sitcom centered on Black characters, premiered in January on NBC. Unlike the other two, this one focused on the relationship between a widowed father and his son. A Norman Lear production, *Sanford and Son* was an American remake of a British sitcom called *Steptoe and Son*. Fred G. Sanford, the junkman Redd Foxx played on the show, may or may not have a tie to the junkman he played in *Cotton Comes to Harlem*, but no matter. The show was a hit. It was also the first show to focus on racism among minorities: Black man Fred hated Puerto Ricans and Asians and ruthlessly made Archie Bunker–style jokes about them. Foxx would return to his Blaxploitation roots a few years later in a very strange, and very gay, movie co-starring Pearl Bailey called *Norman . . . Is That You?*

Whether it was a cocaine dealer, a vengeful Green Beret played by Jim Brown, or (gasp!) a vampire, 1972 was a year of antiheroes in Blaxploitation.

CHAPTER 6

THE *Citizen Kane* OF BLAXPLOITATION

Every genre has its *Citizen Kane*, that is, the greatest movie in its canon. *Super Fly* fits that bill for Blaxploitation. Its screenplay, by Phillip Fenty, is tightly constructed, with hustler characters breathing life into the "one final score" trope commonly found in heist movies. It is very well-acted with few exceptions. The reviews were better than most of the films that preceded and succeeded it. The soundtrack became a best-selling classic soul album. And its fashion sense, inspired by Nate Adams's costume choices and the actors' own closets, started a trend so widespread that it influenced this book's author's mother, who dressed him in a rust-colored "Super Fly coat and hat" ensemble when he was three years old. He looked fabulous.

One of the characteristics that makes *Super Fly* a valid contender for the top of the Blaxploitation heap is its shocking amorality. *Sweet Sweetback's Baadasssss Song* had a similar viewpoint, but its hero eventually realized that the community took precedence over his individual needs. *Super Fly* posits the exact opposite: Youngblood Priest's (Ron O'Neal) actions are done solely for self, with no regard for his fellow man. Gordon Parks Jr.'s film forces the viewer into making a potentially fraught decision about its protagonist. Rooting for him is an act of capitalistic complicity; rooting against him is siding with the corrupt system that made his hustle necessary. "A victim of ghetto demand" is how the film's title song puts it.

Either way, Priest is an antihero whose lifestyle appears seductive even in its most unpleasant moments. He's a gorgeous-looking light-skinned Black man with a straight hairdo to die for and threads that fit the title (*Super Fly* is two words, not one; an adjective, not a noun). He sleeps with the "baddest bitches in the bed," as Curtis Mayfield sings in his brief cameo. He also drives an incredible car and has $300,000 in a safe, all of it made by his team of cocaine dealers. Violating the cardinal rule of drug dealing, Priest partakes in his product, usually via a coke spoon dangling from his necklace. He snorts so much cocaine that the viewer wonders how he can stay upright, let alone unleash karate ass whippings on his enemies. The plot hinges on whether he can turn that $300,000 into a cool million bucks by saturating Harlem with enough coke to make *Scarface*'s Tony Montana look amateurish.

Helping him achieve this goal are his right-hand man, Eddie (Carl Lee), his mentor Scatter (Julius Harris), and Fat Freddie (Charles McGregor), a hapless low-level clocker who meets a tragic end. Giving Priest trouble are assorted Harlem competitors, corrupt politicians, and crooked White cops, one of whom is played by the film's producer, Sig Shore. Providing a small peek into the other major racket in Harlem is a pimp named K.C. The scene with K.C. is completely extraneous, very poorly acted (it's impossible to understand his dialogue), and feels as if it were some kind of mandatory condition hoisted on the filmmakers. Actually, it was—the real-life pimp allowed the use of his customized Caddy in exchange for an onscreen appearance and an "Introducing" mention in the opening credits.

Keeping Priest sexually satisfied are his two main squeezes, one Black (Sheila Frazier, in her film debut) and one White. Priest is introduced in a post-coital scene with the latter, Cynthia (Polly Niles). When she begs him not to go, he offers her a sniff of his product as a trade-off for his having to leave. She turns him down, saying, "Some things go better with coke." That was Coca-Cola's slogan at the time, so this was a product placement the Atlanta-based company probably didn't appreciate.

Frazier's Georgia has more scenes and a more fleshed-out characterization, but she's still reduced to being a booty call for the hero. When she auditioned for the role, the producer, Sig Shore, didn't want her. According to Frazier, he desired a more buxom actress. Aggravated by the runaround she received during the auditions, she gave up, changed her phone number, and moved to a different apartment in New York City. While doing this, Shore had a change of heart, but no one could find her. By sheer coincidence, she ran into someone associated with the production who recognized her. Frazier learned that the filmmakers were frantically searching for her.

To one-up *Shaft*'s shower sex scene, Georgia and Priest get it on in a bubble bath, screwing in slow motion as the audience tries to figure out the logistics of the tub and their bodies. ("I had no idea they were going to shoot it that way!" Frazier said.) More than one review cited this scene, and it surely inspired some folks to discover that bathtub sex isn't as easy as this movie makes it out to be. Especially without the benefit of slow-motion in real life.

Ron O'Neal may be the main character in *Super Fly*, but he's not the true star of the movie. That role went to its score by Curtis Mayfield. Mayfield appears onscreen in the requisite Blaxploitation movie club scene, but his compositions rule the soundtrack so much that *Super Fly* often feels like a music video. *Shaft* may have received the Oscar nomination for Best Score, but *Super Fly* has the better application of its music. And while *Shaft* deservedly won the Oscar for its hero's unforgettable theme song, *Super Fly* ups the ante by giving its hero *two* unforgettable themes, "Pusherman" and "Superfly."

Super Fly's soundtrack, released two months before the film, in June 1972, also sold more copies than the *Shaft* double album in its original release. In fact, *Super Fly* the album made more money than *Super Fly* the movie, paving the way for song-filled soundtracks like 1977's equally successful *Saturday Night Fever*. The album's first single, "Freddie's Dead," was released in July and reached number 4 on *Billboard*'s Hot 100 and number 2 on its R&B chart.

Mayfield's music is in constant conversation with *Super Fly*, underscoring what's onscreen but also occasionally offering up a contrapuntal narration. An example of the former is the opening scene. Two junkies who will later try to rob Priest are shown running the streets of Harlem, angrily discussing their plans. "Little child, running wild," sings Mayfield on the soundtrack, describing the men from his omniscient perch in the theater speakers. He knows what they're up to before the viewer does, and it lends the scene a suspenseful aura. And his soothing, sexy falsetto on "Give Me Your Love (Love Song)" makes the aforementioned tub sex scene even steamier.

Based on his twelve years writing songs for his gospel/soul music group, the Impressions, *Super Fly* might have seemed a bit of a stretch for Curtis Mayfield, in terms of subject matter and language. But his music had already taken a rawer, more sociopolitical turn on his 1970 debut solo album, *Curtis*. Its leadoff song, "(Don't Worry) If There's a Hell Below, We're All Going to Go," opens with a vocally distorted Mayfield yelling "niggers," "crackas," and "whiteys" before condemning everybody to hell.

Additionally, this was a man born into the Chicago ghetto on June 3, 1942, so the salacious material was not going to be foreign to him. "Street living gives you something special," he said of his upbringing. "You don't have to turn out bad. You can learn the rights and wrongs in the street, and sometimes I think the education you get in the streets is more valuable than what you get in school."

The Chicago native who knew the seductive allure of a ghetto hustle is in musical residence, but so is his alter ego, the activist who wrote all those Impressions songs. Long before *Super Fly* would be lambasted for its depiction of drug use, Mayfield pointed out that it played like "a commercial for cocaine" and chose to counter that notion. As a result, there's a tension between what is heard and what is seen. It's explicit in songs like "Eddie You Should Know Better" and "No Thing on Me (Cocaine Song)," and it's implicit in "Freddie's Dead," a song whose lyrics are not heard in the film (costing it Best Song Oscar eligibility), but were well-known by audiences when *Super Fly* opened. A lament for Fat Freddie, who gets killed in a hit-and-run, the song also serves as a warning for anyone who decides to pursue Freddie's lifestyle: "If you wanna be a junkie, wow! Remember Freddie's dead."

Speaking of commercials for cocaine, *Super Fly*'s most controversial sequence is exactly that. Like his father, who directed *Shaft*, Gordon Parks Jr. was a shutterbug of some note. He used his skills to take pictures of numerous people enjoying Priest's product. These stills propel the narrative of Priest's final big score forward and are edited with Madison Avenue–level precision into a montage depicting cocaine-fueled euphoria. In an interview, the comedian Sinbad said a lot of his friends saw this sequence and became convinced selling drugs was for them.

Though this montage is *Super Fly*'s biggest flex of amorality, it still had to contend with Mayfield's voice on the soundtrack. "Pusherman," the most complicated track on the score, is reprised here. On the surface, it's a boastful Blaxploitation hero's song, but underneath its braggadocio is a message to drug users: the dealer owns your soul and he'll use your destruction to fuel his success. "I'm your mama, I'm your daddy, I'm that nigger in the alley," Mayfield sings in his sexy, seductive, and ultimately Satanic falsetto. This is a deal with the devil that won't work out for the junkie. The song is hypnotic, with its relentless percussion distracting from the brutal bluntness of its words. Whether this successfully counters the visual intent of all those happy cokeheads is debatable, but it does at least muddy the waters.

When Deputy Commissioner Sig Shore finally catches up to Priest during the climax, he demands not only a big cut of the profits from this big score but also Priest's continued employment. Priest has outsmarted him, however, by purchasing a Mafia hit on the commissioner in the prior scene. Should anything happen to him, the commissioner gets rubbed out by "the best killers, WHITE ONES!"

"You better take real good care of me," Priest warns. "Nothing, nothing better happen to one hair on my gorgeous head. Can you dig it?"

Like Sweet Sweetback, Youngblood Priest gets away with it at the end. And, like Van Peebles's runaway success, *Super Fly* made a lot of money, 90 percent of it from Black audiences in Black neighborhoods. It successfully fended off *Shaft's Big Score!*, the sequel to *Shaft* that was once again directed by Gordon Parks Sr. and scripted by Ernest Tidyman. Viewers who had already seen that film when it opened in June flocked to *Super Fly*. In one week, it made $65,000 in Baltimore, $43,000 in St. Louis, $40,000 in Kansas City, and $30,000 in D.C. In the last week of August 1972, it outgrossed *The Godfather*, a movie that was constantly being compared to *Super Fly* in numerous articles. The comparison was based not on box office but on outrage. Italian-American groups were livid with Francis Ford Coppola and Mario Puzo's depiction of them, and Black organizations like the NAACP and CORE were equally angry about *Super Fly*.

In a joint statement, the two organizations proclaimed:

> The movie epitomizes, without any hint of retribution, the absolute worst images of blacks. *Super Fly* glorifies the use of cocaine, casts doubt upon the capability of law enforcement officials, casts blacks in roles which glorify dope pushers, pimps and grand theft.

The two groups were adamant about banning this new genre of film, an action that ran counter to the average moviegoer's opinion on the matter. If all the pushback over *Sweet Sweetback's Baadasssss Song* did little to stem the tide of Blaxploitation, why would the same arguments be effective against a far less avant-garde and more polished product like *Super Fly*? As more films of this ilk began to be released, the sense of outrage grew. In October 1972, the Coalition Against Blaxploitation was formed. Like the Catholic Legion of Decency that policed Old Hollywood, this coalition would issue ratings to describe Black movies as "Superior, Good, Acceptable, Objectionable, or Thoroughly Objectionable."

"It seems ironic that black people are flocking to see 'Super Fly' in droves while their own leaders decry the movie as an insult to the black community," wrote Art Peters in the *Philadelphia Inquirer*. Peters clearly overestimated the effect this Respectability Negro Guilt Trip had on viewers, ending his article thusly: "The fact that they have failed to [boycott the film] shows they really don't care." It would be years before viewer support would die out, and not because of any scary article in a newspaper or protest from their leaders.

Such righteousness rarely took into account why *Super Fly* was such a success. "It's everybody's fantasy, to smash a garbage can lid in the face of whatever is making life hell for you and stay cool while doing it," wrote White New York *Daily News* film critic Ernest Leogrande, as succinct an explanation as was needed. Black writer Chuck Stone, in the *Philadelphia Daily News*, saw Blaxploitation as a rite of passage, writing, "The current black film orgy is a necessary, but passing phase for black—and white—changes in attitude."

In his ruthless pan of the film, Stone also referred to *Super Fly* as "the latest in the hysterically exotic super-nigger films" while calling it "sophisticated *Amos 'n' Andy*." "The transformation from the stereotyped Stepin Fetchit to Super Nigger on the screen is just another form of cultural genocide," said Junius Griffin. It wasn't until Youngblood Priest became a household name that Griffin, then the head of the Los Angeles chapter of the NAACP, coined the term "Blaxploitation."

One person who was sick of taking the blame for, and answering questions about, the lack of respectability in *Super Fly* was Ron O'Neal. "I'm accused of everything but the election of Nixon," he said. "I'm held responsible for destroying the Afro haircut . . . as though I can help it that my hair is straight." O'Neal had a point. Even without the movie, people would still be hustling in the 'hood—they were doing it back when reliable, respectable old Sidney Poitier was on movie screens.

Perhaps all this aggravation led O'Neal to make a sequel, 1973's *Super Fly T.N.T.* This time, Paramount handled the release after a skittish Warner Bros. backed out due to anticipated pressure from the Black press. The script was by Alex Haley, co-author of *The Autobiography of Malcolm X* and later his own autobiographical novel, *Roots*. O'Neal took over directing duties, and the film was shot in Senegal and France at the same time *Shaft in Africa* was shooting in Ethiopia.

John Shaft and Priest once again battled at the box office; *Super Fly T.N.T* and *Shaft in Africa* opened in the last two weeks of June 1973. They couldn't have been more different. While Shaft's personality remained consistent, Priest is barely recognizable outside of his flashy duds. Sure, he has an even better car, a Ferrari, and he's now overseas living the good life, but he has pretty much given up his love of coke and his narcissism. His main squeeze, Georgia (again played by Sheila Frazier) wants to have kids and notes that he's aimless and dissatisfied, a nomad roaming from Paris to Rome in search of purpose.

Priest finds that purpose when he meets a distinguished Black gentleman named Jordan, played in his film debut by Robert Guillaume. Long before he achieved TV fame as Benson on the sitcom parody *Soap* and the spin-off that bore his character's name, Guillaume was a stage actor and singer who was at the time touring with a production of *Purlie*, the musical version of Ossie Davis's play *Purlie Victorious*. Priest and Georgia meet Jordan at a nice restaurant where he's so tight with the owners that they allow him to entertain the diners by singing opera.

At the weekly poker game he attends with an international posse of high rollers, Priest meets another very distinguished Black gentleman, Roscoe Lee Browne's Dr. Lamine Sonko. Sonko has personally sought out Priest because he needs a hustler to help him smuggle guns into his war-torn (and fictitious) African nation of Umbria. Though he resists at first, a trip to Umbria changes Priest's mind. Against Georgia's wishes, he carries out the weapons plan, only to be caught and tortured. Turns out Dr. Sonko was an even bigger hustler than Priest was back in Harlem.

Despite the few scenes of war carnage and Priest resorting to murder in self-defense via an impressively graphic electrocution scene, *Super Fly T.N.T.* is a devastating bore. Haley's script takes forever to get started, and its ideas about African wars and global politics lack clarity. The most African thing here is the repetitive score by Ghanaian band Osibisa, which sounds like the incidental music used in many a dubbed-into-English kung fu flick.

The film aims for a level of preachy respectability rather than surrounding its message in the good stuff, the way one would hide a sick cat's medicine in a bowl of tuna. Viewers didn't want a sequel where their hero plays poker, has a pseudo-epiphany of Black pride, and appears in an exploitation film with no sex, no nudity, and no semblance of the character they came to see. As a result, *Super Fly T.N.T.* flopped at the box office while *Shaft in Africa* placed at number thirty for the year.

Gene Siskel thought the lack of everything that made *Super Fly* a hit was a good thing. He ended his positive, three-star review with these misguided words: "But the character of Priest is as significant to the black community as any white movie star-character is to white America, and his transition into a fuller person is much more important than any story line."

As a character, Priest didn't get fuller, he got duller. Adding insult to injury, the *T.N.T.* in the title doesn't even stand for trinitrotoluene. Anybody up on the lingo at the time would have known T.N.T. was an acronym that stood for *'Tain't Nothin' To it*. 'Twasn't nothing to *Super Fly T.N.T.*, either.

"If you want to send a message, call Western Union," goes the famous Hollywood adage. Several movies in the later part of the Blaxploitation era would forget that rule, to their detriment. O'Neal and Haley's attempt to turn a dope pusher into a mature revolutionary and family man was for naught, anyway. The Congress of Racial Equality picketed the New York City theater where *Super Fly T.N.T.* premiered on June 15, 1973.

Some may ask why this book is giving what many consider a disreputable series of films the spotlight. Indeed, Blaxploitation did at times depict unsavory or stereotypical portrayals of Black people, sometimes crossing the line of what was acceptable. Yet looking at these films with contemporary eyes requires adjusting one's mindset to engage with them in the context of the time in which they were made. However, that does not mean that one's outrage is unwarranted if it is still the outcome. Just keep in mind that said outrage is *not a new phenomenon*.

As early as September 20, 1972, a mere month after the release of *Super Fly*, the Associated Press ran an article entitled "CORE Asks Hollywood to End 'Black Exploitation' Movies." CORE, the Congress of Racial Equity, is represented in the AP article by its chairman Roy Innis. At a press conference, he demanded that Hollywood should not release any Black movies unless they had "the CORE seal of approval." "CORE will take all action to stop these films from being produced," Innis said at a press conference. As Paramount Pictures found out at a screening of *Coonskin*, these actions included violence.

Keep in mind that this article ran before *Coffy*, *The Mack*, *Foxy Brown*, and many other well-known Blaxploitation films had been released, let alone made. The article cited *Come Back, Charleston Blue* and *Shaft*, two of the tamest instances of Blaxploitation. Hell, *Charleston Blue* is rated PG. Innis did mention *Super Fly* as a catalyst, which makes sense, as that's the film the term "Blaxploitation" was coined for, but more credibility would have come from a mention of *The Legend of Nigger Charley*, which opened in March 1972 and had that slur in its title.

"We are sick and tired of these bad films being made," said Innis, "destroying the black image and producing the wrong kind of symbol for black youth." But even his outrage wasn't new! Black intellectuals had taken *Sweet Sweetback's Baadasssss Song* behind the woodshed the year before. There's no mention of that movie in the AP article. Instead, the reporter listed the demands CORE was attempting to impose on Hollywood. Innis said these demands were not "censorship," but they damn sure sounded like it.

In fact, CORE was attempting to do to Hollywood what the Hays Code had done forty years prior. CORE wanted the studios to submit all scripts involving Black characters to their board, who had the right to reject them outright and force the films not to be made. CORE also wanted to "pre-edit" any movie before it came out, just in case something got through that they missed. Not even the Hays Code's chief censor, Joe Breen, had the ability to edit a movie that was already in the can, so Innis was clearly chasing rainbows here.

By itself, CORE would not have made much of a difference. But Junius Griffin, the soon-to-be-fired head of the Hollywood–Beverly Hills NAACP and the coiner of "Blaxploitation" was also on board with stopping these films from being made. He complained that kids shouldn't see these films, but he made no mention that perhaps this was a parental responsibility, not Hollywood's. Additionally, Reverend Jesse Jackson said that these movies were a major target of his PUSH initiative as well. These forces came together to form the Coalition Against Blaxploitation.

"We want to show the movie industry how to make class-A black films," said Innis, a man with zero filmmaking knowledge whatsoever. The one good idea he did have was for a portion of successful Black movies' profits to go toward scholarships for teaching Black people how to make films. This would have certainly made a difference and allowed some form of balancing scales to occur.

Shockingly, Hollywood didn't tell these folks to kiss its White ass smack-dab in the crack. In November 1972, another AP article appeared, this one with the title "Minority Groups to Screen Films." Its first paragraph read, "At least

10 percent of the audience at all future film screenings at major motion picture studios will be minority group members who will offer criticism of the movie's relevancy and credibility."

The Coalition Against Blaxploitation (now known as the CAB) would attend all screenings, not just of Black-themed movies, and rate them on a 1,000-point scale. "The studios have never allowed themselves to be censored," the spokesperson for the CAB erroneously stated (see the Hays Code!). "All we want is to give recommendations and to be heard." The article further stated that talks between the studios and the CAB were ongoing, with more concessions possibly granted. Both sides agreed there was no way in hell anybody but the studio or the filmmakers was going to edit a movie. Protesting movies was still an option, however.

In response to the CAB's demands, White film critic Stephen Farber wrote a January 1973 article in *Film Comment* magazine called "Censorship in California." While he agreed that "the civic groups are right to protest the fact that these movies employ so few blacks behind the camera," he expressed concern about what the CAB considered "respectable." He was no fan of the film Innis and company kept holding up, Marty Ritt's *Sounder*, calling it sanctimonious and reminding his readers that, unlike *Super Fly, Melinda, Shaft, Sweetback,* or *Charleston Blue, Sounder* wasn't directed by a Black guy. (It was, however written by the Black guy who wrote *Melinda,* Lonne Elder III.) Farber further states, "According to the protest groups, the fact that black audiences flock to *Shaft* and *Super Fly* is only a symptom of racial oppression. In other words, black audiences don't know what's really good for them . . . the determination of moralists—black or white—should never be underestimated."

Personally, this author agrees with Farber on this one. The "respectability Negroes" who tell Blacks they need to act in a way they approve of in order to be accepted by the majority are a major thorn in my side. Some of the images in Blaxploitation are scandalous, but the CAB and other, more recent people like proven hypocrite Bill Cosby lecturing and guilting Black people into their version of conformity is more offensive than any image on a screen.

Plus, it's not like today, where everything under the sun that's available is at the fingertips of those who probably shouldn't have access to it due to their age. In the Blaxploitation era, one had to either physically go to a theater or wait until the movie showed up on TV in a chopped-to-bits version. The CAB gave no responsibility to parents in terms of policing the habits of their kids. It's the same old argument: Who will protect the children? That shouldn't be a movie's job.

The author was too young to remember anything about the CAB growing up, but he remembers two talk show appearances with the late Roy Innis that ended violently. In the first, Innis knocked over Reverend Al Sharpton on repugnant talk show host Morton Downey Jr.'s show; in the second, he contributed to the near-riot that resulted in Geraldo Rivera getting his nose broken by a chair on his equally repugnant talk show. In both those instances, Innis looked like, well, a Blaxploitation character! So much for respectability. If you can't beat 'em, join 'em!

A Chat About Blaxploitation Westerns and *Buck and the Preacher*

Aisha Harris, host of NPR's *Pop Culture Happy Hour,* wrote the Criterion Collection online essay for their release of 1972's *Buck and the Preacher*. This film reunited Sidney Poitier and Harry Belafonte after their major falling-out over how best to commemorate Martin Luther King's legacy after he was assassinated.

Harris spoke with the author about the film, what it influenced, and how groundbreaking it was. No mention of Harry Belafonte's bare ass, but that's only because the interviewer forgot to bring it up.

When did you first see *Buck and the Preacher*?

I watched it in 2020, right around the [start of the] pandemic. I was going through this phase of watching Sidney Poitier movies, including some I hadn't seen. It may have been on the Criterion Channel. First of all, how did I not know about this film? I hadn't heard about it. When we talk about Sidney movies, we talk about the big ones like *In the Heat of the Night*. I'd seen those. But I had seen films he directed—*Uptown Saturday Night* and *Let's Do It Again*. So I was familiar with Sidney as a director. Of course, those are different films. They're comedies. This is a straight-up Western. He's playing this somber, weary, yet dedicated cowboy hero. By then, there had been a few Black cowboys onscreen…

Like Woody Strode in *Sergeant Rutledge*?

Yes, and *Harlem Rides the Range*. It's funny how many movies back then, even the Westerns, used "Harlem" in their titles to indicate Blackness.

As if there were cattle being rustled on 125th Street.

[Laughs] With *Buck and the Preacher*, it was interesting to see Sidney apply the things he saw the directors on his films do. He was always watching what was going on behind the camera.

In your essay, you mentioned an episode of Ellis Haizlip's groundbreaking Black talk show, *Soul!*, on which Poitier and Belafonte appeared. Was there anything they said that stuck with you?

What struck me the most about it was that [Sidney and Harry] were defensive in terms of trying to establish that they hadn't lost touch with their audiences. And there was also this sense of camaraderie between the two of them.

They speak very highly of one another in each other's memoirs.

They didn't always agree on things, but they were like brothers.

On February 24, 1971, Irv Kupcinet of the *San Francisco Examiner* said that the original director, Joseph Sargent, "stalked off because of differences with the two stars." That gives the impression that Sargent quit. It was my understanding that he was literally fired by Poitier.

Yeah.

Did you find anything in your research that revealed that either Poitier or Belafonte confirmed this firing? It sounded like this White writer was spinning the real story.

I believe I saw proof of that on the Turner Classic Movies site. [Frank Miller's article on the TCM site does indeed say, "So when they fired Sargent, they told the executives that Poitier was only going to direct until the studio men could find a permanent replacement."] Also from my research, I didn't see anything that said Sargent was anything but amicable about the split.

This film deals with the occasionally tenuous relationship between Blacks and Native Americans. Do you think it does a good job of depicting this?

Well, to be clear, the two main Native American characters in this film aren't played by Native Americans. One was played by Belafonte's wife, Julie Robinson, who was Jewish.

Harry played a Jewish angel in Bill Gunn's adaptation of *The Angel Levine*, so turnabout is fair play!

True! But as progressive as *Buck* was in dealing with [the Black–Native American relationship], it wasn't as progressive as it could have been with the casting.

This was Harry Belafonte's first Western and Sidney's second after *Duel at Diablo*. It was also the last Western they did in their careers. Westerns were still very popular at the time, so it seems a bit odd. Did you encounter anything in your research that might explain this?

Well, when you think about it, Sidney didn't do many period pieces. But in most old Westerns, Black people didn't exist. I think that's clearly what *Buck* was pushing back against. It needed to show that we were there and that we were doing shit. Maybe Sidney wasn't getting offered roles like that.

Because they'd have to depict Black people on equal footing in those roles.

Yeah.

The opening credits declare, "This picture is dedicated to those men, women, and children who lie in graves as unmarked as their place in history." You mentioned *The Learning Tree* in your essay. Considering that film's director, Gordon Parks, grew up in Kansas as a result of his ancestors being part of the Exodusters who moved west, do you think the two films are in a historical conversation with one another?

Once you get to the '60s and '70s, Black people become synonymous with "urbanization" in the cultural imagination, and that's all you see. From *Julia* to *The Jeffersons*, Blacks are living in cities. Even today, [the TV show] *Queen Sugar* is an anomaly in that Black people are in the country dealing with country shit. So I can see the two films being in conversation because there were no other films like them. I guess the other exception is *Sounder*. Even when you get to Blaxploitation, everybody is in a city like Detroit or Chicago or New York City.

Unless they're in a Western with Fred Williamson!

Yeah. But even then, they're talking like they're from freakin' Harlem!

Harry Belafonte walks off with not only this picture, but with his second pairing with star-director Sidney, *Uptown Saturday Night*. Both performances have a comic streak and the normally gorgeous Mr. Belafonte garishly changing his appearance. How well do you think he disappears into these performances?

I don't think Harry nor Sidney fully disappear into any of the roles they've played. Like Cary Grant, you always know you're watching *them*. What I do like about Harry's performance in *Buck* is how much fun he seems to be having. When he comes into the brothel and he's shucking and jiving, and the White characters are eating it up without knowing Preacher has a gun in his Bible, it seems like the perfect [rebuttal] to Black characters who were portrayed as super dumb or mere entertainment.

Sidney is still Sidney, even though for a change his nobility and altruism are pointed solely at his Black and brown brethren. Can you speak to this concept? Was it an important turning point for him?

It's really the first time we see that from Sidney. Before that, his only Black cast movies were *A Raisin in the Sun* and *Porgy and Bess*, both of which he's rather powerless in. At this point he has more cachet in his career. He could finally make this movie and do it the way he wanted to, and that's a crucial turning point. It allowed him to make those other movies. It's kismet that the biggest Black movie star at the time was behind the camera for this movie. *Shaft* was a big hit, but it means something that you have [a hit with] this culmination of a Western setting, the trifecta of Harry, Sidney, and Ruby Dee, and it's about Black people doing for themselves with the aid of Native Americans.

Speaking of Ruby Dee, she has been Sidney's wife/girlfriend in practically every movie they made together. How does this relationship differ or stand out? And what is your favorite pairing of them?

What makes this different is that she's the damsel in distress. She's not in a bunch of the movie, but there's glamour for her here. Her hair is a little tussled in that way. To answer your second question, *A Raisin in the Sun* or the movie he made with Cassavetes.

Edge of the City. You know she's kind of the damsel in distress in UpTight, which Dee co-wrote. I think she is really good in a part she wrote for herself. So there's something to be said for that type of role.

I'll have to revisit *UpTight*.

Blaxploitation is full of Westerns, most of them starring and/or directed by Fred Williamson. Have you seen any of his films, like Adios Amigo?

I've seen *The Legend of Nigger Charley*, *Boss Nigger*, and *The Soul of Nigger Charley*. I did a piece on them back when *Django Unchained* came out. The influences for that film weren't just coming from [Italian spaghetti Western director Sergio] Leone, they were coming from these films. I mean, they were basically *Coffy* or *Shaft* in the West. They're not good movies, but they kind of function as like a *Fast and the Furious* type series.

Fred Williamson was the Vin Diesel of those movies! He said, "People want to see me knock a nigger out and then fling my cigar ashes on him." Folks went to those movies because of him. Do you think *Buck and the Preacher* had an influence on the Black Westerns that came after it, like 2021's *The Harder They Fall*?

If you're making a movie with Black cowboys in it, you don't have many prior references. So I do think it is an influence. Even in [Jordan Peele's 2022 California desert horror film] *Nope*, there's a *Buck and the Preacher* poster on the wall.

I saw that! And *Nope* is kind of a Western, when you think about it.

It is very much a Western. I think in a way, the Black Western hero can't be discussed without *Buck and the Preacher*. But *Posse* pulls more from Blaxploitation.

Well, it *was* made by Mario and Melvin Van Peebles!

But when I think about *Buck and the Preacher*, it's a turning point for its stars' careers and for Black filmmaking. It's an anomaly and kind of remains one. It kicked off a new phase of Sidney's career. I think it's a creative move and a strategic one by Sidney. It's a really good movie! I really like it. It's one more people should know about. A very crucial part of American film history.

CHAPTER 2

Dracula was a Redneck

Studio system Hollywood horror films featured Black monsters only when the films were based in "deepest, darkest Africa." There were savages running around, worshipping big gorillas like King Kong or making do as cannibals eager to dine on White meat. The classic Universal horror creatures were far out of reach of the few Black actors big enough to play them. Hollywood would never turn Sidney Poitier into a teenage werewolf like Michael Landon, nor would Paul Robeson be cast as Dr. Frankenstein (though he got close enough to that level of madness in *The Emperor Jones*). Negroes couldn't even play the Invisible Man, not Ralph Ellison's version and certainly not H. G. Wells's. And viewers couldn't even see him! Mummies were also off the table, even if they did come from Africa.

In January 1972, at the same time Warners was making *Super Fly* in New York City, director William Crain was in Los Angeles to begin production on the first monster film to feature a Black vampire. Of course, American International Pictures (AIP) made the title a play on "Black Dracula," calling the film *Blacula*. Inspired by the previously successful idea of casting a stage veteran like Vincent Price to class up their low-budget literary adaptations, AIP hired Shakespearian actor William Marshall to portray Prince Mamuwalde, the man who would be Blacula. Marshall was six feet, five inches tall, the same height as the White guy who held the monopoly on vampires in 1972, Christopher Lee. Like Lee, he was also a classically trained opera singer who rarely got to employ that talent onscreen.

Born in Gary, Indiana, in 1924, Marshall had already been working for almost thirty years before he was cast in his signature role. He made his Broadway debut in *Carmen Jones* in 1944 before being directed by Marty Ritt in Dorothy Heyward's play *Set My People Free* in 1948. In 1950, he understudied the role of Captain Hook for fellow monster movie legend Boris Karloff in *Peter Pan* (in addition to playing Cookson) and, a year later, played De Lawd in a revival of *The Green Pastures*.

It was seeing that Pulitzer-winning racist musical onstage that made Marshall, then eight years old, want to be an actor. He studied at the Actors Studio before journeying to Europe to play in numerous Shakespeare plays, most notably the lead in Othello (no blackface necessary). The London *Sunday Times* called him "the best Othello of our time," which really must have burned Sir Laurence Olivier's ass with a vengeance! Marshall used his deep, bass voice with preternatural precision, whether as the US attorney general in Robert Aldrich's excellent 1977 thriller, *Twilight's Last Gleaming*, or as the King of Cartoons on the '80s children show *Pee-wee's Playhouse*.

Such an awesome voice also made Marshall a formidable bad guy, though in the case of *Blacula*, his villainy is far from certain. The screenplay by Joan Torres and Raymond Koenig has an unusual amount of sympathy for Mamuwalde. His tale is tragic, and his lust for blood is more out of need than desire. Even so, their script doesn't scrimp on the genre goods; *Blacula* has a large body count, even if the bodies don't stay dead for long. It also has an ending that destroys its monster in an unconventional fashion.

"'You're joking,' I said, when I was asked to do it," Marshall told Kevin Thomas of the *Los Angeles Times*. "But I thought it had possibilities. I had damn near many pages of criticism as there were in the script itself." AIP declined most of those changes, but some of Marshall's demands for historical context wound up on the screen: Mamuwalde is African royalty, and he gets to speak a bit of Swahili and educate the viewer on African art and rituals. He never looks less than regal in his human form, carrying himself with a distinguished carriage that matched that incredible voice.

In a pre-credits sequence set in 1780, the powerful Mamuwalde and his beautiful wife, Luva (Vonetta McGee) visit the Transylvanian palace of Dracula (Charles Macaulay). Mamuwalde hopes to get his host's assistance in stopping the African slave trade, but Dracula does not take too kindly to uppity Negroes who don't know their place. To quote Gene Siskel's positive review in the *Chicago Tribune*, "Dracula, it seems, was a redneck."

As punishment, Dracula bites Mamuwalde, but not before lecturing him. "You shall pay, Black prince. I shall place a curse of suffering on you that will doom you to a living hell. I curse you with my name. You shall be Blacula!" An even worse fate befalls Luva; she's left in mortal form to starve and die while listening to Mamuwalde's anguished screams for blood.

A pause here to pay tribute to Charles Macaulay, whose characters were responsible for the creation of two of the first major movie monsters played by Black actors. Before his Count Dracula turned William Marshall into a vampire, his Dr. Gordon turned Marshall's future co-star, Pam Grier, into the Panther Woman in *The Twilight People*. That film, a very-low-budget riff on H. G. Wells's *The Island of Dr. Moreau*, opened in cinemas in June 1972, a month before *Blacula*. Grier told the audience at her 2022 TCM Film Festival tribute that she enjoyed playing a character who was strictly an animal. Her enjoyment is in every frame of her performance. Despite some hideous makeup, Grier is a convincing half-human, half-panther creature who, like Mamuwalde, racks up an impressive body count before her demise.

Blacula's reign of jugular vein puncturing starts when the film jumps to the present day. Two homosexual interior decorators, an interracial couple named Bobby and Billy, buy Mamuwalde's coffin and ship it back to Los Angeles. They both think it looks *fierce*! What's inside it is equally fierce. Mamuwalde has been starving for blood for two hundred years, so the couple become his first victims and, by extension, his first minions.

At the funeral home, Tina (McGee again) and her sister Michelle (Denise Nicholas) mourn their friends. Tina gets Mamuwalde's attention because she looks exactly like his former love, Luva. Bobby's corpse gets the attention of Michelle's man, pathologist Dr. Gordon, because it is completely drained of blood. Gordon is played by the Blaxploitation ubiquitous actor Thalmus Rasulala. Soon after, Bobby disappears from the funeral home, returning home to his master.

Mamuwalde is obsessed with Tina, and she falls for him despite his inability to appear in the daytime. A photographer friend of hers accidentally takes a picture of the two of them, signing her death certificate because vampires cast neither a reflection nor a photographic image. A taxicab driver, Juanita (Ketty Lester) also gets sucked dry after she runs Mamuwalde over with her cab. Now a vampire, she figures in the most terrifying scene in *Blacula*, a slow-motion run down a morgue hallway. Her prey is the hapless mortician Sam, played by film noir legend Elisha Cook Jr. in a cameo.

Despite all that biting and sucking, *Blacula* is a love story where the viewer hopes Tina is indeed Luva reincarnated. She's surprisingly understanding when Mamuwalde explains why he's pursued a relationship with her. It's too bad Dr. Gordon figures out who the Blacula in the title is. Along with Peters (Gordon Pinsent), a cop who gets a sobering lesson in the existence of vampires at Sam's morgue, the good doctor tracks down his foe. Meanwhile, Tina is hypnotized to follow the bat version of Mamuwalde (yes, he turns into a fake bat on a string) to his hideout.

Just when it looks like the two lovers will be reunited forever, Tina is accidentally shot dead by the cops. After bringing her back to "life" with a vampire bite, Mamuwalde puts her in his coffin. When Peters opens that coffin expecting to find its owner, he stakes Tina instead. Having lost his true love twice in one lifetime, Mamuwalde does something unprecedented in horror movie history. He gives up.

Marshall plays his last scene with a haunting dignity and resignation. Here is a tired Black man, done so wretchedly by bad luck that his only recourse is to end it all. "That won't be necessary," he says somberly when Dr. Gordon attempts to stake him. Mamuwalde walks past him and into the daylight, frying himself to death. There's a sense of relief in his demise, for at last the evil curse put upon him by White racism has been lifted. *Blacula* ends with a very lousy (but still gross) melted head special effect.

When it opened on July 26, 1972, *Blacula* didn't do too poorly with the critics. In addition to Siskel, *Variety* gave the film a good review, as did the *Chicago Reader* and the *Miami Herald*. Audiences liked it as well, bringing in $3,000,000 in ticket sales against a $500,000 budget. Along with *Shaft*, it was one of the few Blaxploitation films to win an award, earning Best Horror Film at the inaugural sci-fi- and horror-based Saturn Awards.

Though it featured educated Black characters and a lead that was far from a stereotype, *Blacula* still drew the ire of Junius Griffin. A month before he created the Coalition Against Blaxploitation, he started a beef with Marshall over the actor's dream project, a film version of Martinique poet Aimé Césaire's play *The Tragedy of King Christophe*. King Christophe was a real-life Haitian revolutionary hero, a great opportunity for Marshall, but he was outranked by Anthony Quinn's competing project, *Black Majesty*. The Mexican-American Quinn had intended to play the Black lead role himself, causing all manner of controversy. To everyone's surprise, Griffin endorsed Quinn's project.

"If Black actors can play demeaning roles in *Blacula*," Griffin told *Daily Variety*, "I could hardly oppose Quinn's portrayal." The head of the Los Angeles NAACP did not look good approving a White Latino actor playing a Black character in blackface. As a result, Griffin was forced to resign his post, freeing him up to be a thorn in the side of Blaxploitation. *Blacula*'s director, William Crain, was on record saying Griffin tied him to a chair to prevent him from working on 1976's *Dr. Black and Mr. Hyde*.

Vengefully, Blacula rose again in 1973's *Scream Blacula Scream*. Bob Kelljan took over for Crain, but Torres and Koenig returned as scriptwriters. This time, voodoo is added to the mix courtesy of Pam Grier's Lisa Fortier. It's how Mamuwalde is reborn. He's not happy to return, at least until he casts his eyes on Pam. Marshall is a more brutal vampire this time around, and he's been given a Renfield in the guise of a soul brother named Willis Daniels, played by Richard Lawson in his film debut. Lawson is hilariously over-the-top, going full jive ass at some points before Mamuwalde chews him out for his stupidity.

Like most sequels, *Scream Blacula Scream* is bigger but not better. The plot is muddled, and the audience sympathy is no longer with Mamuwalde. On the plus side, Marshall and Grier were a dream team for fans, and Grier proves herself worthy of being in the same scream queen fraternity as Jamie Lee Curtis. She didn't have to go that route, however, because when *Scream Blacula Scream* hit theaters, *Coffy* was already making Pam Grier a Blaxploitation star.

CHAPTER 8

From *THE ASPHALT JUNGLE* to the CONCRETE JUNGLE

In 1972, the market became saturated with Blaxploitation movies. As Hollywood was wont to do, several of these films were remakes of known material, this time cast with Black actors. This wasn't a new phenomenon, but it became more prominent in 1972, when films like *Get Carter* and *The Asphalt Jungle* were recalibrated and "colorized."

Perhaps the first major instance of this is 1968's *The Split*. With *The Dirty Dozen* the year prior, Jim Brown became the first major Black action star. Robert Aldrich's macho war fantasy put Brown on a team run by Lee Marvin. *The Split* had Brown playing Parker, the same Richard Stark (Donald Westlake's alter ego) character Marvin played in John Boorman's 1967 adaptation *Point Blank*. Brown is called McClain instead of Parker, but Robert Sabaroff's screenplay is based on Stark's Parker novel *The Seventh*. Both were Metro-Goldwyn-Mayer productions.

Like *Point Blank*, *The Split* is as ruthless and violent as Westlake's prose. It became the first film to receive an R rating when the MPAA went live on November 4, 1968. Brown's McClain is cold as ice and icily efficient. Quincy Jones's score and Burnett Guffey's cinematography are willing co-conspirators playing up the danger. In a nod to Brown's football career, *The Split*'s plot involves the robbery of the Los Angeles Coliseum during a Rams game. The thieves start to distrust one another when the money disappears. Real footage of a Rams game was used during the heist scene. In a nice bit of coincidence, Brown's future co-star Bernie Casey would have been a player on the team at the time *The Split* was shot.

In town for the Chicago premiere in October 1968, Jim Brown sat for an interview with Roger Ebert, who had then been at the *Chicago Sun-Times* for just over a year. Brown told Ebert, "What I want to do is play roles as a black man, instead of playing black man's roles. You know? The guy in 'The Split,' for example, could be any color. And I don't make a big thing out of my race. If you try to preach, people give you a little sympathy and then they want to get out of the way. So you don't preach, you tell the story. I have a theory. An audience doesn't need to get wrapped up in blackness every time they see a Negro actor. And a movie doesn't have to be about race just because there's a Negro in it. If there's a bigot in the audience, he has to keep reminding himself, that's a black man, that's a Negro, because the story line has left him 'way behind, man. Away behind. Just tell the story, and before you know it, that cat will be identifying with you, and he won't even know how it happened."

In keeping with the films that reboot the ruthless White protagonist theme, the next exhibit is *Hit Man*, a remake of 1971's Michael Caine classic, *Get Carter*. Both films were based on Ted Lewis's novel *Jack's Return Home*. George Armitage directed, adapting the novel more faithfully than *Get Carter* did. Bernie Casey stepped in the lead. Though this was an MGM production, Roger Corman's brother, Gene, produced the film.

Casey plays Tyrone Tackett, who has "come home" to Los Angeles to attend the funeral of his brother, Cornell. A former police officer, Tackett now works for an Oakland pornographer. Ever paranoid, Tackett finds Cornell's demise suspicious. He was pretty square by comparison, and his drunken drive into the ocean after downing a pint of booze doesn't add up. Cornell's teenage daughter, Rochelle, doesn't want her uncle's protection despite his offers. Meanwhile, Tackett is pursued by several hit men, one of whom is played by *Magnum P.I.*'s Roger E. Mosley. There's also Gozelda, a wannabe porn actress played by Pam Grier, who hopes Tackett can get her a job.

To say *Hit Man* is brutal would be an understatement, but then again, the source material is not for the fainthearted. The film's poster, perhaps the best one in Blaxploitation, features Casey in front of a bullet-ridden target, holding a pistol and a shotgun, the latter positioned at his crotch and pointing at the viewer in a cool 3-D style effect. "He aims to please," says the pun-filled tagline. Tackett uses those guns to shoot several people point-blank in the face. His niece winds up raped during a porn shoot and is later shot in the head to ensure her silence. The entire adult film subplot is as sleazy as possible, and no one in Tackett's orbit is trustworthy. As for Gozelda, she ends up locked in a trunk before being driven to an animal wildlife park, where she is eaten by a mountain lion. "Run," Tackett tells her before leaving her helpless in the middle of nowhere. Like everyone else Tackett executes, she had it coming.

(It should be noted that the mountain lion was the last character to win a battle against Blaxploitation-era Pam Grier.)

It's not known if the Coalition Against Blaxploitation had *Hit Man* on their radar when it opened on December 20, 1972. Picking up their slack, however, was the Catholic Legion of Decency, which rated the film O (morally objectionable, aka "watch this and you'll automatically burn in hell"), stating that the "dizzying spectacle of raw sex and supergraphic violence would horrify the Marquis de Sade." This is just slightly hyperbolic.

Before *Hit Man*, Gene Corman produced *Cool Breeze*, a take on 1950's *The Asphalt Jungle*, which itself was based on W. R. Burnett's 1949 novel of the same name. There's a different Lord Jones to be liberated this time, master thief Sidney Lord Jones (Thalmus Rasulala). He's just gotten out of San Quentin and is itching to return to his old ways. A $3 million diamond heist is on the agenda, with the intent to create a community bank that will serve the public as well as provide a money-laundering front.

As in *Jungle*, the architect of the crime recruits a motley crew of fellow criminals who excel in one of the skills needed to pull off the heist. Lord Jones hires a reverend who cracks safes when he's not preaching the gospel; gets an untrustworthy criminal to serve as the group's muscle; reunites with his old bookie friend, Stretch; and tries to find a fence for the jewels.

Stretch sends Lord Jones to get financing from millionaire real estate mogul Bill Mercer, an older man who is secretly insolvent and not-so-secretly carrying on an affair with a much younger woman played by Margaret Avery thirteen years before she got an Oscar nomination for *The Color Purple*. If *Cool Breeze* has a tragic figure, it's Mercer, and that juicy role goes to Raymond St. Jacques. St. Jacques gives an excellent performance; he seems so much more broken down than Coffin Ed or his militant in *UpTight*. St. Jacques and Rasulala were consistently good during the Blaxploitation era, even when the movies they made were not worthy of their talents.

Long before the thieves in *Point Break* wore Reagan masks to commit their robberies, *Cool Breeze* put its crooks in Nixon masks and had them hijack a city bus as part of their crimes. The heist is genuinely exciting and suspenseful, well shot by cinematographer Andrew Davis in his first job. After serving time in Blaxploitation, Davis would go on to direct *The Fugitive* and the movie that put Steven Seagal on the map, *Above the Law*.

Cool Breeze reunites St. Jacques with his *Cotton Comes to Harlem* co-star Judy Pace. As in that film, she's a tough woman who will do anything for her criminal man. Paula Kelly is also here, as are Stack Pierce and Lincoln Kilpatrick. Each of these actors will show up in films of this era. Even Pam Grier shows up briefly, unfortunately used as exposition in a thankless role as a sex worker who sleeps with Lord Johnson.

Writer-director Barry Pollack ends *Cool Breeze* on a note of ambiguity. Does Sidney Lord Jones get away with the crime? Or does the freeze frame mean the cops have gotten him? Either way, the wonderful smile of Thalmus Rasulala ushers in the closing credits. Audiences enjoyed the film when it opened in March; the million-dollar box office take led Corman to tackle *Hit Man*. Box office lightning did not strike twice, presumably because an equally violent, more polished film called *Across 110th Street* opened that same week as *Hit Man*.

Yaphet Kotto had been acting for thirteen years before he landed his first starring role in a movie. The son of a Cameroonian immigrant who had royalty in his ancestry, Kotto was raised Jewish (his name means "beautiful" in Hebrew) and was raised in Harlem. His time at the fabled Actors Studio gave him the ability to play all types of roles, but that doesn't mean he didn't spend time in a few Blaxploitation movies.

Before Kotto immortalized his neighborhood as the co-lead in *Across 110th Street*, he teamed up with future Blaxploitation writer-director Larry Cohen to make 1972's *Bone*. *Bone* was Cohen's first film, but not Kotto's. It was, however, the largest role the actor had to date when the film started shooting in July 1971. His titular character is one of the leads alongside Joyce Van Patten, Andrew Duggan, and Elaine May's daughter, Jeannie Berlin. (May's mother, Ida Berlin, is also here in a profane cameo!)

"Love Bone before he LOVES you," the tagline read under a smiling, physically intimidating Kotto holding a dead rat. Like many exploitation films of the 1970s, *Bone* existed under several alias titles, including *Dial Rat for Terror* and *Beverly Hills Nightmare*. It was not a box office success like Cohen's later films *Black Caesar* and *It's Alive*, but *Bone* has a reputation as one of the director's biggest cult classics.

Bone tells the story of rich White couple Bill and Bernadette (Duggan and Van Patten) whose house is "invaded" by a Black criminal named Bone. They think he's the exterminator they called to kill the rat in their pool, which he does. But he believes they have a lot of money, as Bill does ads for the car dealership he runs. When Bill says he has no money in the house, Bone sends him to the bank, threatening violence to Bernadette if he doesn't return within an hour. Bill goes to the bank but gets no money. Instead, he runs into the Girl (Berlin), whom he proceeds to have a fling with while his endangered wife is at home. This takes longer than an hour.

Meanwhile, Bone and Bernadette play nasty mind games, culminating in her decision to murder Bill when she discovers he hasn't retrieved any money from the bank. Bone and Bernadette sleep together, then embark on the plan to have him kill Bill. This noirish twist doesn't go as expected. At the end, Bone disappears as mysteriously as he arrived.

In an interview with Josiah Howard, Cohen described his directorial debut as "an over-the-top, kind of wild story" and blamed its initial failure on the audience being sold an incorrectly defined bill of goods. "Well, the response was odd because the distributor who bought the picture released it as a black exploitation movie," Cohen said, "even though I told him it was a comedy."

Anyone who has seen this complex, almost avant-garde provocation would be hard-pressed to call it a comedy, even a dark one. *Bone* contained attempted rape, racism, threats of murder, child molestation (complete with a seduction based on the victim's incestuous abuse), and climaxes with Bernadette beating her husband unconscious before smothering him to death. She plans on blaming Bone—the cops would believe a large Black man committed such a physical murder—but he's gone before she can call the cops.

In a 1978 *Film Comment* article, film critic Robin Wood compared it to Godard's 1968 bourgeois nightmare, *Weekend*. "It is Cohen's most difficult work," he wrote, "an example of . . . the attempt by an American director at the equivalent of a European art-house movie." He also called it "virtually inaccessible." Adding to his moviegoing experience, Wood was temporarily thrown out of a Museum of Modern Art screening scheduled specifically for him, an act that syncs perfectly with the film's strange goings-on.

Before casting Kotto, Cohen caught his performance as the violent avenging angel of the cuckolded, castrated, and killed Lord Byron Jones in *The Liberation of L.B. Jones*. "He embodied the fantasy image that many people had of what a black man looks like," Cohen explained. "Since [*Bone*] was about people's fantasies, I thought he was just perfect." Kotto's competition for the role was Paul Winfield; the loss of the role led Winfield to make the more respectable *Sounder* with director Marty Ritt—and to an Oscar nomination for Best Actor.

Winfield may have starred in a movie the Coalition Against Blaxploitation championed, but he still managed to do time in the genre they despised. When 20th Century–Fox wanted skin in the Blaxploitation game, they hired Black director Ivan Dixon and White *Shaft* co-screenwriter John D. F. Black to concoct a tale of a stylish Los Angeles fixer. The fixer gets involved with two crime syndicates who each pay him as he plays one side against the other. Dixon shot the film in Los Angeles in March 1972. Assisting the actor-turned-first-time-director behind the camera was an editor working on his fourth film, future Steven Spielberg collaborator Michael Kahn.

Trouble Man starred Negro Ensemble co-founder Robert Hooks, whose son, Kevin, had just played Paul Winfield's son in *Sounder*. Now Winfield was playing Robert's boss, a man named Chalky. It took real balls to name a character of Winfield's complexion "Chalky." The elder Hooks's character was named Mr. T, and he did not pity any fools. He also drove a badass Lincoln Continental Mark IV, a steel boat of a Detroit-built automobile making its debut in 1972. Mr. T's wardrobe was untouchable, with suits so stylish and distinguished that they stoked the audience's envy. And he had the lovely Paula Kelly waiting for him at home.

Most importantly, Mr. T had theme music provided by Motown legend Marvin Gaye. The *Trouble Man* soundtrack was his follow-up to his masterpiece, *What's Going On?* The mostly instrumental score was Gaye's only soundtrack, but it gave the world the title song, easily one of the artist's best compositions. Opening with a massive statement by several types of drum (the instrument Gaye played on Motown songs in the 1960s), the song falls into a jazzy piano groove that leads into a bluesy shuffle. It's accompanied by horns and a flawless falsetto by Gaye, which he drops only to scream, "Got me singing YEAH! YEAH!" in the bridge between the first and second stanzas. There's also an unforgettable vocal run in the middle, where Gaye's lyrical wordplay matches his quick, breathless delivery.

Good Lord, this song is fantastic . . .

At least the version that's *on the soundtrack* is! The version of "Trouble Man" that plays over the actual opening credits of the film is vastly different. There's no falsetto, for starters, and the arrangement is different. Compared to the more widely known remastered version, it's as if the filmmakers replaced filet mignon with White Castle. At least both versions of "Trouble Man" have the good sense to keep one of the greatest lyrics of the twentieth century: "There's only three things that I'm sure of: taxes, death, and trouble." Gaye leans into the word "trouble," letting it breathe as if to tell us Mr. T is going to get into a lot of it. Winfield; his partner in crime, Ralph Waite (the dad from the TV series *The Waltons*!); and the ubiquitous Blaxploitation star Julius Harris will see to that. The body count on this one is high. Stitching all the carnage together, Kahn's editing job is a far cry from *Raiders of the Lost Ark*, but he managed to get more work in this era than one might expect.

"Mr. T is cold hard steel!" read the ads when *Trouble Man* opened on November 1, 1972, at the DeMille Theater in Times Square. A week later, it opened at the Roosevelt in Chicago. In the New York *Daily News*, Wanda Hale's three-out-of-four-star positive review tells readers, "The language is rough, and Hooks gets as many closeups as Marilyn Monroe did." She was in the minority for liking the movie. Over at the *New York Times*, Vincent Canby wrote, "I'm not sure if it wants to be described as cool or uppity" before ending his review with a kicker: "*Trouble Man* is a horrible movie, but it's worth thinking about." Canby's rather despicable review also calls Kelly's character "a house slave."

Trouble Man isn't very good, but it is far less embarrassing than Hooks's prior film, 1967's Otto Preminger howler, *Hurry Sundown*. In that one, "Southerners" Michael Caine, Jane Fonda, and Faye Dunaway match wits with Hooks and Beah Richards over who owns plots of land. The *New York Times*, represented by Canby's predecessor, Bosley Crowther, called it "an offense to intelligence." Hooks appeared sparingly in films over the next several decades. Like Paul Winfield, who did *The Wrath of Khan*, he eventually wound up in a *Star Trek* movie, *The Search for Spock*. He was also directed by his son, Kevin, in Wesley Snipes's pseudo-Blaxploitation crowd pleaser *Passenger 57*.

A month after *Trouble Man*'s release, Yaphet Kotto returned to theaters alongside Anthony Quinn in the aforementioned brutal crime drama *Across 110th Street*. The dynamic between Quinn's Captain Mattelli, an aging Italian cop, and Kotto's much younger potential replacement, Lieutenant Pope, mirrors the relationship between the Mafia and the Black gangsters wrestling for control of Harlem. Pope is a new breed of cop who doesn't trust Mattelli because he's a racist, a cop on the take, and is prone to beating up those he arrests.

As in these Black cop/White cop "buddy" movies, Mattelli and Pope will join forces against a common enemy. It's not just the corrupt police force, it's also the criminals who work for D'Salvio (an excellent Anthony Franciosa) and Doc Johnson (Richard Ward). *Shaft* briefly covered the tensions between Black and Italian mobsters, but that film is child's play in the violence department. Director Barry Shear and screenwriter Luther Davis open their film with a drug money transfer between the two criminal factions gone awry due to robbery. The robbers machine gun everybody in the room before jumping into a car driven by Jackson (Antonio Fargas). Cops get shot and run over in the getaway.

Much of the violence—and it's preternaturally nasty—stems from D'Salvio trying to outdo himself in the cruelty department. He's not happy about the robbery that opens the film. He hangs one former henchman by the ankles from a great height on a construction site, then lets him fall to his death despite getting the information he needs. After discovering Jackson drove the getaway car, he has him beaten mercilessly, castrated, and then crucified. Jackson is still alive when Mattelli and Pope find him, but all he can do is scream when they try to question him before he dies. Fargas, a vet in Blaxploitation, has died in several films, but this is easily the most gruesome way he's kicked the bucket. It's a harbinger for the later films of the era, ones that were primarily concerned with sadism. As a gritty film made in the '70s, *Across 110th Street* is guaranteed not to have a happy ending; it ends with one of its protagonists suddenly getting shot in the head by a sniper.

Quinn and Kotto are excellent, and *Across 110th Street* earns a place not only in the Blaxploitation genre but also in the super-violent cop genre ushered in by *The French Connection*. Satisfying the former is the memorable and superb theme song written by Bobby Womack and J. J. Johnson. Womack sings of the dangers that exist in the titular location, and his forceful growl, coupled with the pulsating beat of the music, make this a fan favorite and one of the best theme songs. Twenty-five years later, Quentin Tarantino would use it to underscore Pam Grier's return to a big-screen starring role in his best film, *Jackie Brown*. QT loves Pam, and the world was about to learn why her fans did.

CHAPTER 9

What's Happening in the Clean World?

1972 wasn't just the year Blaxploitation emerged as a full-fledged entity. It was also a year when Black history was being made in mainstream Hollywood. When the Academy Award nominations were announced on February 12, 1973, several categories contained never-before achievements by the Black talent involved in *Sounder* and *Lady Sings the Blues*. While it would be erroneous to call these films Blaxploitation, they are important enough to warrant a few words about their use as "counterprogramming." They are also damn good movies shot by the legendary Mexican-American cinematographer John A. Alonzo.

Directed by Martin Ritt and adapted from William H. Armstrong's 1969 novel by Black writer Lonne Elder III, *Sounder* tells the story of the Lees, a sharecropper family led by Paul Winfield as Nathan Lee and Cicely Tyson as his wife, Rebecca. Kevin Hooks plays their son, David. Sounder is the Lee family dog. He gets his name in the title but does little to deserve that honor. Well, he gets a nonlethal bullet wound, but that's far from the indignity Nathan suffers.

Nathan Lee and Rebecca do backbreaking work as sharecroppers beholden to an uncaring White landowner, but moments of fun occasionally arise. Nathan Lee pitches for an all-colored sharecroppers baseball team, horsing around with his friend Ike (blues singer Taj Mahal, who also contributed to this film's soundtrack). Ike's antics are as enjoyably loose as the score. He flirts with Rebecca and ribs Nathan Lee the way any good friend does.

Sounder opens with the titular dog, Nathan Lee, and David hunting raccoon for dinner. Unfortunately, the raccoon escapes and they return home empty-handed. Nathan Lee's feelings of desperation lead him to commit petty theft that night, stealing food to feed his family. Rebecca and David are happy to eat the sizzling sausage and ham they awaken to, a respite from the cold mush they'd been eating for months. But questions about the procurement of this feast are ignored. Rebecca gets her answer when the police arrive to arrest her husband.

In that same instant, David is separated from his father and his dog. Rebecca tries to put in a good word for her husband, but the law is uninterested in any explanations. As the sheriff rides off with Nathan Lee, Sounder gives chase. Another cop aims his rifle at Sounder, but Nathan Lee kicks the gun away as it fires. Wounded in the ear, Sounder runs off into the woods. His owner ends up in a brutal prison, suffering a permanent leg injury before returning to his family. (It's a nicer fate than in the book, where Nathan Lee dies.)

Throughout *Sounder*, there is a sense of long distances between the places the characters travel to; a lot of walking occurs through gorgeous, wide-open vistas in the outdoors. Ritt's understated direction and Alonzo's stunning widescreen cinematography give the actors space—literally and figuratively—to communicate all manner of subtle emotions, quietly imbuing *Sounder* with an unshakable moral outrage. The geography is so familiar that, by the time Nathan Lee hobbles home, the distance he travels seems endless.

Sounder contains two exceptionally heartfelt hugs that elicit well-earned tears. The first is between father and son, with David accepting a freedom of sorts from his father. The second is the primary reason to watch *Sounder*, a reunion scene played brilliantly by Tyson and Winfield. The intense physicality of her emotional response nearly stops the viewer's heart. Tyson runs with reckless abandon toward Winfield, grabbing him so fiercely one can feel her enveloping arms. The camera almost drops out of frame, a mistake left in the film because this particular take was so powerful.

Opponents of the fast-growing Blaxploitation genre were quick to laud *Sounder* and to demand more films like it. The film was a critical success, earning numerous rave reviews and four Academy Award nominations. Winfield and Tyson became the first Black actors to be nominated together as Best Actor and Best Actress, and Lonne Elder III became the first Black screenwriter to be nominated for adapting a screenplay. *Sounder* was also a Best Picture nominee, the first for a film predominantly cast with Black characters. But the Academy was not yet done with making history. The Billie Holiday biopic *Lady Sings the Blues* would also earn Oscar nods.

One could debate the merits of casting Diana Ross as Billie Holiday. She doesn't sound like the jazz singer, and more than one purist hit the ceiling with rage and protest when she was announced. Yet few film critics could deny that she gives one helluva performance. And the box office numbers didn't lie; the film finished at number 10 on 1972's box office chart. Her covers of Holiday standards like "Good Morning Heartache" were also wildly successful, so much so that Ross sang them in concert for decades to come.

Regarding her acting performance: for a diva so concerned with fashion and beauty, Ross was never afraid to look her worst on the big screen. Her opening scene is fearless, an intense howl of drug-withdrawal fury, and she's equally adept at other feelings of desire, passion, and longing. Her songs aren't approximations so much as interpretations, and they're not as objectionable as the initial uproar indicated. Ross anchors the film with a performance that earned her an Academy Award nomination for Best Actress, an award she was robbed of by its eventual winner, Liza Minnelli, for *Cabaret*. Ross did win the Most Promising Newcomer–Female award at the Golden Globes.

Cinematographer Alonzo and costume designers Bob Mackie, Norma Koch, and Ray Aghayan give *Lady Sings the Blues* the kind of old-school studio system glitz and glamour heretofore unseen in a film about Black people. The resulting visual bling-bling is pure movie magic, even when a frazzled Miss Ross is threatening someone with a straight razor while demanding money for a fix.

As the love interest, Billy Dee Williams provided a still-unsurpassed blueprint for Black male suaveness. Williams was so debonair that he was referred to as "the Black Clark Gable" in the *New York Times*. (Williams said when he saw himself onscreen making his character Louis McKay's memorable entrance, "I fell in love with myself.") He and Ross have such spectacular chemistry together that producer (and Motown legend) Berry Gordy reteamed them in a more appropriate entry for this book, 1975's *Mahogany*.

As Piano Man, Holiday's sidekick and eventual drug partner, Richard Pryor gave the true definition of a supporting turn, one that was worthy of Oscar consideration yet ignored. His comedic chemistry with Ross was effortless, so much so that his brutal, tragic demise had a horrific, bitter sting to it. Pryor, who grew up in a whorehouse not unlike the one Ross's Holiday works in early in the film, knew more about the environment and drugs than director Sidney J. Furie or anyone else on the set. Ross said that he taught her how to properly shoot up so her heroin scenes would look realistic. Pryor, Williams, and Furie would reteam a year later for 1973's *Hit*.

These two predominantly Black films received nine Oscar nominations in total. Were things finally looking up for minority talent? Of course not!

1973

1973

PLENTY TO SEE IN '73

1973

1973

Blaxploitation made one of its two forays into television by shoehorning one of its biggest R-rated heroes into a neutered, tame television series that lasted a surprising seven episodes. But in theaters, 1973 was the year for Blaxploitation movies. The market became saturated with them, including four classics of the era. Several stars of the genre either came into their own or were introduced to audiences. Box office was good, and release dates were swift enough to cause "traffic jams" of films opening on the same day.

My first exposure to the era's movies was a film made in 1973, though I didn't see it until the summer of 1974. That film, *The Exorcist*, started what we think of as "a blockbuster movie." The concept of blockbuster films will have some bearing on the downfall of the Blaxploitation era, but not yet. Right now, Blaxploitation is popping at all the urban theaters in Los Angeles, Detroit, the Chicago Loop, and New York City's Times Square.

Speaking of theaters, there are a few names you'll become quite familiar with in these pages. The same theaters played Black movies over the years, and they were usually located in downtown "urban" areas. In Chicago, there's the Roosevelt and the Oriental; in Philly, there's the Milgram. Detroit had the Grand Lake.

In New York, the Cinerama often peddled films for soul brothers and their foxy ladies, as did the RKO 86th Street Theatre uptown. Even the Penthouse, on 47th and Broadway, had a turn (*Coffy* played there). But if you really want a good laugh, keep count of how many times the DeMille in Times Square shows up in this book.

More Black folks were on TV, and in roles that weren't humiliating—well, almost. *A Charlie Brown Thanksgiving*, the follow-up to the *Peanuts* Christmas special, aired for the first time on CBS in 1973. It introduced Franklin, the token Negro of Charlie Brown's neighborhood. Even as kids, we cast a suspicious eye on Franklin. He was clearly bussed in. The table seating of the Thanksgiving dinner was an insult—Franklin is forced to sit in a broken chair *and* he's the only one on that side of the table. That would never have happened on *Fat Albert*.

Also on CBS: Sherman Hemsley finally made his first appearance as George Jefferson on *All in the Family* on October 20, setting the groundwork for one of the longest-running Black sitcoms just two years later. Norman Lear had kept his word to wait for Hemsley to finish his role in the musical *Purlie*, which is why George was often mentioned on the show but never seen before this. Additionally, a Black detective series created by the makers of *Columbo* found its way to television. That show got cancelled with a quickness. Adding insult to injury, he was the second Black detective by virtue of debuting one day after the first Black detective show featuring a familiar movie character.

In January, CBS sold my beloved New York Yankees baseball team to their most famous and memorable owner, George Steinbrenner. On April 6, Yankees player Ron Blomberg became the first major leaguer to bat as a designated hitter, a controversial position created by the American League. Yankees fans were forced to cringe as our team played at Shea Stadium (home of the evil New York Mets) while the House that Ruth Built underwent a much-needed renovation.

Richard M. Nixon was sworn in for his second term, making him the first person to be sworn in twice as vice president and president. The first year of his new term was filled with the messy business of the Watergate scandal. Nixon's White House counsel John Dean got fired. Attorney General Richard Kleindienst resigned with H. R. Haldeman and John Ehrlichman. In October, vice president Spiro Agnew resigned and got three years of probation. The so-called Saturday Night Massacre that same month beget calls for the president's impeachment.

In November, the president famously said, "I am not a crook." He lied about that, but Nixon did keep one of his election promises. The United States' involvement with Vietnam ended in 1973, when the Paris Peace Accords were signed. While the war would inspire several movies of the 1970s, including Oscar winners *The Deer Hunter* and *Coming Home*, a full movie about the many Black veterans of the war would not be made until Spike Lee's *Da 5 Bloods* in 2020.

Since Black folks didn't trust the government from jump street, Watergate had no effect on the Black films of the era, though there was a Blaxploitation film that scared the government so much that it was eventually withdrawn from theaters. Watergate did usher in a slew of "paranoid thriller" films like 1974's *The Parallax View*, shot the same month the shit hit the fan with Dean and Ehrlichman.

It was a good thing that Blaxploitation movies played in theaters that were easily accessible by public transportation like the subway. The Organization of the Petroleum Exporting

Countries, or OPEC, issued an embargo on several countries including the United States in October. This lasted until March of the following year and caused all manner of havoc. The price of oil went up 300 percent. If you relied on your car, you were screwed six ways until Sunday. All that White flight to the suburbs had a downside after all.

Everyone's favorite future grill salesman, George Foreman, knocked Joe Frazier out in the second round of their January 22 bout to become the heavyweight champion of the world. Though Blaxploitation wouldn't see a boxing movie until Jamaa Fanaka's 1979 film *Penitentiary* (and that would be just outside the era's end), Foreman, Frazier, and Muhammad Ali would have a tie to the era in a very odd way. In a more suitable for sports way, Ali had his jaw broken in a losing match with the man who would later star in the Blaxploitation classic *Mandingo*, Ken Norton.

Bruce Lee's swan song, *Enter the Dragon*, opened in June but wasn't the first martial arts hit. That honor went to *Five Fingers of Death* (original title: *King Boxer*). Its success led to the boom of the so-called chop socky films, a genre whose rise ran in parallel with Blaxploitation releases. *Enter the Dragon* crossed that line between martial arts films and Blaxploitation, introducing Jim Kelly and his awesome Afro to American audiences. The Black cinematic history of 1973 would include Kelly, Pam Grier, Max Julien, Richard Roundtree, Ron O'Neal, William Marshall, Tamara Dobson, and even Sidney Poitier.

CHAPTER 10

NUrse COFFY and CLEOPATra Jones

Women in Blaxploitation pictures were often disposable characters who served two purposes: screw the hero and bring him information or a weapon. There were exceptions, from Judy Pace's performer in *Cotton Comes to Harlem* to Diana Sands's activist in *Willie Dynamite*. And while Black women were making strides as leads in Blaxploitation-adjacent films like *Sounder* and *Lady Sings the Blues*, they had yet to showcase their talents by carrying a Blaxploitation film the way Richard Roundtree and Ron O'Neal had done.

Pam Grier's starring role in *Coffy* in 1973 changed all that. After several supporting roles, she landed the co-lead in *Black Mama White Mama*, an American International Picture with a story by future Oscar-winning director Jonathan Demme. Demme would cut his teeth on "chicks in chains" movies, making his directorial debut in 1974 with the humanistic women's prison movie *Caged Heat*. For *Black Mama White Mama*, he, Joe Viola, and screenwriter H. R. Christian paid homage to—or rather, blatantly ripped off—Stanley Kramer's 1958 race drama *The Defiant Ones*. In that film, Tony Curtis and Sidney Poitier are chained together and must work through their hatred for one another in order to survive.

This time, Grier's moll, Lee Daniels (like the director!), and Margaret Markov's revolutionary, Karen Brent, are the interracial prisoners chained together. Markov had just come off a prior prison film written by Viola and Demme and shot in the Philippines, 1972's *The Hot Box*. A hot box fits into *Black Mama White Mama* as well, when the duo gets sentenced to time inside it by the angry lesbian guard who fancies them both. When their prison convoy is ambushed by machine gun–toting criminals, Karen and Lee escape. Just like Poitier and Curtis, they get into a fistfight while tethered. Unlike the men, the ladies also do a nude shower scene and steal food from the house of a couple who are too busy having sex to notice. "I hope he can last," Lee says to Karen as the lovers' moans become more intense. Unfortunately, he cannot.

Markov got top billing on the poster, but Grier got top billing onscreen. As they would do for much of their careers, both actresses did their own stunts. The chemistry between them, and their penchant for looking like they're having a great time, makes one wish they'd done more movies together. New World Pictures did have the good sense to reteam them for the violent 1974 gladiator spectacle *The Arena*, where their stunt work would have been even more impressive if Grier had been granted her wish to be totally nude in her battle sequences. ("See Pam's bush!" is how Grier described this in her interview at the 2022 TCM Film Festival.) Both films were among the first to open in their respective years. Markov would retire from film after *The Arena*, just as Grier was becoming a major action star with *Coffy* and its pseudo-sequel, *Foxy Brown*.

Coffy was director Jack Hill's third collaboration with Grier, shot in Los Angeles in January and February 1973. It wastes no time in establishing its premise. Grier's character, Coffy (short for Coffin!) is a nurse who despises drug dealers, and she's willing to lure them to their violent ends by any means necessary. By day, she's an angel of mercy; by night, she's the angel of death. As the film opens, she entices two heroin pushers with the promise of a one-night stand at their apartment. As one guy strips down to his purple boxers, the other watches while prepping his fix. Horny viewers expecting the requisite nudity and intertwined bodies were in for a big surprise.

Coffy pulls out a sawed-off shotgun, calls the half-naked guy a motherfucker, and blows his head clean off. The effect is so outrageously graphic that it jolts the audience into wicked levels of applause. Then Coffy demands that the other guy shoot up with an enormous amount of horse. "This will kill me!" he pleads. "Maybe it will and maybe it won't," she says. "But if it do, you gonna fly through them pearly gates with the biggest fucking smile St. Peter ever seen!"

Coffy is an unapologetically nasty piece of work. Its protagonist is one of Blaxploitation's meanest heroes, as tough as most of the men, if not tougher. "The baddest one-chick hit squad that ever hit town," crowed the poster's tagline. "She'll cream you!" *Coffy* kicked off a long series of films where the ladies got to whip as much ass as the men, with Grier at the forefront of these roles.

Jack Hill described her as "having that something special only she has. She has *it!*" It's the same kind of "it" Clara Bow displayed in her silent masterpiece, *It*, but a lot rougher and earthier. Whatever "it" was, it earned *Coffy*'s rightful place in the Holy Trinity of Blaxploitation alongside *Super Fly* and *Shaft*.

Having a female hero wasn't *Coffy*'s only deviation from the genre. The negative portrayal of drugs was also unusual, especially after *Super Fly*. Coffy's eleven-year-old sister has gotten hold of some bad smack and is now comatose at the hospital where Coffy works. She takes her cop ex-boyfriend, Carter (William Elliott), on a tour of the pediatric drug ward, pointing out that some of the patients are under ten years old. Carter is the rare honest cop, uninterested in being on the take like the rest of the department. When he backs out of the latest shakedown, his colleagues beat him like a piñata while Coffy helplessly watches. This is a crucial mistake, because Coffy knows how to keep—and settle—a grudge.

Meanwhile, Coffy's current boyfriend, Howard Brunswick (Booker Bradshaw), is a smooth politician running for Congress. He's suave and sexy, satisfying his leading lady in a nude sex scene mere minutes after he's introduced to the audience. Howard may be a stud, but he's also corrupt as shit and stupid as hell. Like most of the men in this picture, he will underestimate Coffy at his own peril. But the demands of Howard's campaign give her time to plan and execute her revenge undetected.

After gleaning his whereabouts from a former employee (and evading her very angry lesbian lover), Coffy goes undercover as a sex worker for King George (Robert DoQui), the pimp whose bad heroin her sister injected. King George wears the eye-searing yellow outfit that influenced Antonio Fargas's threads in the 1988 Blaxploitation parody *I'm Gonna Git You Sucka*. His theme music, like Coffy's, is by vibraphonist Roy Ayers. "George, King George," repeats a smooth-voiced brother over Ayers's music as George surveys his stable of women.

Jack Hill uses this location to stage one of the great catfights in exploitation film history. Bare breasts and broken glass fly everywhere, and in one of Grier's script contributions, Coffy's coif gives new meaning to the term "good hair" when one unlucky vixen discovers it's loaded with razor blades. This display of feminine ferocity gets Coffy her first client for George, a freaky, racist Italian guy named Arturo—King George's benefactor. It also affords her the opportunity to replace George's heroin with sugar, which will save her when she's later forced to inject a large amount of it.

If the Coalition Against Blaxploitation were going to complain, at least

Coffy gives them a moment when they have a point. After a botched assassination attempt on Arturo, Coffy tells him King George hired her. As retribution, Arturo's henchmen, one of whom is played by Sid Haig, tie George to the back of his own car using a noose. They then proceed to drag him behind it for what feels like an eternity. Though the gory aftermath looks far from realistic, the dragging scene itself is preternaturally vicious, hinting at some of the more gruesome moments that will occur in later Blaxploitation films. Granted, the audience is baying for blood and rooting for Coffy's revenge, but this scene temporarily throws the film off-kilter. On the TCM podcast *The Plot Thickens*, Grier said she wanted this scene to be even *more* graphic.

Despite giving its audience the gore-filled, vengeful goods, Coffy's climax is quite nihilistic. Howard, who's supposed to be running for office to help Black people, turns out to have no such good intentions and is in cahoots with Arturo. A distrust of authority figures is a running theme in Blaxploitation, as is the character of the turncoat Negro willing to sell out his own people for a seat at the White man's table. Howard's betrayals are particularly egregious, considering he knows what Coffy has been through. In a hiss-worthy scene, he orders her death.

Since *Sweet Sweetback* spoiled audiences into demanding their Black heroes survive to the end credits, Jack Hill wasn't going to disappoint them. After surviving the aforementioned sugar-filled fake overdose, Coffy dispatches Haig's henchman with a jab to the jugular, causes another henchman to be splattered all over on the LA freeway, then drives a car through Arturo's house (crushing his one-eyed bodyguard in the process). She kills everybody before returning to Howard's beach house, the site of the one sex scene in the film. Howard is there, and he tries to sweet-talk Coffy into "his loving arms."

"You always were a good talker," she tells him while aiming the same sawed-off shotgun she used on those dope pushers in the first reel. But before she can succumb to the full effect of Howard's silver tongue, they are interrupted by a naked White woman asking when Howard will be returning to bed. Mirroring her first use of the shotgun, Coffy shoots Howard in the head. Unfortunately for Howard, it's not the one on his shoulders.

As she stumbles out onto the beach, alone and spent, Roy Ayers serenades Coffy with a song about how righteous she is. However, Grier's lonely image in the frame visually questions the price of retribution. Like Charles Bronson's vigilante in *Death Wish*, Coffy feels traumatized by her first killing, so much so that she takes people out only in self-defense afterward. It's a satis-fying ending, but one is left wondering what will happen to Nurse Coffin after the credits roll.

As expected, reviews for *Coffy* were not so hot when the film opened on June 13, 1973. In New York City, it played at the Penthouse in Times Square, where New York *Daily News* critic Ann Guardino saw it before filing her one-star review. In Chicago, it blew the roof off the Oriental ("the Oriental is Y'Ori-ental now!" read an ad for the theater), which is where Roger Ebert saw it. Coincidentally, Grier briefly appeared in the movie Ebert wrote for Russ Meyer, *Beyond the Valley of the Dolls*.

Ebert's two-star review was one of the nicer pans of the film. Of course, the man who loved buxom women loved watching Grier. "She is a young actress of beautiful face and astonishing form," he wrote, "who has previously been seen in the kinds of movies frequented only by demented creeps and movie critics." Those demented creeps came out to say, "Wham! Bam! Thank you, Pam!" *Coffy* was a hit, making $2 million at the box office, four times its original budget.

Helping put asses in seats were the dynamic movie posters, which showed multiple pictures of Grier's outfits and hairstyles. Another, more famous poster featured a gloriously Afro-crowned Grier wearing a red shirt tied above her midriff. That shirt was a happy accident; the poster photos were shot without much preparation or warning, forcing Grier to improvise on clothing. The red shirt she found was too small to be worn over her entire torso, so she tied it under her cleavage. An iconic image was born.

Coffy wasn't the only 1973 movie to feature a baadasssss woman in the lead. That year, Max Julien created two more Blaxploitation classics, one as an actor and the other as a writer. The latter film, *Cleopatra Jones*, shared some similarities with *Coffy*, including an anti-drug theme, an iconic poster, and a statuesque heroine (Tamara Dobson) who was a major fashion plate who could handle a gun. But *Coffy* was a very hard R while Cleo wore her film's family-friendly PG rating with pride. Julien and his co-writer Sheldon Keller wrote a lighter, funnier script that matched *Slaughter* director Jack Starrett's deft touch. *Cleopatra Jones* also had a two-time Academy Award–winning actress, Shelley Winters, as its villain, fresh off her Oscar-nominated turn in the campy disaster epic *The Poseidon Adventure*.

Tamara Dobson's pre-stardom arc was different from Pam Grier's. Born in Baltimore on May 14, 1947, she was two years older and got her start in 1969 as a fashion model for magazines like *Ebony* and *Jet*. Before her career began, she did fashion shows at the Maryland Institute College of Art before receiving her degree in fashion illustration. Dobson also worked as a beautician between fashion shoots. At six feet two inches, she struck quite a figure, managing to get into the Guinness World Records at the time for being the tallest leading lady in cinema. "6 feet 2″ and all of it Dynamite!" screamed the *Cleopatra Jones* posters.

Starrett and costume designer Giorgio di Sant'Angelo took full advantage of Dobson's skill set, dressing her in eye-popping costumes and enough fur to give animal rights activists conniptions. In her opening scene, federal agent Cleopatra Jones wears a fur with numerous animal tails on it while visiting the Afghani desert to witness the airborne destruction of poppy fields worth $30 million. Upon her return, she has to outwit and shoot assassins sent to kill her, all while looking like she stepped off the pages of Gordon Parks's *Essence* magazine. Grier would get her multi–costume change opportunities in later films like *Friday Foster*, but *Cleopatra Jones* set the standard for Blaxploitation actioners.

Like Youngblood Priest, Cleo drives a jaw-dropping car, and like Priest's Caddy, it's a custom-made version viewers can only dream of owning. The US government must pay extremely well for an employee to drive a 1973 Corvette Stingray. Five were made for the film, each with a roof that automatically lifted whenever its owner opened the door, because no automobile would dare muss the gigantic Afro of Cleopatra Jones as she's exiting it! Also like Priest, Cleo gets a great love scene theme song: the masochistic soul hit "It Hurts So Good" by profanity-loving R&B singer Millie Jackson.

Shelley Winters clearly understood the assignment when she took the role of Mommy, Cleo's nemesis. The actress who once acted opposite Sidney Poitier in 1964's *A Patch of Blue* (and won an Oscar for it) had entered into her second career phase as a genre-film goddess. She had conquered the disaster epic and was making time in Blaxploitation's neighboring genre, Hagsploitation, when Mommy came along. She's a larger-than-life caricature, a tough lesbian who singlehandedly controls the drug trade, and Winters is damned if she's going to be upstaged by anybody. She's as over-the-top as her preternaturally red dye job, and equally as violent. When one of her henchmen fails to kill Cleo, she cusses him out and beats him to a pulp with her fists. Winters also gets as many wardrobe changes as Tamara Dobson, though her outfits veer comfortably into drag queen territory.

Part of the fun of this hilarious, terrifying performance is listening to the real-life big ol' liberal Winters spout her outrageously racist dialogue. She bursts on the screen screaming obscenity and outrage, fuming that Cleo's desert visit put a dent in her earnings.

"That bitch! That goddamn Black bitch!" Mommy screams. "How dare she mess around with my poppies?! My God! Everyone in Turkey must be flyin'! I'll kill her! I *will* kill her! Thirty million dollars up in smoke! Goddamn her, that troublemaking coon!"

Coffy visited a drug treatment facility, but Cleo's main squeeze, Reuben (Bernie Casey) runs a place that helps community kids avoid or detox from drugs. When corrupt cops raid it at Mommy's behest and plant drugs on a recovering addict, Reuben's pet project is in danger of being shut down. Cleo's police chief frenemy, whom she calls "Lieu," gives her seventy-two hours to clear the kid's name and prove Mommy's handiwork. She's assisted by her faithful comic sidekicks, karate experts Matt and Melvin Johnson aka the Johnson Brothers, played by Albert Popwell and Caro Kenyatta, respectively. Popwell had already achieved exploitation movie immortality by playing the recipient of Clint Eastwood's infamous "Do you feel lucky, punk?" speech in 1971's *Dirty Harry*, and 1973 also saw him playing opposite Eastwood in the *Dirty Harry* sequel *Magnum Force*.

Julien and Keller's script also gives a plum role to Blaxploitation staple Antonio Fargas, who plays the aptly named Doodlebug. He's Mommy's main dope pusher, a guy with an Afro shaped like a trapezoid and enough money from his dealing to afford a White chauffeur/valet. "What's next, Doodlebug?" asks Cleo upon meeting the chauffeur. "Two White iron jockeys on the lawn?" What's next is his departure from Mommy's employ to start a competing business. That goes over as well as one expects: in the film's one moment of brutality, Mommy has Doodlebug squashed by a tow truck.

Mommy will crush several more of her henchmen before the big showdown with Cleopatra Jones. It's here where the movie disappoints; a villain like Mommy deserves a better fight scene than she gets. After teasing the audience with the possibility of a long hand-to-hand combat scene, Cleo dispatches Mommy far too easily. Reuben's center is saved, and Cleo drives off into the sunset—and into a fun, though inferior, R-rated sequel, 1975's *Cleopatra Jones and the Casino of Gold*.

When *Cleopatra Jones* opened at the DeMille in New York City on July 4, 1973, it was in direct box office competition with *Coffy*. At year's end, *Cleo* emerged victorious, earning $3 million to *Coffy*'s $2 million. That PG rating may have contributed to the extra tickets, but another theory is that there were plenty of other Blaxploitation movies in the summer of 1973 vying for the pocket change of the "demented creeps." Just that week alone, viewers also had *The Mack, Super Fly T.N.T.*, and *Shaft in Africa*, not to mention Sidney Poitier's latest film, a tragic love story called *A Warm December*, and the Blaxploitation poseur that was James Bond's *Live and Let Die*.

Black media outlets like *Ebony* and *Jet* seized upon the fact there were two beautiful Black women headlining films, and they were, as the Southerners say, "finna start some shit" between them. *Ebony* published an article in their November 1973 issue entitled "The Battle Among the Beauties." It so offended Tamara Dobson that she wrote a letter to the editors. In it, she stated that she and Grier had been friends since 1969 and were also neighbors. There was no beef between them, as the article alluded. "I would respectfully request that the facts be set straight," she wrote.

In her autobiography, *Foxy*, Pam Grier mentioned her attempts to shop around Hollywood an *I Spy*–inspired buddy comedy starring her and Dobson. It would have been the first one of its kind starring two Black women. Despite the success of their films, nobody in Hollywood wanted to finance this movie. This was a great loss if ever there were one.

CHAPTER 11

Pimps Are Everywhere, even on *Sesame Street*

Remember Richard Zanuck, the guy whose famous dad, Darryl F. Zanuck, fired him from the family studio 20th Century-Fox? Well, that traumatic event forced him to consider pimping.

Not as an occupation but as a film subject. Truth be told, Zanuck and his partner David Brown were also producing the Paul Newman–Robert Redford con artist caper *The Sting* when *Willie Dynamite* started filming in New York City in February 1973. A year prior, the duo set up shop at Universal Pictures under the banner of Zanuck/Brown Productions, with *Sssssss*, a horror film about a man turning into a snake, as their first feature. Their names would later appear on Steven Spielberg's first two films, *The Sugarland Express* and *Jaws*. They would also win their own personal Oscars for producing the film that is the antithesis of Blaxploitation, *Driving Miss Daisy*.

In addition to the anti-drug diva duo of *Coffy* and *Cleopatra Jones*, 1973 gave viewers two competing pimp movies: *The Mack* and *Willie Dynamite*. They shared the similar plot of a pimp who wants to be the number one hustler in his 'hood. *The Mack* was the first film to be released. Though both films were rated R, Zanuck's production is by far the tamer of the two. By comparison, it's rather quaint; there is very little nudity, and violence is limited to two gnarly but not overly graphic knife wounds. Additionally, where *The Mack*'s protagonist, Goldie (Max Julien) is fighting against the Man, *Willie Dynamite* has a nemesis in the guise of a former sex worker who wants to take down the titular pimp. She is played by the late, great Diana Sands in her last film role.

Willie Dynamite is a "day in the life" look at its hero. Willie D is having a very bad day indeed. He is tired of being the second-greatest pimp in New York City, yet his plans to ascend to the top are consistently thwarted by the cops, by his fellow pimps, and by Sands's Cora, a self-proclaimed "Ralph Nader for hookers." The film is a litany of darkly comic events that prove the Big Daddy Kane adage that "pimpin' ain't easy." Tony-nominated Black director Gilbert Moses went from staging Melvin Van Peebles's incendiary Broadway musical *Ain't Supposed to Die a Natural Death* to directing White writer Ron Cutler's screenplay. They fashioned an entertaining though rather puritanical cautionary tale for pimps and the women who choose them.

Playing the role of Willie, in his film debut, was Roscoe Orman, a character actor and singer who once played Stepin Fetchit in a one-man stage biography written by the first actor to play Gordon on *Sesame Street*, Matt Robinson. Coincidentally, after starring in *Willie Dynamite*, Orman became the third actor to play Gordon, a role he held for forty-two years. In 1976, however, Orman resumed his onscreen pimp ways as Tyrone on the ABC soap *All My Children*. Tyrone was terrifying, and he confused the hell out of the kids at home with the mothers, aunties, and grandmothers who religiously watched their "stories." Orman mentioned getting letters from kids begging him not to beat up Big Bird, a not-so-far-fetched request. After all, *Sesame Street* did have a workable corner.

For all its flashy furs, cars, and women, *Willie Dynamite* is primarily a character study, a pas de deux between Cora and Willie. Cora keeps getting in Willie's hair (figuratively, as the man is bald) by pulling his women aside to lecture them about getting out of the life. To Willie, she's akin to one of those former smokers who vehemently turns against cigarettes once they quit. Cora isn't that extreme; she tries to convince his stable to abandon prostitution, or at the very least to go into the sex business for themselves. "He's ripping you off!" she says. Cora's assisted by her district attorney main squeeze, Robert Daniels, played by the ubiquitous Blaxploitation star Thalmus Rasulala. While Cora just wants to put Willie out of business, Daniels wants to put him in jail.

Though he often winds up in darkly hilarious situations and is dressed in over-the-top attire, Willie D is no clown. He also isn't a nice guy, threatening his women with violence and worse. Character actor Orman makes him equally charming and menacing, but also desperate and, late in the film, a completely destroyed figure who finds an ironic joy in retirement. After Cora destroys his livelihood with help from the IRS; the brutal throat-slashing of his best worker, Honey; and the untimely death of his beloved mother (Royce Wallace), Willie is a hollow shell of a man who literally gets religion. The film ends with him walking away from pimping for good.

For his trouble, the film's composer, J. J. Johnson, gave Orman one of the great, underrated Blaxploitation theme songs, "Willie D," sung with verve and funk by Motown legend Martha Reeves. "He's commercialized and he's selling lies," Reeves tells us before singing the hell out of the era's catchiest chorus. (Twist the author's arm, and he might admit this is his favorite theme song.) Johnson gives Reeves a set of quality songs that weren't hits but wound up in more than one soul brother's album collection.

Diana Sands turns in an excellent, committed performance, standing up to Willie when he tries to intimidate her. Cora looks at him with a "been there, done that" expression, as if to say, "I've been scared by a better grade of monster than you." Once she vanquishes her foe, Cora feels a form of sympathy and compassion toward him. By no means should her change of heart work, because it makes no sense. Yet it's worth evaluating her performance and considering her intent.

With her early death from cancer at thirty-nine, Sands was a tragic loss. As an actor, she had mystery. There was always the sense that she kept something from the viewer, something she held just for herself. It's an odd mixture of pride, self-preservation, and balls. It drew in the audience and added to her complexity. She was never just what she presented onscreen; she was always smarter than she let on. The real danger was in not knowing just how much smarter. Even when she played a character trying to find her identity, as in *A Raisin in the Sun*'s Beneatha, it shone through. She also had a Swiss timing to her delivery, imbuing her line readings with the right note at the right time. No matter how dopey the line was, she could make it work in service to her character.

Her last professional act was to recommend Diahann Carroll for 1974's *Claudine*, a role she was originally scheduled to play before she fell ill. She left behind an impressive slew of stage performances, including originating the role of the sex worker opposite Alan Alda in *The Owl and the Pussycat*, the aforementioned *The Landlord*, and her one starring role in 1972's obscure, hard-to-find, Maya Angelou–scripted *Georgia, Georgia*. Sands gets to sing and fall in love with a White man, but *Georgia, Georgia* is fatally wounded by Minnie Gentry, whose role can best be described as a bigoted, psychotic Mammy character. Gentry commits murder in the film's incredulous climax, then spends the closing credits ruthlessly brushing the deceased's hair. It does not play as Angelou intended.

Though it opened in Chicago during the last weeks of December 1973, *Willie Dynamite* is classified with the 1974 films as it opened everywhere else in that year. New York City got it in January, nine months after *The Mack* debuted at the Cinerama in Times Square, and three months before the Zanuck/Brown Company got respectable: on April 2, 1974, *The Sting* won seven Oscars, including Best Picture.

Like Willie D, *The Mack*'s Goldie has run-ins with the cops and steps away from pimping for good after the death of his mother. Before that, however, director Michael Campus and screenwriter Robert Poole put him through a much grittier ringer, one replete with graphic violence, nudity, and the ne plus ultra of '70s pimp attire. Goldie's realm is the Oakland of 1972, a city split by two distinctly different factions: the Black Panthers and the criminal underworld. The former is represented by actor Roger E. Mosley, who plays Goldie's righteous brother, Olinga. The latter is played by the genuine article, real-life kingpin and pimp Frank D. Ward.

Ward appears in a few scenes. In one, he's laying down pimp game in a real Oakland barbershop on Forty-Eighth Street and Telegraph Avenue. In the film's famous Players Ball sequence, he comes in second place as Mack of the Year. (It's easy to guess who wins that contest.) Ward told producer Harvey Bernhard, "I should be Mack of the Year in this scene!" The principal players in *The Mack*, from Campus on down, all agreed that without Frank Ward, there would have been no movie. Not just because he was technically one of the film's inspirations; he also put up money and provided protection for the filmmakers. According to all sources, Ward was immensely likable and could win people over easily. "Frank Ward was the real Goldie," said Campus.

"But he was a criminal," said Julien. "A serious criminal."

The Mack begins with a title card that read, "In Memory of a MAN, Frank D. Ward." In the middle of filming, Ward was gunned down in his car along with a woman. He was shot in the back of the head. Conspiracy theories abounded. A guy that big would have made plenty of enemies on his way to the top. One of the more nagging theories was that the hit was commissioned by Huey Newton. "Huey liked Frank," Julien said, expressing disbelief about his involvement. The Black Panthers knew *The Mack* was being filmed; Newton sent for Bernhard at one point, and when he didn't acquiesce, he got a visit from Bobby Seale. Seale kicked in his hotel door, telling him, "The man wants to see you!" However, they weren't against the movie.

There's none of *Willie Dynamite*'s glossy Universal Pictures sheen on *The Mack*. It looks made on the run, primarily because it was, and the low budget of barely $300,000 is evident in every frame. At times, it mimics a documentary, not surprising as Campus had been a nonfiction filmmaker. There's a realism that remained out of reach for its numerous imitators. *The Mack* knows its universe, and the actors bring some of their own real-world experience to their roles. "My brother was a pimp," said Dick Anthony Williams, citing the inspiration for his character, Pretty Tony. And when Julien portrayed excitement over winning Mack of the Year, Frank Ward pulled him aside and told him that no pimp would lose his cool no matter how great the honor. Julien reshot the scene with nary an indication that he was glad he won. He acts like he expected it.

Once again, co-star Richard Pryor called upon his expertise with pimps and whores to infuse his role with realism. Though much of the dialogue was improvised, Pryor rewrote the final drafts of *The Mack* with input from Poole and Julien. It was Julien's idea to cast Pryor, who by then had a reputation for being difficult and unreliable due to his drug habit. In *The Mack*, it's often painful to watch him, and not because he gives a bad performance. (It's good work.) Pryor is extremely high on cocaine in almost every scene. His face is puffy, and his eyes are glazed over. It goes with the mise-en-scène, to be sure, but he's clearly not acting. Because of Pryor and Ward, *The Mack* had verisimilitude to spare.

And then there were the clothes! Goldie's iconic white fur coat and his hats were Max Julien's idea. The unforgettable pimp and ho attire was designed by two Black Los Angelenos Julien heard about, June and Mr. Marcus. Their handiwork is on full display in the scene *The Mack* is most famous for, the Players Ball. This is a real event, one the author once attended wearing a purple suit with matching purple hat and alligator shoes. (He looked fabulous.) Goldie and his "bottom bitch" Lulu (Carol Speed) show up in their fanciest threads and his custom-made Cadillac. Campus uses handheld cameras to capture the event, giving it a you-are-there immediacy. Everyone wanted to go to the Players Ball after this, and the scene influenced rappers from Too $hort to Outkast to Snoop Dogg to Nas, who once rapped, "Mack like Goldie, it's the same story."

Rappers also sampled Motown recording artist Willie Hutch's score for *The Mack*, specifically its two most famous cuts, "I Choose You" and "Brothers Gonna Work It Out." Before Hutch composed his debut film score, his most notable achievement had been co-writing the Jackson 5's number one hit "I'll

Be There." His theme for *The Mack* is a funky, five-and-a-half-minute freak-out that "tells the story of the Mack!" He also composed the sensitive "Mama's Theme" that plays under Goldie's return home. Hutch's work on this movie earned him the job scoring *Foxy Brown*.

The allure of *The Mack* for viewers lay in the possibility that it will answer a question Goldie himself poses: "How do you convince these women to sell their bodies on the street?" "Anybody can control a woman's body," Goldie is told. "But the key is to control her mind." To run his game, that is, the smooth talk that seals the deal and gets women to "choose" him, Goldie uses the local planetarium space show! "In this organization, there's a president, a director, and a teacher," he seductively states over the PA system to the women staring up at the stars. "All of these offices are held by me." The unusual methodology does nothing to hide the sting of misogyny inherent in this power dynamic. Instead, it highlights why the pimp character has come to be revered by so many men.

The plot of *The Mack* is its least memorable feature. The initial draft of the script was written on toilet paper in Poole's jail cell while he was incarcerated. Goldie gets out of jail and arrives in Oakland on a bus. He decides he wants to be the number one pimp, a desire expressed in a fantasy sequence where Goldie makes it rain money in his own room. It's one of the rare times Goldie smiles. Afterward, he reconnects with his right-hand man, Pryor's Slim, and former flame Lulu. She tells him she needs a daddy to look out for her on the street. Though Pretty Tony disses Goldie by calling his operation "a rest haven for hos," he still becomes a raging success.

Unfortunately, Goldie is constantly harassed by extremely racist cop Hank (Don Gordon) and Hank's equally racist partner. He also has to deal with the Fatman (George Murdock), a low-level thug who wants in on his earnings. These White characters are responsible for a lot of the violence in *The Mack*; the rest comes from the Black characters re-creating real-life events. A scene where a rival pimp is tossed in a trunk with a bag full of rabid rats echoed a story Julien heard in Oakland, as did another scene where Goldie forces Pretty Tony to stab himself repeatedly with his pimp cane sword. The Fatman's fate—death by an injection filled with battery acid—was also based on an actual execution.

As she did in *UpTight*, Juanita Moore plays the mother of Max Julien's character. The only time Goldie fully lets down his guard is around her. He wants to get her out of the 'hood, buy her a house and set her up so she can relax and retire. She wants him to follow the more righteous path of his brother. There's a hint of sadness in Julien's eyes for the duration of *The Mack*. Nowhere is it more prevalent than when he's opposite Moore, and it isn't acting. On April 27, 1972, Max Julien's mother was murdered. Her shocking demise haunted the actor throughout filming. When Mother dies from injuries sustained from a beating by Hank, Goldie's anguish is almost too real.

The relationship between Goldie and Olinga mirrors the tenuous conflict that existed between the hustlers and the revolutionaries. They argue about each other's goals and how they are at odds about them. Olinga calls Goldie by his government name, John, and refuses to compromise. But Olinga eventually violates his code of ethics, stepping into Goldie's world to protect his brother and avenge their mother's murder. Though he kills in self-defense, he sees the act as a corruption of his belief system. The vanquishing of his enemies is the last play in Goldie's pimp game. The film ends with him leaving town on a bus similar to the one he came in on, with Hutch singing about how the brothers are gonna work it all out.

The Mack had its West Coast premiere at Oakland's Roxie Theater, with the proceeds going to the Black Panther Milk Fund. The lines were around the block. In addition to New York City and Oakland, the film played in eighteen other predominantly Black markets. Audiences stood up and cheered. So did a few critics. "Makes *Superfly* look like a gnat!" proclaimed World News Syndicate's Bill Lane. The *Los Angeles Times*' Kevin Thomas called the Players Ball "a sight as spectacular as it is ephemeral and is likely to linger in the memory long after the movie is over."

But for the most part, critics sounded like the New York *Daily News* review: "*The Mack* is dishonest!" *The Hollywood Reporter* accused Campus and Bernhard of being two White men exploiting Black people. In the documentary on the DVD release of *The Mack*, Max Julien defended the movie and the filmmakers. He also pointed out that pimps aren't just in the streets. They're in the boardroom and the courtroom. It only looks more elegant on the surface.

CHAPTER 12

WHEN BOND MET
BLAXPLOITATION

Live and Let Die was Roger Moore's first appearance as Ian Fleming's Agent 007, James Bond. Based on the quality of the film, it should have also been his last. That Bond's longest-running canonical portrayer began his tenure in a Blaxploitation rip-off constitutes some kind of Hollywood ouroboros; by the time it opened on June 27, 1973, *Live and Let Die* was surrounded by Blaxploitation movies paying homage to 007. Shaft was "hotter than Bond, cooler than Bullitt," according to the trailers. *Shaft's Big Score!* climaxed with a massive, Bond-inspired boat chase. Jim Brown's Slaughter, who had a sequel in 1973, went to exotic locations and tangled with dangerous women. Cleopatra Jones was a federal agent herself, pitted against a cartoonish supervillain. Sweet Sweetback was an even bigger super stud than Sean Connery could conjure.

But, as Melvin Van Peebles once said, "Hollywood has an Achilles pocketbook." Blaxploitation movies were kicking ass and taking names at the box office, and Hollywood wanted to capitalize by incorporating its biggest franchise into the mix. It's not known if Black audiences had flocked to prior Bond films; a familiarity was more likely to come from their numerous airings on *The ABC Sunday Night Movie*. Nevertheless, with a new actor assuming the role, producer Cubby Broccoli needed a sexy twist to make people forget, to use George Lazenby's words from his sole Bond outing, "that other fellow."

That other fellow had just unretired from playing Bond to do 1971's *Diamonds Are Forever* before retiring again until 1983, when he would once more do battle with his successor for box office dominance. Moore's *Octopussy* won that battle over Connery's non-canon *Never Say Never Again*, but Moore's goofier

Bond was on his last legs. He lasted one more feature, 1985's *A View to a Kill*, which has a tie with *Live and Let Die* in terms of the type of Bond Girl both films employ.

Live and Let Die was the second Bond novel to be published. Fleming wrote it in 1954 at his estate in Jamaica, the island where some of the action takes place. Bond is also roaming around Harlem, making this the one 007 novel that could easily lend itself to a faux-Blaxploitation spin. It also helped that the novel was racist, advancing the idea that the Black Power movement and the NAACP were communist fronts that threatened America. There's even a chapter called "Nigger Heaven," just in case the author's prejudices weren't blatant enough. Screenwriter Tom Mankiewicz left all that commie business out of his script, opting instead for a plot that included heroin, repeated use of the word "honky," and a White voodoo woman.

Every generation gets the 007 they deserve. In November 1972, Generation X got forty-five-year-old Roger Moore. Ten years prior, as Connery was becoming Bond, Moore was portraying another famous and successful series character, *The Saint*'s Simon Templar. Templar was a much looser, Robin Hood–style take on spies and their agencies. This looseness carried over into Moore's performance as Bond and, considering the ridiculousness of the stories he had to carry, it served him well. One cannot imagine the far meaner and more stoic Connery Bond dealing with Dr. Kananga, the villain of *Live and Let Die* played by Yaphet Kotto.

Kananga is the corrupt dictator of San Monique, a fictional island in the Caribbean where one of Bond's fellow agents meets his demise in a pre-credits sequence. Kananga is at the UN when another agent is murdered mere feet from him by one of his agents. A pair of Black hands are seen committing the crime. This is intercut with footage of a somber parade in New Orleans. After a third agent is murdered, the streets of the Big Easy erupt in a dancing frenzy, as if to celebrate the murder of this White man by scary Negro forces.

Kotto seemed like perfect casting for a Bond villain. He's big and intimidating and has a voice he uses with a terrifying authority. Unfortunately, all that is undermined by his second role as Mr. Big, a Harlem gangster. Mr. Big looks like Yaphet Kotto trapped in an atrocious makeup job. Since the actor is such a distinctive-looking man, it's easy to figure out that Kananga is Mr. Big in disguise. Making matters worse, while Kananga speaks like an educated, power-mad psychopath, Mr. Big sounds like Sapphire, the Kingfish's wife from

Amos 'n' Andy. Kotto spoke about how ridiculous and stereotypical he thought this role was and how he did his best not to look ridiculous. He did not succeed.

M sends Bond to Harlem to investigate the aforementioned murders. Throughout his investigation, Bond is assisted by a series regular, CIA agent Felix Leiter (*The Fly*'s David Hedison) in America, and in San Monique by Rosie Carver (Gloria Hendry). *Live and Let Die* missed a grand Blaxploitation opportunity to cast Bernie Casey as Leiter, a role he would play in *Never Say Never Again*. It does, however, introduce the first Black Bond Girl three decades before Halle Berry's Jinx did her Ursula Andress imitation exiting the ocean in *Die Another Day* and twelve years before Moore did battle with Grace Jones's May Day in *A View to a Kill*.

Unlike Jinx and May Day, Rosie Carver is offensively incompetent. Imagine Butterfly McQueen's Prissy from *Gone with the Wind* as a secret agent. Hendry spends most of her screen time reacting with big-eyed terror at what the White filmmakers assume would pass for voodoo symbolism. Bond even scares her into a sexual encounter by capitalizing on her oversize superstitions about "cursed" hats and dolls. Carver's ineptitude is an insult to Hendry. When she was filming this role, Hendry was already on the screen with Yaphet Kotto in *Across 110th Street*. When *Live and Let Die* was released, she was simultaneously appearing in *Slaughter's Big Rip-Off* and as Fred Williamson's brutalized moll in *Black Caesar*; neither were roles to write home about, but she still fared better than she did here.

Live and Let Die fares better with its Black henchmen. As Tee Hee, Julius Harris gives the franchise one of its most memorable and dangerous baddies. He loves crocodiles and has an artificial metal arm to prove it. That metal arm and its clawlike hand are cooler and more impressive than any gadget Q gives Bond. Tee Hee bends Bond's gun on their first meeting, a visual neutering, and is far more menacing than Kananga. This is why he gets the last fight sequence in the film, one of the most brutal battles between Bond and a nemesis. With his steely accoutrement, Tee Hee is the Black counterpart to Richard Kiel's Jaws, the metal-mouthed killer who would later torment 007 in *The Spy Who Loved Me* and *Moonraker*.

Also out to spoil Bond's success is acclaimed choreographer Geoffrey Holder, best known for playing Nasty Nelson in Eddie Murphy's sex comedy *Boomerang* and for pitching 7UP for years. Tony Award winner Holder plays Baron Samedi, Tee Hee's sidekick and the one character in *Live and Let Die* who looks like he was airlifted in from a Blaxploitation movie. He gets the last shot of the film, hinting that he might return in other Bond movies. Nearly naked save for a white top hat, tailcoat, and face paint, Holder laughs that wonderful laugh of his while dancing his own choreography and scaring the hell out of San Monique residents. Baron Samedi is a well-known character in Haitian lore, a spirit of the dead who guards the past and is often seen as a Black man dressed as Holder is, but with a skull painted on his face. Without that history, which is left unexplained by Mankiewicz's script, Baron Samedi must have come off to viewers as some kind of Voodoo Alvin Ailey.

There's another Bond Girl in *Live and Let Die*, the soothsayer Solitaire. Though Black in the book, she's played by Jane Seymour. Seymour gets an "Introducing" credit despite this not being her first movie. Originally, the producers considered Diana Ross, who was just about to be nominated for Best Actress for *Lady Sings the Blues*. Ross would have made a better Kananga. Speaking of Kananga, he seeks advice from Solitaire (a Black man going to a White woman for voodoo?!) until she runs afoul of James Bond's pecker. Apparently, the source of Solitaire's power was located in her hymen; once deflowered, she's practically useless and becomes a damsel in distress who needs to be saved from these unruly Negroes.

Though they covered Chuck Berry and were influenced by Little Richard, nobody would consider the Beatles for a Blaxploitation soundtrack. Regardless, Cubby Broccoli got George Martin to do the score for *Live and Let Die*. Producer Harry Saltzman wanted a Black woman to sing the theme song, but Martin got the Cute Beatle, Paul McCartney, to write and sing it instead. McCartney and his wife Linda received the canonical Bond series' first Oscar nomination for Best Song, and while there's no argument it is one of the best of the Bond themes, it is done a major disservice by Maurice Binder's opening credits sequence.

Binder's titles were part of the Bond movie DNA, with their nipple-less naked women writhing around and flying through the air while cats crawl from between their legs and guns become phallic symbols. This time, Binder supplemented his writhing dames with an actual Black woman whose eyes are wider than studio system–era coon's Willie Best. Symbols are painted on her body with white paint. Every so often, she bursts into flames and turns into a skeleton. The entire endeavor looks cheap, like the opening credits of a movie from low-budget Dimension Films or one of the lesser New World Pictures.

It does resemble a Blaxploitation production, especially something horror-related like *Blacula*. It might have worked better with Black songstress Brenda Arnau's cover version of the theme song, which Saltzman managed to sneak into the film.

It's safe to say director Guy Hamilton was no Jack Hill and that Mankiewicz, Cubby Broccoli, and everyone else behind the cameras had no clue about what made Blaxploitation films click. They did, accidentally or otherwise, manage to give Kananga the most Blaxploitation-style plan of any Bond villain. Like Youngblood Priest, he wants to get America hooked on his drug product. The only difference is, Priest wants to sell his dope, while Kananga wants to hook customers by temporarily giving it out for free!

Kananga's entire plan is to scare island natives away from his poppy fields via voodoo while simultaneously impersonating a Harlem gangster named Mr. Big to sell his product. Even Priest had pushers to do his work for him, yet someone as big as Kananga couldn't manage the lowest-level clocker to look a brother out?

This is a Bond villain?

What happened to crazy world domination? Where are the active volcano lairs and sharks with, to quote Austin Powers's nemesis, Dr. Evil, "frickin' laser beams attached to their heads"? Kananga even *has* sharks, but alas, they're laserless. How bootleg is this shit? Making matters worse, Kotto wasn't allowed to do any publicity for the film as United Artists thought there would be protests if audiences discovered the villain was Black before the film was released. Viewers should have rioted because Kananga's plan was *beyond ratchet*.

Imitation is the sincerest form of flattery, and it also can be quite lucrative. *Live and Let Die* made more money than any of 1973's Blaxploitation films, coming in at number 7 for the year. Roger Moore made six more Bonds, all better than his first and each showing his age in more noticeable fashion. As for Bond himself, he has yet to revisit Harlem.

A much better example of spy movies gone Blaxploitation came out in December 1973. Fred "The Hammer" Williamson starred in *That Man Bolt*, a Hong Kong–based actioner with espionage elements. As Jefferson Bolt, the world's best courier of currency, Williamson dressed in a tuxedo, bedded beautiful women, blew up a lot of shit, got involved in international intrigue, and squared off against a baddie who had a slew of kung fu assassins. Throughout the film, assorted characters refer to the protagonist as "Mr. Bolt," which sounds a lot like "Mr. Bond." As if the 007 similarities weren't evident enough, the tagline for *That Man Bolt* was "He's 'Bonded'!"

The villain here is bank owner Kumada (Masatoshi Nakamura), who, in addition to suspect financial dealings, has a stable of women he watches like a hawk. Bolt is assigned to deliver a large amount of money to Kumada, based on the instructions of a shady Brit named Griffths (Byron Webster). Bolt carries the loot in a suitcase handcuffed to his wrist, using some of it in the requisite casino gambling scene. Turns out the money is counterfeit, but that's the least of Bolt's problems. After sleeping with Kumada's main squeeze, Dominique Kuan (Miko Mayama), Bolt must deal with a slew of assassins out to get him.

Unfortunately, *That Man Bolt* doesn't do right by its Black Bond girl, either. She's given a great Ian Fleming–like name, Samantha Nightingale, and is played by the charismatic and beautiful future star of the TV series *Get Christie Love!*, Teresa Graves. A professional singer, Graves performs two musical numbers at the standard-issue Blaxploitation movie night club before hooking up with her former flame. Her love scene with Williamson featured a rare occurrence of nudity by the actress (who was against appearing naked onscreen). Their lovemaking is interrupted by assassins, and in a nod to *Thunderball*, she's shot in the back when Bolt uses her for a human shield.

With Williamson running around in LA, Vegas, Mexico City, and Hong Kong, *That Man Bolt* aimed more for an international flavor than a Blaxploitation one. It's the rare film to be directed by two people, Henry Levin and David Lowell Rich, and its script was co-written by Ranald MacDougall, who also scripted *Mildred Pierce* and *Cleopatra*. All this studio system firepower, plus the frugal Universal Pictures of this era was willing to spend money on this one in the hopes of starting their own spy franchise. Williamson signed up for three films, but Universal allegedly got cold feet at the thought of a Black superspy and reneged on the deal.

Williamson was paid for two Bolt films, but this is the only one that got made. Largely forgotten, and unfairly so, *That Man Bolt* is notable as being the movie that kept Williamson's appearances in the film he was concurrently filming, *Hell Up in Harlem*, to a minimum despite his being the lead.

CHAPTER 13

Payin' the Cost to Be the Boss

Director Larry Cohen entered the Blaxploitation game by writing 1973's *Black Caesar*, an homage to Mervyn LeRoy's famous pre-code Warner Bros. gangster drama, *Little Caesar*. That 1931 classic put Edward G. Robinson on the map as a force with which to be reckoned. A brutal crime drama based on W. R. Burnett's novel (he also wrote *The Asphalt Jungle*), its box office success spawned the type of gangster films Warners became synonymous with during the 1930s. Eddie G. and his fellow tough guy, Jimmy Cagney, lit up the screen in films like *The Last Gangster* and *The Public Enemy*, shooting up their nemeses, living fast, and dying hard. In a blatant nod to the Warner Bros. director stable and its ties to his film, Cohen cast William Wellman Jr., the son of *The Public Enemy* director William Wellman, in a pivotal role.

LeRoy had Robinson's Rico as his antihero. Cohen had Fred Williamson's Tommy Gibbs. Gibbs is a Black street hustler who will eventually follow in the footsteps of real-life Harlem gangsters like Bumpy Johnson and Frank Lucas. The film opens in September of 1953, with young Tommy (Omer Jeffrey) using his shoeshine box to set up a mob hit. His work with the criminal underground leads him to his future nemesis, a corrupt, racist cop named McKinney (Art Lund). McKinney brutally beats Tommy's legs, permanently injuring him before sending him up the river for eight years. Revenge is one of the things on Tommy's mind when he returns to Harlem in 1965.

Casting the six-three Williamson was an inspired choice, as he looked great in the old Warners gangster uniform of suit and hat. Plus, he could easily convey menace as well as charm. The actor was also a known cinematic commodity by this point, having played Dr. Oliver "Spearchucker" Jones in Robert Altman's *M*A*S*H*, a sexy Black cowboy in the Blaxploitation Western *The Legend of Nigger Charley*, and a boxer in the Blaxploitation drama *Hammer*. Those residing in the clean world knew Williamson from his stint as Diahann Carroll's love interest in her groundbreaking 1969 sitcom, *Julia*.

Like Bernie Casey and Jim Brown before him, Fred Williamson was a former NFL player. He began his career as a defensive back with the Pittsburgh Steelers before spending four years with the Oakland Raiders and three with the Kansas City Chiefs. The Gary, Indiana, native has the distinction of being the only Blaxploitation star to play in the Super Bowl. The first Super Bowl, to be exact, which his Chiefs lost to the Green Bay Packers 35–10 on January 15, 1967. During his time with the Chiefs, Williamson began referring to himself as "The Hammer," a name derived from a comment by the coach of the San Francisco 49ers earlier in his career. The Hammer liked to hit his opponents upside the head as if they were nails, a move the NFL would eventually ban.

The nickname followed him into his movie career, giving many the erroneous notion that it derived from B. J. Hammer, the character he played in *Hammer*. That Hammer also went upside people's heads—he was a dockworker-turned-boxer working for a corrupt Black boss and the Mafia. Director Bruce Clark's film was an odd mishmash of Elia Kazan's *On the Waterfront* and the boxing subplot of Jamaa Fanaka's 1979 film, *Penitentiary*. The star of the latter film, Leon Isaac Kennedy, even has a cameo. Boxers who don't follow the rules of fight-fixing, or who ask too many questions about their bigwig overlords, wind up murdered. B. J. Hammer eventually becomes the next target for extermination. It does not end well for the bad guys.

Vonetta McGee provided the love interest in *Hammer*, and Bernie Hamilton played a frenemy cop. The ubiquitous Blaxploitation star D'Urville Martin also had a small role. While convincing as a boxer, Williamson had to contend with a mediocre, confused script by Charles Johnson and a shockingly dull and repetitive score by soul legend Solomon Burke. Hammer may have the least memorable theme song for a Blaxploitation action hero.

Black Caesar had just finished filming in Harlem when *Hammer* opened seventy-eight blocks farther south, at the DeMille, on September 22, 1972. *Super Fly* and *Shaft's Big Score!* were waiting for *Hammer*, siphoning off money that might have gone into its box office numbers. Jim Brown's *Slaughter* was also playing. Both *Super Fly* and *Slaughter* would eventually go to number 1 on the nationwide US box office charts during their respective runs, proving the grow-ing audience craving for Blaxploitation. *Hammer* got lost in the shuffle.

No such fate befell *Black Caesar*. It was a hit when it opened in February 1973 at the Cinerama in New York City and the Roosevelt in Chicago. Never mind that it was harshly panned by many critics. Kathleen Carroll called it "revolting" in the New York *Daily News*. Kevin Thomas in the *Los Angeles Times* wrote it was "utterly unconvincing" but "suggests its fast-rising star Fred Wil-liamson possesses the emotional range and stamina to sustain a large-scale role." One critic who enjoyed the film was Jean Dietrich of Louisville, Ken-tucky's *Courier-Journal*. Dietrich found it "well-acted and action packed" with "super bloody violence. Much foul language. One brief scene of upper frontal, and full back female nudity." Those are the building blocks of a hit!

In keeping with the dark themes of its Depression-era influences, Cohen wrote Tommy Gibbs as a mean and ruthless piece of work, a man to be revered and hissed at in equal measure. Upon his return to Harlem, Gibbs's first act is to execute a doomed mobster he hadn't been contracted to kill. Bringing the dead man's severed ear to Mafia kingpin Cardoza (Val Avery), he brokers a deal to work as a hired killer. Cardoza tells him he doesn't hire spooks but changes his mind when he hears Gibbs's mastery of Italian. "My cellmate was a Sicilian," he says.

The payment for services rendered is control of the shittiest block in Harlem. From that location—127th and Edgecombe—Tommy Gibbs builds his empire. He and his associates mow down their enemies in a montage of machine gun massacres. Eventually, he takes over Cardoza's territory. In a gruesome, exciting scene, Gibbs's crew murders an entire pool party, filling the pool with enough bloodied bodies to turn the water completely red.

As he rises to the top, Gibbs has little time for pleasantries, and he's as brutal to his enemies as he is to his love interest, Helen (Gloria Hendry). Hendry's singer-turned-mobster-moll role is rather thankless. In an ugly scene, Gibbs rapes her. Whenever she stands up for herself, he hits her. Later, there's a nude, consensual sex scene that does little to erase those prior violations. When she vengefully turns on Gibbs in the third act, she's still seen as a victim.

Any hope for Helen's happiness is dashed. For example, when she finds love with Gibbs's nerdy childhood friend, Joe, he's subject to a brutal beating to show how weak he is. Later, he forgives Gibbs and offers to help him escape the most dire of straits, only to have the top of his head blown off for his trouble.

Gloria is left widowed with two kids and, since Gibbs ruined her singing career, no way to make any money.

Julius Harris plays Gibbs's father, with whom he has daddy abandonment issues. Papa Gibbs reappears once his son has hit the big time. "Did it ever occur to you that I've waited twenty-five years to kill you?" his son asks before blaming the extreme poverty he endured on his father walking out on the family. Papa Gibbs manages to escape being shot. When his son needs him, however, he once again abandons him.

Gibbs's mother, played by Minnie Gentry, is a maid working for William Wellman Jr.'s Alfred Coleman. Coleman is unaware of this when he becomes Gibbs's lawyer and partner in a legitimate business of stock portfolio investments. Gibbs uses that money to line the pockets of McKinney in order to keep the cops at bay. He also has the upper hand courtesy of some stolen ledgers that list, with names, all sorts of payoffs and corruption. "I want McKinney nice and fat before I kill him," he tells Coleman.

Once their partnership is successful, Gibbs buys Coleman's house, and everything in it, paying him an ungodly sum of money that Mrs. Coleman demands he accept. When Mama Gibbs discovers her son bought the house she slaved in for decades, she rejects his gift outright. "I've always been a maid," she tells him. He offers to have some White women be her maid. Incredulously, she says she wouldn't know what to tell them to do.

Gentry's character is a real throwback to the studio system portrayal of older Black women as overly religious servants of man and God. She falls on her knees in front of Reverend Rufus (D'Urville Martin), begging him to pray for her son. As a character, Reverend Rufus is a strange mix of con man beholden to Gibbs and religious zealot. At one point, he prays so ridiculously that Gibbs slaps him silly in a failed attempt to stop him. Prayer is the good reverend's response when Gibbs wants him to help get a bullet out of his side. Unfortunately, he'll carry that bullet with him into his final showdown with McKinney.

Cohen writes antiheroes, and *Black Caesar* features one of his more fearsome and fleshed-out creations. The filmmaker's penchant for provocation is also very much in evidence. In the film's climax, McKinney has turned on all of his cronies, including Coleman, whom he shoots in the forehead as a means to frame Gibbs. When he arrives at Coleman's office, McKinney punches him in his wounded side before forcing him to get on his knees and shine his shoes. (Where McKinney got an old-fashioned shoeshine box is never addressed.)

Gibbs starts buffing and polishing before gaining the upper hand. He forces McKinney to put black shoe polish on his face and sing Al Jolson's "Mammy" before beating him to death with the shoeshine box. Cohen intercuts this beating with the one McKinney dispensed on Gibbs's legs in the first reel. Satisfied with his revenge, he hobbles back up to the Harlem neighborhood where he was born and raised. The building he grew up in is condemned, just like Gibbs's soul.

In his first gangster role, Fred Williamson struts confidently through Harlem in his finest threads; he looks like a million dollars. The hat that Cohen took credit for putting atop his head was memorable enough for it to be featured prominently on the film's poster. Williamson even looks super fly as he's stumbling down the street after being shot in broad daylight on Fifth Avenue. Part of that swagger comes courtesy of *Black Caesar*'s soundtrack, sung by the Godfather of Soul himself, Mr. James Brown. Several of these songs would later become beats sampled by hip-hop DJs and MCs.

Brown and Fred Wesley wrote *Black Caesar*'s score with no regard to the usual way movies are scored. Brown's music had to be edited into the film wherever the beats fit. Cohen was frustrated, as was AIP head Samuel Arkoff, but the score works very well no matter how it got into the picture. "Mama's Dead," a mournful lament featuring Brown's anguished vocals, plays in Mama Gibbs's funeral scene. Brown's superb composition, "The Boss," is most memorably used twice. "Paid the cost to be the Boss," he sings thrice in succession while his horn section did what James Brown's horn section always did.

"The Boss" first plays during that montage of Gibbs machine-gunning his foes. It gets a reprise in the aforementioned shooting sequence. In the former scene, it's a magnificent boast, sung from the chest and carried along by hot guitar licks and brass section blasts; in the latter, the irony is as delicious as the song is catchy. The *Black Caesar* soundtrack is one of Brown's masterworks, but the best song on it wasn't written by the soul singer.

Black Caesar opens with a song sung by Brown but written by Barry De Vorzon (of the disco film *Xanadu* fame) and Bodie Chandler. "Down and Out in New York City" is not only the film's theme, it's its thesis statement. As he later would do for Dan Hartman's "Living in America" in *Rocky IV*, Brown turns another writer's song into something that sounds like it sprung from his own pen. As the opening credits follow young Tommy Gibbs running through Harlem after the mob hit, the song tells the story of his rise from shoeshine boy to

King of Harlem. Brown's vocals are so compelling that Cohen could have had them play over a black screen and they would have lost none of their power. "Down and Out" is a fan favorite; in a Twitter poll of favorite Blaxploitation songs conducted by the author, it placed number two, higher than "Theme from *Shaft*" and "Freddie's Dead."

"Mother of Mercy, is this the end of Rico?" Edward G. Robinson asks at the end of *Little Caesar*. It was! And it was the end for Tommy Gibbs just before the closing credits of *Black Caesar*. In what might be considered an anticlimax, Gibbs is taken down not by rivals but by kids, a batch of future Black Caesars, who rob him in front of his childhood home and beat him to death. Critic Robin Wood wrote that this finale was unlike the one that ended Rico, because it was "not the reimposition of established values but a reminder of the social roots of the evil and an acknowledgment that nothing has been achieved."

Regardless, it was a fitting end, a biblical "live by the sword, die by the sword" style demise. Unfortunately, that scene was witnessed only by the audience at *Black Caesar*'s test screening in Los Angeles. That audience wasn't happy with seeing their "hero" get killed, something Sam Arkoff warned Cohen against doing. So, before the film premiered in New York City, Cohen introduced himself to the audience, then went into the projection booth and physically cut the ending out of the last reel. Since the VHS version restored the original cut, no one besides audiences in 1973 saw the film this way.

Despite its abrupt end, *Black Caesar* was such a hit that a sequel was immediately commissioned. This presented a problem: neither Larry Cohen nor Fred Williamson was available to do an impromptu sequel. Williamson was in Hong Kong making *That Man Bolt*, and Cohen was in LA at Warners making his killer mutant infant film, *It's Alive*. Cohen turned out a screenplay on the fly for *Hell Up in Harlem*, then shot it whenever he had a break and on weekends when Williamson was doing the Los Angeles scenes for *Bolt*. *Hell Up in Harlem* opened in December 1973 at the same New York City theater *Black Caesar* did, the Cinerama.

The resulting film was, in the author's opinion, a disaster. Though Tommy Gibbs is in much of *Hell Up in Harlem*, Fred Williamson is not. He was replaced by a stand-in whenever he wasn't available, which was often. No one seemed to notice in 1973, though it is quite evident now, thanks to high-definition media players and the like. Also, unless a viewer saw the movie at that preview in 1973, they are confused by the sudden reappearance of a dead man.

Cohen disavows his protagonist's original death scene and expands the roles of Papa Gibbs, Reverend Rufus, and Helen (again played by Julius Harris, D'Urville Martin and Gloria Hendry, respectively). It opens with a rewrite of its predecessor's ending: Helen runs up on corrupt DA DiAngelo (Gerald Gordon) to tell him that Tommy Gibbs is about to be shot by a cop on Fifty-Seventh Street and Fifth Avenue. She tells him she's the one who dropped a dime on her ex-husband and mentions the ledgers that, unbeknownst to her (or anybody who saw *Black Caesar*), feature DiAngelo's name on their pages.

Meanwhile, clips from the shooting in *Black Caesar* and the subsequent taxi chase scene are recycled over the opening credits. Added is narration by Williamson, stating that he called several members of his crew (who were all clearly shot to death in *Black Caesar*) and his papa to assist him. They rush him to Harlem Hospital and force a surgeon to operate on him. The cops don't arrest Gibbs because he still had the ledgers. All of this retconning is done in the sloppiest of ways.

Since his star was barely available, Cohen turns *Hell Up in Harlem* into the story of how Papa Gibbs inherits his son's empire. He also introduces a new nemesis, Tony King's Zach, to cause trouble. Harris is convincing as a tough guy, but the dynamic is different. He's all menace and lacks Williamson's charm.

Also different is the way the film treats Tommy Gibbs's new love interest, Sister Jennifer (Margaret Avery, a dozen years before *The Color Purple*). She's a member of Reverend Rufus's church who knows what Gibbs is yet falls for him anyway. Avery is docile and doesn't have much of a character to play, though she convinces her man to get out of the business. Her excuse for being in the picture is so Cohen can shoot the requisite sex scene, this time with more nudity by Williamson than his leading lady. At least she's treated better than Helen.

The thankless nature of Hendry's role in *Black Caesar* is not only repeated, it's served with a heaping side order of cruelty. DiAngelo beats and sexually assaults her after her confession. Papa Gibbs takes away her two children as punishment for her betrayal. She chases after Gibbs, begging him to kill her as she has nothing else to live for besides her kids. Eventually, she's strangled by Zach, her body left in a crumpled heap in an alley. Cohen pulls his camera away from her body slowly, as if trying to evoke some sympathy for this poor woman. Ultimately, this leads to endless shootouts as Tommy Gibbs returns to take back his territory and avenge her death.

Hell Up in Harlem is no fun at all, makes little sense, and is barely watchable despite Harris's performance. The biggest miss, however, had to do with Cohen's desire to have James Brown score the sequel. AIP refused to work with him. Instead, the mediocre score is sung by gravel-voiced Motown singer Edwin Starr, whose most effective contribution is entitled "Big Papa."

Now, the legend goes that Sam Arkoff was so angry at how Brown delivered the score for *Black Caesar*, and the extra money it cost to fit it in, that he did not want to work with Brown again. The real story is that AIP did work with Brown again after *Black Caesar*, on the Jim Brown sequel *Slaughter's Big Rip-Off*. It was on that film that the singer fell out of favor with AIP, causing them to put the kibosh on Cohen's request for Brown to do a *Hell Up in Harlem* score on spec.

This was a big, big mistake. Brown took his composition and released it as a stand-alone album. That album, *The Payback*, was not only Brown's biggest seller, but its title song became one of the building-block samples of hip-hop. "So now, ya punk, ya gotta get ready for the big payback," sang Brown. One can imagine that was dedicated to American International Pictures' head honcho.

CHAPTER 14

YOU CAN'T JUDGE A MOVIE BY ITS COLOR

Record companies like Stax and Motown provided soundtracks for Blaxploitation films. Their artists also appeared in two documentary films, *Save the Children* and *Wattstax*, that were part of the era but served as counterprogramming. They chronicled two major concerts in Chicago and Watts, Los Angeles, respectively, and provided a real-life look at the communities that so many Blaxploitation films dramatized.

Concerts like these were not uncommon at the time. They served as a way to channel the anger resulting from racism, assassinations, and segregation into a positive event that celebrated the resiliency of Black people. The first concert that influenced future events was held in Harlem in 1969, yet the footage didn't see the light of day for decades.

In 1969, the Harlem Cultural Festival took place at the same time Woodstock was occurring one hundred miles to the north. It, too, was a concert filled with plenty of Black talent, from Nina Simone to the 5th Dimension. It came about as a response to uprisings and a desire to give struggling Black folks something they could enjoy for a few hours. Admission was free, and the venue took place in what is now Marcus Garvey Park in Harlem. Though the event was covered and sponsored, very little of it saw the light of day outside of a television broadcast on WNEW-TV in New York City. Decades later, Ahmir "Questlove" Thompson took the footage recorded by Hal Tulchin and fashioned it into the Oscar-winning 2021 documentary *Summer of Soul*.

Back in 1973, Stan Lathan's *Save the Children* featured Stax and Motown artists performing at Jesse Jackson's 1972 Operation PUSH Exposition in

Chicago. In between acts, there was footage of speeches, other exhibitions within the event, and commentary from Black attendees. Motown put out the soundtrack album.

Mel Stuart's 1973 film *Wattstax* had the Stax record label behind it, their first foray into film production. It was a recording of the Watts Summer Festival, an event created by neighborhood activist Tommy Jacquette after the Watts Uprising of 1965.

In the opening moments of *Wattstax*, the film's master of ceremonies, Richard Pryor, spoke about how the attendees "heard, felt, sang, danced, and shouted the living word in a soulful expression of the Black Experience." The concert occurred on August 20, 1972. The admission was $1, a price most people in Watts could afford. One hundred twelve thousand people attended. Their buck bought them a full day of performances by artists on Memphis's Stax record label, culminating in a set by its biggest star, Oscar-winning singer Isaac Hayes.

The Stax label had a reputation among Black denizens in Memphis. Stax president Al Bell and executive Larry Shaw were well-known for their community-based humanitarianism. Their company presented itself not only as an entertainment vehicle but as a charitable organization that Memphians could always count on to help with fundraising, promotion of local events, and even neighborhood financial disputes. In his book, *Soulsville, U.S.A.: The Story of Stax Records*, music historian Rob Bowman tells the story of the IRS attempting to shut down a Memphis business. The owner of the Afro shop pulled a gun, made the IRS agents take off their clothes, and demanded to talk to Isaac Hayes. Word got back to Stax, and Hayes actually showed up to help defuse the situation.

So it was no surprise that Stax wanted to be involved in the Seventh Annual Watts Summer Festival. Their West Coast rep, Forest Hamilton, brought the event to the label's attention. Stax paid to rent the venue and, since Bell had seen what Berry Gordy had done with Motown producing *Lady Sings the Blues*, he contracted with David Wolper's production company to do *Wattstax*. There were also album tie-ins and live concert (and staged studio) recordings of the artists who appeared at the festival. Stax's contract gave 50 percent of the US film profits and 50 percent of net revenues from merchandise to the festival in exchange for exclusive film and recording rights to the next five Watts Summer Festivals. That exclusive part of the contract was never executed. However, the most interesting part of Stax's deal with Wolper was the one thing of which Al Bell and Larry Shaw demanded total control: according to Bowman, Stax had final approval over any type of narration related to "words or phrases having a special Black connotation."

In other words, Stax had the right to ensure *Wattstax* would be unapologetically Black, from the musical numbers on down to the language. That latter element earned the film its R rating; though none of the performers (save the obvious Pryor) worked blue, the interviews with Watts denizens and comedy bits interspersed throughout the film are filled with "motherfucker"s and "nigga"s and other colorful bits of vernacular familiar and natural to anyone who ever lived in the 'hood. To assure skittish parents afraid their children might see any sex or violence, Stax explained that the MPAA's decision was based solely on profanity. They claimed *Wattstax* was "rated R for Real."

Stax's marketing department had a detailed plan for *Wattstax*. In addition to the record tie-ins and radio ads targeting the urban market, the label ensured that the film opened in theaters that were equidistant from Black and White neighborhoods. There would be no relegating to the usual "Black movie" theaters. Larry Shaw called this "the company's spearhead for the young white market of middle America." The film even had a catchy tagline designed to appeal to, and guilt, White folks: "You Can't Judge a Movie by Its Color."

After Pryor's introduction, *Wattstax* begins with a sequence that explains why the title is a combination of "Watts" and "Stax." The 1971 hit "Whatcha See Is Whatcha Get" by Stax recording artists the Dramatics plays as the title appears over the neighborhood's most famous landmark, the Watts Towers. As the credits roll, clips of Watts from the uprising to the present day are shown, often edited in time with the song. Shots of burning buildings and police cars are intercut with scenes of people going about their daily routines. Folks are shown going to church, having a beer, shooting dice on the street, and catching a bus. For fun, a kid rolls a tire through a vacant lot.

Instead of going into a musical number, *Wattstax* immediately cuts to its first of many conversations between natives of Watts. The topics (sex, relationships, the riots, life in Watts, racism) were chosen by the filmmakers, but the responses are all unscripted. These rap sessions take place in barbershops, restaurants, and community centers. Among the talking heads are future actors Raymond Allen and Ted Lange. The former got a job on *Sanford and Son*, Redd Foxx's NBC sitcom set in Watts, where he played the perpetually drunk husband of LaWanda Page's Aunt Esther. The latter wound up in much more dire straits as Isaac the Bartender, the token Negro on ABC's *The Love Boat*.

Stuart alternates between these vignettes, Pryor's running commentary at what appears to be a bar, and live musical numbers. Pryor had already shot *Lady Sings the Blues* at the beginning of 1972, and at this point in his career, he had gravitated away from the tame humor he brought to *The Tonight Show* and toward the profane comedy and characters with which he would become synonymous. Throughout *Wattstax*, whenever one of the Watts denizens said something completely off the wall, there's a cut to the comedian saying, "Now that nigger's crazy!"

Pryor's association with Stax Records would lead to the Grammy-winning comedy record that thrusted him into full stardom, *That Nigger's Crazy*, in 1974. The genesis of some of the routines on this album can be found in his onscreen *Wattstax* riffs. Despite the excellent record sales, Stax abruptly closed soon after, halting any further pressings. Thankfully, Pryor was able to buy his masters and transfer them over to Warner Bros. Records.

The Staples' "We the People" plays over scenes of concertgoers entering and paying their buck. A plethora of 1972 fashions fill the screen, along with a parade of massive Afros, pigtails, cornrows, processes, and hats atop people's heads. Cinematographer John A. Alonzo can't help but keep finding a woman's ass to focus his camera on, a feat he will carry throughout the film. People, including Miss Watts 1972, are asked their opinion on the upcoming concert. To a fault, everyone says, "It's beautiful!"

Wattstax isn't a document of the entire concert. Instead, specific numbers were chosen. A few were either re-created after the festival or shot in an obviously different location for a variety of reasons, including time or artist unavailability. The Emotions, six years away from their Grammy-winning biggest hit, "Best of My Love," suffered the most as a result of not being at the Coliseum. Mel Stuart staged a gospel number for them in a small neighborhood church.

Conversely, Johnnie Taylor's performance at the Summit Club was not only a showstopper in the film, he got a live album out of it separate from any of the live *Wattstax* recordings Stax put out. Sweating profusely and flirting with the women in the audience, Taylor ran through his hit "Jody's Got Your Girl and Gone," a song about a guy who slips into men's houses while they're out at work, screws their women, and leaves remnants of his cuckolding just to add insult to injury. Speaking of songs about infidelity, Luther Ingram's performance of "If

Loving You Is Wrong, I Don't Want to Be Right" was so passionate and intense that the camera found women in the audience enraptured by the song. Turns out this entire segment was staged to look like it occurred at the Coliseum.

While those digressions are entertaining, the concert footage that Stuart and Alonzo shot live is the film's main draw. Melvin Van Peebles introduced the Staple Singers, who performed "Respect Yourself." Winning the award for the most theatrical performance were the Bar-Kays, with their giant white Afro wigs and clothes made out of jewelry. Their song "Son of Shaft" was the most recent hit performed at the concert, and their original plans to enter the arena on horse-drawn chariots was nixed because it would upstage the "father of Shaft," Isaac Hayes, who was slated to appear last.

An artist's standing with Stax influenced their placement in the show. So it made sense that the penultimate spot was reserved for Rufus Thomas. Thomas's daughter, Carla, appeared just before him. She had been responsible for writing and singing Stax's first big hit, 1961's "Gee Whiz (Look at His Eyes)" when she was fifteen years old. She famously duetted with Otis Redding on his hit song "Tramp" and had several hits of her own. *Wattstax* shows her singing "Pick Up the Pieces."

Rufus Thomas had been around since the early 1950s, long before Stax's existence. He had a slew of hits, including several novelty dance records that he sang well into his eighties. A comedian, disc jockey, dancer, songwriter, and performer, Thomas was the complete package. In *Wattstax*, he was as shameless as he was fearless. Here was a fifty-four-year-old man doing a dance called "The Funky Chicken" in front of 112,000 people who were dancing with him.

Thomas clowned around, but he was a serious musician, singer, and showman. Taking the stage in thigh-high white boots with a pink shorts suit and cape—an outfit that was extreme even by 1970s clothing standards—he posed and asked the audience, "Ain't I'm clean?" It was a throwback to his DJ days, and the line elicited a hearty response from an audience that knew it was coming. His set would show just how much the fans loved and respected him. During Thomas's first song, the 1971 hit "The Breakdown," John Alonzo's horny camera zeroed in on a woman in a very short red-and-white polka-dot dress dancing as if her life depended on it. Of all the people the film shows dancing, this unnamed woman was the most memorable.

Dressed in a knee-length shirt made of gold chains, Isaac Hayes cut quite the figure of gaudy machismo. Plus, it was the singer's thirtieth birthday, and this show was his present. Hayes closes out *Wattstax* with "Theme from *Shaft*" and "Soulsville," playing the saxophone on the latter.

During the closing credits, the West Coast rep who brought Stax the idea for this film got the greatest onscreen credit in cinema history. It read, "Associate Producer: FOREST HAMILTON, Hnic."

For the film's premiere on February 4, 1973, Stax went full old-school Hollywood. Outside the Dorothy Chandler Pavilion (where the Academy Awards would be presented a month later), they had red carpets, celebrities, TV cameras, and klieg lights. *Wattstax* got a lot of publicity and played like gangbusters. Something this seemingly perfect was bound to go wrong, and the next day, it did.

Doug Netter, the vice president of MGM, informed Stax and David Wolper that they planned to sue over the use of songs from *Shaft*. Contractually, songs from the *Shaft* soundtrack could not be performed in any other film until 1978. Like *Black Caesar*, the ending of *Wattstax* suddenly got lopped off after its Los Angeles premiere. However, Stax provided a replacement. They flew Hayes back in from the Netherlands, made a soundstage look like the Coliseum, and had him perform his upcoming single, "Rolling Down a Mountainside." It felt anticlimactic—here was the biggest star singing some song nobody had heard before rather than the hits they loved. But until the director's cut restoration that played at the 2004 Sundance Film Festival, that's what anyone who wasn't at the Chandler Pavilion got to see.

No matter. *Wattstax* was a critical and box office hit. After a Manhattan benefit screening for the Schomburg Center on February 15, 1973, the film opened at the Loews Orpheum (not the DeMille!) the next day. The ads were filled with blurbs from critics singing its praises. Roger Ebert gave it four out of four stars in his review, writing, "The sense of spontaneous joy fills the film." In *World* magazine, Hollis Alpert wrote, "Finally a film has been made that gets close to the contemporary black experience." Joy Gould Boyum, a Black critic, wrote in the *Wall Street Journal*, "*Wattstax* shows us blacks laughing at themselves and inviting other blacks to laugh with them . . . its images will carry white viewers closer to its understanding." Mel Stuart received a Golden Globes nomination for Best Documentary in 1974.

Fulfilling Al Bell and Larry Shaw's dreams of taking Stax global, *Wattstax* played in Nigeria and was so popular, theater owners raised ticket prices to deter people from seeing it multiple times. In May, the film played at the snooty and revered Cannes Film Festival, where it was well received alongside another unusual choice, Bill Gunn's Black vampire art house film, *Ganja & Hess*. And it was rediscovered the way nature, God, and Columbia Pictures intended when the restored version of *Wattstax* played Sundance thirty years after its initial release.

All this joy for a company that would go bankrupt and dissolve by 1975.

As for Bell's wish to produce movies like Berry Gordy (who would go on to produce several more), that didn't go so well. The only films Stax was involved with that got a release were *The Klansman*, a piece of trash starring Lee Marvin and O. J. Simpson, for which Stax did the score; and 1975's super-obscure *Darktown Strutters*. The Dramatics appear out of nowhere in that film to sing "Whatcha See Is Whatcha Get." Ironically, the producer on this film was the same Doug Netter who threatened to sue Stax over the *Shaft* songs.

Strutters is worth a brief mention here. It's not the worst thing the Blaxploitation era produced, but it certainly is the weirdest. In his review, Roger Ebert called it "the first black motorcycle gang rock scifi musical, which would seem to be saying a lot." The leader of the motorcycle gang, played by Trina Parks, is looking for her mother, who was an abortionist. That is, when she and her equally sexy lady bikers aren't eating chicken and ribs at a faux Kentucky Fried Chicken outlet. The owner of that outlet, who is clearly modeled on Colonel Sanders, pretends to be a benefactor to the Black community. In reality, he's an evil genius turning out clones of Black leaders who will do his evil bidding. (The makers of *Undercover Brother* have definitely seen this movie.)

That plot exists alongside numerous dance numbers, motorcycle chases, and slapstick-like pie fights and people flying through the air as if defying gravity. There's also a guy who runs a drug-infused ice cream stand, years before Cheech and Chong would do it in *Nice Dreams*. He sells Quaalude Pies, Cough Syrup Milky Ways, Downer Dream Pies, and, of course, the Pot Sicle. *Darktown Strutters* doesn't make one damn bit of sense, but there's something about its desire to offend and its willingness to try anything, no matter how outdated, to earn a laugh.

Larry Shaw hated this movie, and he tried to get Richard Pryor to record some bumpers for it that they could edit in in order to salvage the picture. But during the screening, Pryor suddenly disappeared. Shaw found him crawling out of the theater on his hands and knees, attempting to sneak out unnoticed. He begged Shaw to let him leave, citing that he'd do a lot of things for the man, but watching this was not an option. One hopes that the gods of fate immediately cut to Pryor's famous retort in *Wattstax*: "Now, that nigger's crazy!"

CHAPTER 15

ONCE AGAIN, INJUSTICE FOR BILL GUNN

Bill Gunn made a career out of not doing the predictable, most subversively when it came to depicting Black characters onstage, in print, and onscreen. He helped shatter the long-standing, antiquated Hollywood ideal of two-dimensional Blackness by making his characters messy, complex, neurotic, intelligent, flawed, jubilant, petty, and, most of all, recognizably human.

This may have been due to the way he saw himself and his upbringing. Born in 1929 and raised in a middle-class White neighborhood, Gunn once told his friend Chiz Schultz that his family raised him as if he were White and middle class. "Bill didn't feel he'd been brought up as an African-American man," Schultz told *Cineaste* magazine. And yet, he would be viewed as a Black artist. Unfortunately, this would interfere with his art.

Though *Stop!* never saw the light of day, the next film he directed got butchered *after* it was released.

During its run, Blaxploitation begat numerous horror films with acting leads of color. Asked to do a film in the same vein as *Blacula*, Gunn returned with 1973's decidedly different *Ganja & Hess*. After a less-than-stellar box office, his producers responded by notoriously gutting the film in the hopes of reshaping it into the standard exploitation flick its director intentionally avoided. The movie is demanding, slow, meditative, and not particularly scary. It is also very effective, at least in the original cut that resurfaced decades later.

As fellow independent filmmaker Abel Ferrara would later do in his 1995 vampire film *The Addiction*, *Ganja & Hess* used vampirism as a metaphor for being strung out on something, quite possibly the notion of assimilation. Hess

(Duane Jones) is a wealthy anthropologist who rides in a chauffeured Rolls-Royce to his estate in Westchester County, an area that probably benefitted from the White flight that once struck *The Landlord*'s Brooklyn neighborhood. This connection seems intentional, a sort of ironic location swap, as if to say, "Send the rich White guy to the 'hood and the rich Black guy to the 'burbs, then give both the illusion of inclusion."

Beau Bridges's landlord is almost murdered in Hal Ashby's film, but Jones's Hess actually does get killed by Gunn himself, playing George, a suicidal, self-described "neurotic" who believes in the blood-drinking curse of an ancient African tribe led by Mabel King, who played Steve Martin's adopted mama in *The Jerk*. (Gunn's acting credentials go way back to when he appeared on Broadway with James Dean.) As a result, Hess develops a taste for blood that will entangle him in sex, religion, and madness. Soon, George's wife, Ganja, shows up looking for her husband. She finds him in Hess's freezer, but she's still willing to let Hess turn her into a fellow bloodsucker.

Eventually, Hess tires of this new lifestyle and dies by suicide. Ganja continues on, however, and in the film's dreamlike last scene, the victim she and Hess previously killed for food is seen emerging naked from a body of water and running toward her.

Clearly, this was going to be a hard sell to anyone looking for exploitation.

Three years before Michael Schultz's *Car Wash* and sixteen years before Spike Lee's *Do the Right Thing* did it, *Ganja & Hess* went to Cannes. This was an unprecedented step for a film made by a Black director. There, it won the critics' prize and seemed headed for the type of artistic success most Black films were not afforded.

However, its debut at the ritzy Playboy Theater on Fifty-Ninth Street in New York City (no DeMille or Cinerama for *this* Black movie!) was cut short after three days. "The white critics just demolished it, because they had never seen anything like it," Schultz told *Cineaste*. "They had never seen a black millionaire in a mansion, with a limo and chauffeur." The Black newspaper *The Amsterdam News* called it "the most important Black movie since *Sweetback*," but it was panned by outlets like the *New York Times*, which published a negative, error-filled review by A. H. Weiler.

That review pissed Gunn off so much that, like Gordon Parks before him, he wrote a letter to the editors of the *Times*. It was published in the May 13, 1973, edition under the headline, "To Be a Black Artist." In it, he ripped Weiler's review and wrote, "It is a terrible thing to be a black artist in this country . . . If I were white, I would probably be called 'fresh and different.' If I were European, 'Ganja & Hess' might be 'that little film you must see.' Because I am black, I do not even deserve the pride that one American feels for another when he discovers that a fellow countryman's film has been selected as the only American film to be shown during 'Critic's Week' at the Cannes Film Festival . . . Not one white critic from any of the major newspapers even mentioned it."

In an attempt to recoup his $350,000 in losses, Quentin Kelly, the producer of *Ganja & Hess*, sold it to a distributor that recut the film and renamed it *Blood Couple*. The ads, and the cover for the VHS tape that the author's video store would rent out fifteen years later, promoted it as a Blaxploitation horror quickie. Butchered, the film made little sense and even less money. Kelly had originally offered recut rights to Bill Gunn, but the director destroyed Kelly's office in a fury, saying, "You cannot change my movie."

Eventually, *Ganja & Hess* was restored and received the praise and attention it deserved. A side effect of that was it caught the attention of the prolific director from Da People's Republic of Brooklyn, Spike Lee. The general freakiness and meditative nature of *Ganja & Hess* made it a perfect fit for an admittedly terrible remake by Lee in 2014 (he called it *Da Sweet Blood of Jesus*, paraphrasing a line from a song in the film). Truth be told, however, Gunn's influence on Lee is evident even in his earliest scripts. Scenes in Lee's films where the characters simply sit and shoot the shit longer than cinematically expected pay homage to Gunn's style, as does Lee's penchant for unconventional or even weird endings. Lee also relocated *Ganja & Hess* to Brooklyn, acknowledging a symbolic tie to *The Landlord*.

Unfortunately, Gunn never got to see this newfound appreciation for his work. He died on April 5, 1989, long before he could see how the fruits of his labor influenced so many.

CHAPTER 16

SHAFT IN AFRICA ... AND ON TELEVISION

Moviedom wasn't done with John Shaft. After *Shaft's Big Score!* turned the Black private dick into a 007 clone, whizzing through the water in an exciting boat chase and blowing shit up as if MGM were made of money, another movie was commissioned. It also helped that director Gordon Parks and screenwriter Ernest Tidyman's follow-up to *Shaft* was a box office hit. Neither of them returned for the third film, but on paper it appeared to be in good hands. MGM hired *In the Heat of the Night*'s Oscar-winning screenwriter, Stirling Silliphant, to pen this iteration. To direct, they got John Guillermin, who helmed the successful Jim Brown–Lee Van Cleef adventure film, *El Condor*. Guillermin was the first, and thus far only, White director on a *Shaft* film. He and Silliphant turned the titular character into, of all things, *a slave*.

Well, an itinerant worker in Africa would probably be more accurate, though when Shaft asks what the job is, his new employer simply says, "A slave." That new employer won't take no for an answer, either. Shaft is kidnapped by Osiat (Frank McRae), an enormous Black dude he shoots several times to no effect. This "bulletproof" brother drops Shaft off at a mysterious compound, where the private dick's privates are suddenly public. Butt-nekkid Shaft has to battle 120-degree heat in a room full of sand (he buries himself for protection) after engaging in a stick battle with Osiat. Fans of the male form get several opportunities to enjoy Roundtree's bare ass, though there's a gaffe that shows Roundtree is clearly wearing underwear at one point.

After successfully fending off Osiat, Shaft is met by Wassa (Debebe Eshetu), the agent who ordered him brought to the compound. An African government wants him to go undercover to take down the evil conglomerate that's mistreating and murdering migrant workers. Overcoming the trials set before him while being physically and psychologically vulnerable, Shaft more than qualifies for the job. "The emir will be pleased," Wassa tells Shaft. "Also, by the fact you're already circumcised." Viewers now have an answer to *that* particular question!

In the pre-credits sequence, the emir's son is brutally murdered by the Eurotrash group Shaft needs to destroy. Their White leader, Amafi (Frank Finlay), is introduced getting a blow job in his car from "the only woman I can get it up for," Jazar (Neda Arneric). Jazar is more than a little freaky, and she has a penchant for Black men. Thankfully, Amafi has a thing for hearing about Jazar sleeping with Black men. Later, he orders her to record her rendezvous with Shaft for his listening pleasure. She gets it on with the cat who won't cop out but tragically gets the knife in the ribs intended for him.

Before all that transpires, Shaft hooks up with another woman, the emir's daughter, Aleme. Played by Vonetta McGee, she engages him in a discussion about her upcoming female circumcision. Their conversation is perhaps the first time a mainstream movie used the word "clitoris." Shaft offers to show her what she's missing once tradition takes hold in her nether regions. As usual, McGee portrays the perfect package of beauty and smarts, something she strived to do throughout her appearances in films of this era.

Shaft in Africa shows the plight of itinerant workers being forced to work "sixteen hours a day, seven days a week." There's a heartbreaking scene of a fire that kills many of the men Shaft bonded with throughout the film, which leads him to enact a very violent revenge. During the exciting explosion- and gunfire-filled finale, John Shaft lives up to the Four Tops theme song that plays under the opening credits. The superb song, "Are You Man Enough" is driven by Levi Stubbs's gruff vocal and tough, clever lyrics by Dennis Lambert and Brian Potter.

Richard Roundtree agreed to do *Shaft in Africa* because "the change in atmosphere is a very good thing, a real shot in the arm. Also this time, the script is better." Roundtree also discussed taking the trip to Ethiopia in a ship. "There was me going back to Africa using technically the same route as a lot of slaves used," he told reporter Molly Johnson. "It was a weird experience." He also got to meet the emperor of Ethiopia, Haile Selassie, who spoke fluent English but conducted his interviews in Aramaic. Selassie gave producer Roger Lewis and the crew easy access to filming locations.

Silliphant's script had a lot of truth to it regarding how workers were kidnapped and basically enslaved by Europeans looking to minimize costs and maximize exploitation. But, as with *Super Fly T.N.T.*, which was also shot in Africa at the same time, audiences didn't want Afrocentric messages with their Blaxploitation. The reviews were lackluster as well; Jerry Oster in the New York *Daily News* called it "just another noisy fantasy" when it opened at the Cinerama on June 20, 1973. *Shaft in Africa* was a box office flop, making $1.5 million on a $2.1 million budget, but it wasn't the end for John Shaft just yet.

While *Shaft in Africa* was being filmed, MGM sold the rights to bring John Shaft to the small screen. The pilot was the original *Shaft*, but edited for television. CBS added it to a wheel (rotating series) of shows that included *Hawkins*, a mystery series starring Jimmy Stewart as Billy Joe Hawkins, a crusty, West Virginia lawyer who solved crimes. The wheel ran in the 9:30 to 11:00 p.m. Eastern time slot every Tuesday. A promo reel for the CBS 1973 fall season hilariously shoehorns a clip of Shaft walking down 125th Street between shots of sitcom characters Mary Richards, Maude Findlay, and Archie Bunker.

Shaft: The TV Movies joined the then current slate of shows about detectives in urban locales. Los Angeles's *Columbo* and San Francisco's *McMillan & Wife* were on NBC. Two weeks after Shaft's TV show premiered, fellow New Yorker Theo Kojak would join him on the same network. And a month after Shaft's last episode ran on February 19, 1974, *The Rockford Files*' Jim Rockford would join the ranks of private dicks on NBC.

Unlike John Shaft, none of these memorable dudes was originally R-rated, often profane, and frequently, explicitly laid. Regardless, CBS and MGM thought a neutered Shaft would appeal to the masses. He was no longer "a sex machine to all the chicks," and he was in cahoots with the police, helping them solve cases. With two exceptions, his clients were White. And as *All in the Family*'s George and Weezy Jefferson would do two years later, Shaft moved on up to the East Side, exchanging his Greenwich Village pad at 55 Jane Street for a deluxe apartment at 2160 East 67th Street. That fictional address would, in reality, be located in the middle of the East River.

Neither Gordon Parks nor Ernest Tidyman was associated with the TV series. Tidyman was busy writing the gruesome and weird Western *High Plains Drifter* for Clint Eastwood. Like Parks, his association with the MGM Shaft franchise ended with *Shaft's Big Score!*, though he would continue to write several more novels featuring the character. Instead, the small-screen adaptation was a collaboration between William Read Woodfield and his writing partner, Allan Balter. Coincidentally, Woodfield worked as a photographer for *Life* magazine during Parks's tenure before branching out into writing for television. He was smart enough to keep Isaac Hayes's Oscar-winning theme song, but the series was scored in a sound-alike fashion by Johnny Pate, the composer for *Shaft in Africa*. In keeping with Blaxploitation's penchant for giving people their start, three episodes of the series were edited by one of the genre's most prolific editors, George Folsey Jr. Folsey would later cut most of John Landis's biggest hits, including *National Lampoon's Animal House* and *Coming to America*.

CBS's John Shaft wouldn't offend the White viewers who stumbled upon his show. The *Los Angeles Times*'s Cecil Smith wrote that "Shaft on TV makes Barnaby Jones look like Eldridge Cleaver." Roundtree himself found the endeavor to be "a lifeless, watered-down version of the films." Trouper that he is, the actor acquits himself nicely despite the odds. Bastardized or not, Shaft was still the smoothest and the slickest cat in the room, matching wits with villains like Robert Culp, Clu Gulager, and, in the show's biggest get, a very game Tony Curtis.

Surprisingly, Shaft wasn't the only Black crime fighter on the telly at the time. *Tenafly*, a show featuring a far more bougie Black detective played by James McEachin, debuted in a wheel on NBC the day after *Shaft* debuted on CBS. Tenafly, a former cop, lived in the 'burbs, was happily married, and appeared far more palatable to Middle America than Roundtree's suave urbanite. He also had a bigger TV pedigree as a product of *Columbo* creators William Link and Richard Levinson. None of that mattered; his show lasted five episodes before it got the ax.

A *Cleopatra Jones*–inspired TV show called *Get Christie Love!* debuted on ABC in 1974, just as CBS was canning *Shaft*. It starred the strikingly beautiful former *Laugh-In* regular Teresa Graves as a female undercover cop. This series lasted twenty-three episodes, more than three times the number of *Shaft*s. Adding insult to injury, Graves's co-star for the first half of the season was Charles Cioffi, aka Vic the frenemy cop from the first *Shaft* movie. In addition to being as charismatic (and as action-oriented) as Richard Roundtree, the tragically gone-too-soon Teresa Graves had the distinction of being the first African-American woman to have a drama show on TV. She was also the first TV crush the author ever had.

Shaft: The TV Movies had a generic structure from which it rarely deviated. Shaft would somehow get roped into a case, usually through an implausible friend the show clearly pulled out of its ass. This would require him to collaborate with NYPD Lieutenant Al Rossi (Ed Barth). The character Rossi is a holdover from *Shaft's Big Score!*, where he was played by Angelo Gnazzo. Fans of the first film will recognize Barth as one of the Mafia goons, so it's a bit jarring to see him get all kumbaya with Shaft. Roundtree and Barth have genuine chemistry together.

In her New York *Daily News* review, TV critic Kay Gardella wrote that viewers of *Shaft: The TV Movies'* first episode should "turn the dial fast" if they were expecting the same level of excitement they got from the movies. "The script is like a Fourth of July explosion," she continued, "with bits and pieces flying all over the place before it's all neatly wrapped up by Shaft 90 long tedious minutes later." "Long" and "tedious" are the perfect adjectives; to pad out the fixed runtime and (presumably) to keep things cheap, each episode featured stretches of driving through New York City and, in one case, rural Connecticut. The endless driving montages made viewers long for someone to just take the subway.

The episode Gardella reviewed, "The Executioners," features Robert Culp as a respectable man whose wife is put in a psychiatric ward after she is raped. Culp brings together a slew of other supposedly law-abiding professionals— lawyers, judges, cops—and convenes them in a gym. To that location, he brings people he believes have failed society. Their first victim angered Culp by defending an assumed cop murderer in court. He is drugged and kidnapped, then tried by Culp in a fake court. He's found guilty with zero chance for a defense, then executed by drowning in the gym's swimming pool. His body is then tossed into the East River. Every victim meets this fate.

Shaft's scenes of harassing Culp, and Culp's aggravated reaction, have a *Columbo* vibe to them that is at odds with the Black private dick's usual temperament. Eventually, Shaft is brought before the executioners' court and sentenced. This occurs after Roundtree climbs several walls and structures like Spider-Man. The show climaxes with his being threatened with drowning, something that happens more than once in this series. (Kidnapping and abuse of women are also repeated plot devices.) It's hard to imagine anyone watching the series beyond this lackluster debut.

Ja'Net DuBois, Willona on *Good Times* and the singer/composer of *The Jeffersons'* theme song, has a dramatic role in "The Killing," the series' second episode. It's one of the aforementioned two times Shaft's client is Black. This is the only episode where the word "nigger" is uttered (the later scripts prefer "spade"). It's also the sleaziest of the bunch, and the one that most approximates a Blaxploitation vibe. There are pimps fighting over territory while dressed like preening peacocks. The show is still not very good at this point, but until the absurd happy ending, it hints that it may go in a nastier direction.

The best of the guest stars, Tony Curtis, matches wits with Shaft in episode 3, "Hit-Run." Curtis really leans into his "Noo Yawk" accent here, and his scenes with Roundtree are quite entertaining. Until Clu Gulager in the series finale, no other actor correctly senses the absurd tone of the show and responds by chewing major holes in the scenery.

The fourth episode, "The Kidnapping," is the best that *Shaft: The TV Movies* has to offer. It opens with the biggest action sequence, featuring Shaft's pursuit of a heroin distributor while the distributor's cronies shoot at him from a helicopter. The 'copter chases him into an abandoned warehouse while Pate speeds up Hayes's theme song on the soundtrack to match Folsey's furious editing. It's genuinely exciting, evoking the grandiosity of the climax of *Shaft's Big Score!*, especially when Shaft singlehandedly shoots the helicopter out of the sky. It falls to the ground in a massive fireball.

As awesome as this sequence is, it has nothing to do with the main story except to put Shaft on the kidnappers' radar. Perhaps CBS had some money to burn and Woodfield and Balter, who wrote this one, decided to take advantage. The main plot involves a kidnapping where the criminals asked for Shaft by name. They want to "throw some work a brother's way" because they're Black themselves.

Turns out they're a trio of White guys using stereotypical Black voices and enough jive to impress Barbara Billingsley's character from *Airplane!* Their rationale is to have the cops looking for three Black men while they get away scot-free. This is subversive enough to generate interest, even if involving Shaft makes little sense.

The best part of this episode is how Shaft confirms his suspicions that "these cats are White." During a phone call, Shaft lays on these fools some deep-in-the-'hood slang, shit they don't say anymore but any adult would have known. His line is met with confusion. The kidnappers' amateurishness and racism are the reasons Shaft eventually shoots them.

Shaft helps out a Black character once again in "Cop Killer." Familiar character actor James A. Watson Jr. plays Officer Tyler, who is framed for extortion by his White co-workers in the opening scene.

Shaft must avenge him, so he assumes another persona, an even faster-talking hustler from Chicago. Roundtree has a lot of fun with this role. He also gets a few scenes with a pre–*Kolchak: The Night Stalker* Darren McGavin playing a captain who may or may not be on the take. Ken Kolb's script has some very pointed sentiments about bad cops, but they never cut deeply enough to leave a mark. And he ends it with Rossi learning that, while in surgery, Shaft donated some blood to him. Based on the one-drop rule, Rossi is now Black! "So if you feel a sudden craving for black-eyed peas and cornbread," warns Shaft, "don't worry, baby, it's OK."

Episode 6, "The Capricorn Murders," is the series' weakest, an odd, extremely convoluted tale of arson, double-crosses, and diamonds. It's an Agatha Christie plot crossed with an episode of a nighttime soap opera, and Shaft doesn't really fit in here.

However, the next episode, "The Murder Machine," emerges as the show's second best. Clu Gulager plays Richard Quayle, a hit man leading a double life. He's so efficient and ruthless, he does only two or three jobs a year. He's also a family man with a house in the suburbs, two kids, and a doting, unsuspecting wife played by Fionnula Flanagan (whose name is misspelled in the opening credits). It should be noted that Quayle is the only character in the entire series who gets laid. Imagine Shaft saying, "Ain't this a bitch? It's my show and *he* gets lucky?!"

Quayle's involvement in the death of someone close to Shaft brings out the darker side of the detective. This time, it's personal. *Finally*, we get the lean, mean, vengeful John Shaft we remember from the cinema! He breaks ranks with Rossi, ventures out on his own, is unapologetically violent, and has a very formidable opponent in Quayle. Plus, there's a cameo from Pam Grier's frequent co-star, Sid Haig! The fire is finally lit under Roundtree's performance, just in time for the show to get canned.

On April 22, 1974, CBS officially cancelled both *Shaft* and *Hawkins*. They were in good company; CBS also cancelled *Here's Lucy* (at Lucille Ball's request) and the top-rated *The Sonny and Cher Hour* (at their divorce's request). For all its timidity, *Shaft: The TV Movies* wasn't a total disaster. But it didn't teach CBS any lessons about leaving Black movie heroes in the R-rated movies they immortalized. On April 4, 1975, the network aired a pilot for *Black Bart*, a TV show based on Mel Brooks's raunchy masterpiece, *Blazing Saddles*. Thankfully, it was not picked up.

CHAPTER 12

WHEN BLAXPLOITATION
SPOOKED THE GOV'MENT

In March 1969, South Side Chicago native Sam Greenlee published his debut novel, *The Spook Who Sat by the Door*. Rejected by numerous American outlets, the book was printed by British publishers Allison & Busby as one of their first works. The Busby from the company's name, Margaret Busby, designed the cover of the book herself, slapping quotes by Black activist/comedian Dick Gregory and Brit spy novelist Len Deighton on the back cover. Also on that back cover was this synopsis: "The CIA needs a Negro: there have been accusations of racial discrimination. So black Dan Freeman begins his lone career in an all-white world. Dan Freeman—tame, conspicuous, harmless. But behind this mask he coolly develops his subversive expertise in judo, guns, women, strategy ..."

No wonder the novel had a hard time finding an American publisher! (It was eventually released by the Richard W. Baron Publishing Company.) For starters, its title was a play on two separate vernacular definitions for the word "spook"—in espionage terms, a spook was a spy, and in racial terms, spook was an epithet for Black people. Greenlee put his main character, Dan Freeman, in the role of the CIA's Token Negro, a man they put at the forefront for maximum visibility as a sign of "progress." In other words, he's sitting by the door so that whoever looks in can see him. When US senators tour the facility, Freeman is their tour guide. He's trotted out for these types of ceremonial events, even after the organization had done everything in its power to prevent him from passing the tests that earned him his credentials.

Greenlee knew something about how government organizations worked. In 1957, he became one of the first Black agents of the United States Information

Agency (USIA) to work overseas. The USIA was created by then president Dwight D. Eisenhower "to understand, inform and influence foreign publics in promotion of the national interest, and to broaden the dialogue between Americans and U.S. institutions, and their counterparts abroad." In other words, propaganda was one of its duties. In his eight-year tenure, Greenlee served in Iran, Pakistan, Greece, and Indonesia. He was awarded the Meritorious Service Medal in 1958.

Greenlee also knew something about segregation and racism of the Midwestern variety. Born to Samuel Greenlee, a Black man of Native American descent, and Desoree Alexander, who was light enough to pass for White, his entrance into the world stunned the doctors who thought they were delivering Chicago's latest Caucasian. He wrote that the medics were surprised "when a mocha-colored infant emerged from between my mother's ivory thighs. Perhaps the doctor gave me an extra hard slap on my ass and I've been mad at white folks ever since."

After retiring from the USIA, Greenlee lived in Mykonos, Greece, which is where he ran into Margaret Busby. In her *Observer* obituary for Greenlee, she quoted his poem "Felony," a verse that could serve as the thesis statement of *The Spook Who Sat by the Door*: "A free / black mind / is a concealed / weapon!"

Busby paid Greenlee a £50 advance and got *The Observer* to publish excerpts from the book, none of which included the book's plotline about the protagonist using his skills to train citizens for a Black revolution against America. The novel became a hit and was translated into multiple languages, including French, Italian, and German. Greenlee's then wife did the Dutch translation herself. Despite all this overseas success, Greenlee pointed out that the American press expressed little interest in the novel.

A 2016 paper by J. M. Berger, a writer and researcher on extremism, cited *The Spook Who Sat by the Door* as a literary influence on the far more incendiary (and racist) *The Turner Diaries*, a 1978 dystopian novel written by neo-Nazi William Luther Pierce. This was the work that influenced Oklahoma City bomber Timothy McVeigh, who photocopied pages of the book as part of his manifesto. Pierce tells the story of Blacks and Jewish people confiscating guns from White people and taking over. As in *The Birth of a Nation*, a White supremacy group decides to "restore order" by waging a race war. It ends with their victory and a global genocide of non-Whites.

Berger wrote, "Like *The Turner Diaries*, [Greenlee's novel] declines to put a label on its ideology. It describes intense efforts to create propaganda, but gives little insight into its contents."

Greenlee's expertise in propaganda may have been enough to make the film version of his novel the only Blaxploitation movie yanked from release. He certainly thought so. Of his novel, he said, "It's a training manual for guerrilla warfare. That's why it scared the white folks so much. I wanted to show a brother who had an objective and a plan."

In 1973, *Trouble Man* director Ivan Dixon and Greenlee teamed up to turn *The Spook Who Sat by the Door* into a feature film, with Greenlee adapting his novel with Mel Clay. The two men raised $750,000 of the film's $1 million budget from Black investors. To earn the rest, Dixon shot several high-action sequences and showed the reel to studios. United Artists ponied up the rest of the money and distributed the film.

Working once again with editor Michael Kahn, Dixon fashioned a film that was more like a training manual than a standard actioner. The film's philosophy on revolution, and some of the tricks of this trade, were explicitly defined. Remember, this was a film about Black people starting a revolution in ten major cities. There are scenes that discuss sniper measurements, how to make explosives, and what body parts to aim for in knife combat. Some of the aforementioned action scenes feature the film's heroes waging successful battle against the National Guard. Blaxploitation movies had a reputation for misrepresenting militants; this felt like the real deal, a "training manual for guerrilla warfare."

The Spook Who Sat by the Door opened on September 21, 1973, at (surprise, surprise!) the DeMille in Times Square. Perhaps what led to the mysterious disappearance of the film in many locations less than a week after that premiere was the notion that the government itself created the blueprint Dan Freeman (Lawrence Cook) used to direct his rebellion. As in the novel, *The Spook Who Sat by the Door* begins with a senator whose low polling among Black people will cost him the election. He devises a plan to target the CIA for its lack of diversity. If he can get one Black spy, he can use that as a diversity chip to play.

The government has other ideas. The CIA brings on forty potential subjects, all of whom the agency thinks are too weak to survive the grueling entrance tests. Freeman, a Korean War vet, consistently surprises the naysayers. He's quiet, never prone to anger, is able to whip the ass of the huge White judo trainer hired to take him down, and is athletic enough to survive every physical fitness test. Most importantly (and the movie positions it this way), he's blatantly heterosexual; the CIA observes that he has a girlfriend back in Chicago and has dalliances with a sex worker played by Paula Kelly.

It's interesting to note that, decades before the Dora Milaje were depicted in *Black Panther* and the Viola Davis film *The Woman King*, *The Spook Who Sat by the Door* mentioned the kingdom of Dahomey and the Agojie warriors for which it was famous. Kelly's character is billed as "Dahomey Princess" because Dan tells her she looks like the picture of an Agojie warrior in a book he read. Kelly later resurfaces as a spy of her own design, bringing information from Freeman's former CIA boss with whom she's been sleeping.

After he serves his purpose as the Token Negro, Freeman retires from the CIA and returns to Chicago to execute his real mission. After five years in the CIA, he's trained and ready to pass on what he knows to the young brothers he'll recruit as his army. These guys are part of a gang called the Cobras. A theory exists that posits the Cobras were an influence on the Symbionese Liberation Army (SLA), the group that kidnapped Patty Hearst five months after *The Spook Who Sat by the Door* was released.

Freeman reestablishes contact with his married ex-girlfriend, Joy (Janet League), and Dawson (J. A. Preston), the Chicago cop who once ran the streets with him back in his more militant college days. Both will complicate matters for Freeman and the viewer in the film's climax. Before that happens, Dixon and company repeatedly hammer home how easy it is for Black people to use against White America its underestimation of Black intelligence. In a line guaranteed to glue itself into the mind of any viewer, Freeman tells one of his minions that "a Black man with a mop, tray, or broom in his hand can go damn near anywhere in this country. And a smiling Black man is invisible." To prove this point, he has a guy posing as a janitor rob a CEO's desk *while the CEO is sitting at it*.

In another scene that must have drawn audience cheers, Freeman finances his operation by staging a bank robbery with men who can pass—"all the yellow niggas," says the very light-skinned Pretty Willie (David Lemieux), who also gets a speech railing against people who don't think he's Black. As expected, the witnesses and the cops think "six Caucasian men" held up the bank. Watching Pretty Willie and his crew pick out their Afros and "return" to Blackness in the back of a van post-robbery is one of the funniest sight gags the Blaxploitation era has to offer.

Freeman's plan to train similar gangs in other cities goes over well, but his timeline is escalated in Chicago when a riot occurs after the police shooting of a fourteen-year-old girl. The cops sic dogs on the protestors, as if this were 1965, leading to a three-day rebellion that draws the National Guard. As soon as they show up, Freeman and his army combat them in scenes of machine gun fire and explosions. They even blow up Mayor Daley's office. "The mayor's office now has air conditioning!" the group's spokesperson, Uncle Tom (actually Freeman), announces over the radio airwaves they've commandeered.

More violence ensues, including a murder Freeman doesn't want to commit but has no other choice but to do. *The Spook Who Sat by the Door* ends, as the novel does, in the middle of the Black revolution. It has spread to multiple cities armed with Freeman-trained soldiers, but the ultimate outcome is left unknown. It does sound like the Black folks are kicking the government's ass, however.

With its score by Herbie Hancock, written just before he hit the big time as a film composer with *Death Wish*, its provocative theme, and scenes that look like they were shot on the fly and without permission (because they were), *The Spook Who Sat by the Door* is one of the best and most effective Blaxploitation films. One wouldn't know that from the reviews. Boy, did this one get under the skin of all those White critics!

When *The Spook Who Sat by the Door* opened in the Chicago Loop two weeks before it hit the DeMille in New York City, Gene Siskel gave it one star out of four. He did cite Lawrence Cook's performance as a bright spot, writing, "In the face of many embarrassing scenes, Cook maintains a dignity that recommends him for more challenging roles. In an odd juxtaposition, right under the review, Siskel eulogized director John Ford, who had kicked the bucket a few days before.

The Big Apple's best had a field day of faux outrage. Jerry Oster in the New York *Daily News* was either feigning ignorance of slang or was really that dense when he wrote, "*The Spook Who Sat by the Door* is not a ghost story." He also misrepresented the final scene between Dawson and Freeman and said that the film "begins as a comedy, middles as an adventure and ends as a tragedy."

At least the *New York Times*' Vincent Canby owned up to his confusion. He wrote that the film "is a difficult work to judge coherently. It is such a mixture of passion, humor, hindsight, prophecy, prejudice and reaction that the fact that it's not a very well-made movie, and is seldom convincing as melodrama, is almost beside the point. The rage it projects is real," before ending his review by saying the movie equates hating White folks with freedom. Canby also referred to Sam Greenlee as "Dan Greenlee."

About the film being yanked from release: there are listings in the New York papers for screenings as late as October 1974. But in most places, *The Spook Who Sat by the Door* virtually disappeared. Greenlee said in a 2003 interview that he blamed the FBI, which "characterized the film as subversive." He also said this ruined his career and put a damper on Dixon's. Truth be told, Dixon never directed another movie again, and he only came out of cinematic retirement to act in 1976's *Car Wash*. He did, however, have a long career in directing for television, one that extended until 1993.

In 2003, five years before Dixon's death, *The Spook Who Sat by the Door* got a DVD release courtesy of actor/comedian/activist Tim Reid's production company. Dixon expressed pride in the film at the time, saying that "it expressed everything that I felt about race." Reid called it "arguably one of the most significant Black movies ever made." Eight years later, a documentary called *Infiltrating Hollywood: The Rise and Fall of* The Spook Who Sat by the Door chronicled the film's history, and a year later, it was accepted in the National Film Registry of the Library of Congress, the rare Blaxploitation film to be added.

CHAPTER 18

JIM KELLY'S TOO BUSY LOOKIN' GOOD

"Introducing Jim Kelly," read the credit for the martial arts champion at the beginning of Bruce Lee's classic last film, *Enter the Dragon*. This was a misnomer; Kelly's first film was 1972's *Melinda*, the directorial debut of Hugh A. Robertson, the Oscar-nominated editor of *Shaft* and *Midnight Cowboy*. Perhaps this particular introduction was being extended to viewers outside the Blaxploitation sphere. By the time *Enter the Dragon* opened on August 19, 1973, the movie market was as saturated with Blaxploitation films as it was with the so-called chop socky karate flicks. And the "fighting against a dangerous and corrupt system while seeking revenge" plot fit in with similar Blaxploitation plots.

Putting Kelly in a film with Bruce Lee was not an unusual move. In several Blaxploitation films, Black heroes would team up with an Asian hero or do battle against an Asian villain. As seen in films like *That Man Bolt* and *The Big Doll House*, low-budget filmmakers capitalized on the cheaper filmmaking that Macao, the Philippines, and Hong Kong could buy. Also, several Blaxploitation movie protagonists employed some form of martial arts as a defense, from Cleopatra Jones to Youngblood Priest to Dolemite (though his skill set was quite questionable). Unlike those characters, every role Jim Kelly took came front-loaded with his formidable fighting skills.

James Milton Kelly was born in Paris, Kentucky, on May 5, 1946, barely a year after the end of World War II. Like his future co-stars Jim Brown and Fred Williamson, his football prowess initially brought him success, earning him a scholarship to the University of Louisville. However, he left the school after hearing a coach use racial slurs when addressing a fellow player. To fill the void, Kelly took up Shorin-ryu karate in 1964. He won the International Middle-weight Karate Championship in 1971. While John Shaft was strolling through Harlem and Sweet Sweetback was running from the law, Jim Kelly was planning to join them. In a 2010 *Salon* interview with Bob Calhoun, Kelly detailed his decision-making: "In 1969, after I got my black belt from Sgt. LeRoy Edwards in San Diego, I had to make a decision about what I wanted to do with my life. I said, 'What will make me happy?' I said, 'I need to make a lot of money, I need to be very famous, and I need to be motivational for kids.'"

Kelly continued. "Since I wasn't going to play professional football, and I was a very good football player. I played college football and I could have gone on to play pro. Since I wasn't going to do that, how was I going to get these needs of mine met? I said, 'Why don't I become an actor?' What I had to do was become world karate champion and use that as a stepping stone and maybe get into the movies."

In Los Angeles, Kelly opened a dojo that was frequented by Hollywood celebrities who noticed his charisma. It's how he got the acting gig on *Melinda*. Robertson wanted him to train Calvin Lockhart, who was playing a radio DJ framed for murder by a corrupt millionaire. During their sessions, Kelly snared the role of Charles Atkins, a sensei who fights alongside the heroes during the film's climactic battle.

"Your Kind of Black Film," read the tagline for *Melinda*, a bold statement that worked as both a marketing statement and a description of what was going on behind the camera. This was the first studio film that had a Black writer, pro-ducer, and director who were all different people. Robertson was hired to direct at MGM during the editing of *Shaft*, using a script by Lonne Elder III, *Sounder's* Oscar-nominated screenwriter (Elder also appears as a cop). Production duties were overseen by Pervis Atkins.

With his smooth, wonderful speaking voice, Lockhart was perfectly cast as Frankie J. Parker, a very egotistical DJ who spits game on the radio and in real life. New York City–area viewers may have wondered if Lockhart's moniker was an homage to Frankie Crocker, the pioneering Black disc jockey who ruled the soul/R&B radio airwaves at the time. Crocker would turn WBLS into a ratings powerhouse in the 1970s, creating a blueprint for others who ran Black music stations.

More likely, Lockhart's cocky character was a parody of the actor's prickly reputation; he had publicly been deemed a problem on the set of his first leading role, 1970's *Halls of Anger*, a film about student bussing produced by Walter Mirisch. Mirisch had plans to turn Lockhart into a clone of the actor's fellow Bahamian, Sidney Poitier, and he was very invested in using this particular film as the vehicle to do so. He hired Paul Bogart, then a TV director for CBS's *All in the Family*, to direct. "He made my life absolutely miserable," said Bogart. "I had the feeling Mr. Lockhart just didn't want to be there."

Melinda was a more interesting feature than *Halls of Anger*, primarily because of its complex mystery story and its performances. Vonetta McGee played the title character, a beautiful, mysterious woman who entices Frankie into a whirlwind affair. (Their sex scene is one of the most erotic in all of Blaxploitation, staged in semidarkness and juxtaposed with the reactions of a hilarious audience stand-in who's listening on the other side of the door.) Unfortunately, Melinda ends up brutally murdered and Frankie is framed for the crime. A shady friend played by Rockne "Black Samson" Tarkington may be involved in the cover-up.

Kelly's role is small, and his performance is somewhat stilted, but he wasn't expecting perfection his first time out. "I didn't even know what a movie camera looked like," he told *Black Belt* magazine. Regarding the role he played, he said, "I thought to myself 'I'm not ready for this.' But I said 'OK.' It was a great break." If nothing else, *Melinda* provided an introduction to the fighting style and skills he would utilize throughout his film career. Audiences took notice, but it was six months before Kelly was considered for his next role, Williams in *Enter the Dragon*.

Billed as "the first martial arts film made by a major Hollywood studio," *Enter the Dragon* was produced at Warner Bros. by Fred Weintraub and Paul Heller. "As far back [as 1970], I was interested in doing a martial arts film," Weintraub said. "Everybody laughed at me when I said I wanted to put a Chinese actor's name [Bruce Lee] above the title. That had never happened in the history of Hollywood."

It should not have seemed unusual to put Bruce Lee's name above the title. He had more movie experience by 1973 than many top-line actors, having starred in Hong Kong films as a kid. His career started in 1946, in fact. In 1966, he became well-known in America when he portrayed Kato, the ass-kicking valet to Van Williams's Green Hornet on the eponymous television series and its parent show, *Batman*. In 1969, he made his American film debut in *Marlowe*, a violent adaptation of Raymond Chandler's *The Little Sister*, starring Jim Garner as Philip Marlowe. Lee's appearance as a villain is physically electrifying, but the film disrespects him by dispatching his character in an insulting, offensive fashion. (Quentin Tarantino would insult Lee further in a similar scene in *Once Upon a Time . . . in Hollywood*, when the audience is expected to buy Brad Pitt kicking Bruce Lee's ass.)

Though Lee was born in San Francisco and was therefore an American citizen, his cinematic legend was forged when he returned to Hong Kong for the first time since he'd left in 1959. He had a much bigger fan base among his Chinese brethren. As such, he accepted an invitation from the famous producer Raymond Chow to resume the Hong Kong movie career he had started at five years old. The 1971 film, director Wei Lo's *The Big Boss*, was a hit. Lo and Lee followed that with 1972's *Fist of Fury*. Lee himself helmed *The Way of the Dragon* after that, the film that teamed him with an antagonistic Chuck Norris. These films, released in the US with confusing titles (*The Big Boss* was called *Fists of Fury* while *Fist of Fury* became *The Chinese Connection*), increased Lee's visibility with American audiences, leading him back to the States.

Kelly wasn't the first choice for the role of Williams. In fact, he wasn't even considered. He was working at his studio when his agent sent him down to Warners to interview for *Enter the Dragon*, though she cautioned it was simply for exposure. As Kelly told *Salon*, "She said, 'You won't get the part, but go out there. I want you to meet the producers . . . They have a guy they want already, but they're just having a little problem with him so they're interviewing other people.' So I went out there and talked to Fred Weintraub and Paul Heller and looked at the script for a second. They asked me what I thought of the script. I said, 'I love it. I think it's a great script.' They said, 'How soon can you leave for Hong Kong?'"

The plot of *Enter the Dragon* sounds like the beginning of a bar joke: "A Black guy, a White guy, and an Asian guy walk into a madman's island battle royale . . ." The White guy was actor John Saxon, cast because he was, in Warners' estimation, a bigger and more recognizable name. Thankfully, he made a convincing fighter; he had some karate training in the shotokan system with Japanese master Hidetaka Nishiyama. Saxon's character, Roper, had so much chemistry with Kelly's Williams that viewers continued to associate the two of them in real life with their onscreen partnership.

In the film, Roper and Williams are competing in a karate tournament on a mysterious island run by a suspected crime lord named Han (Shih Kien).

Roper hopes to win to settle his gambling debts, debts that will be held over his head when Han later asks him to join his criminal empire. Bruce Lee plays Lee, a sensei hired by the Brits to investigate Han's criminal endeavors and report his findings. Lee also discovers that Han's henchmen were responsible for his sister's brutal death, adding revenge to his itinerary.

Williams is on the island because he's a cool soul brother who wants to win. With his impeccable Afro, masterful karate moves, and considerable swagger, he represented a figure Black audiences could identify with and root for (besides Bruce Lee, of course). He's also the tie to Blaxploitation, echoing a sexual prowess not unlike the era's biggest studs. When offered a choice of "company for the evening," Williams selects multiple, very willing women to sex up.

Screenwriter Michael Allin gives Williams the most quotable lines in *Enter the Dragon*, delivered by Kelly in a better performance than he gave in *Melinda*. He describes Han as a figure "right out of a comic book," which is a nicer description than *Philadelphia Inquirer* critic Barbara Wilson's observation that "he resembles both Richard Nixon and Chou En-Lai." Williams also states that "ghettoes are the same all over the world—they stink." And his dialogue with Han sums up Kelly's modus operandi so well they became his signature lines.

> **Han:** *It is defeat that you must learn to prepare for.*
> **Williams:** *I don't waste my time with it. When it comes, I won't even notice.*
> **Han:** *Oh? How so?*
> **Williams:** *I'll be too busy looking good!*

Defeat comes for Williams, unfortunately. He gets beaten to death by Han, then has his battered body unceremoniously dumped in front of his pal, Roper. It's an ignoble death, but it spurs the audience to cheer even harder when Bruce Lee avenges him by slaughtering Han in a fantastic final battle set in a hall of mirrors.

Sadly, Lee never got to hear those cheers; he died on July 27, 1973, three weeks before *Enter the Dragon* opened in Los Angeles. "Bruce was the greatest," Kelly remembered when asked about his time with Lee. "He had soul. He had rhythm. He had style."

Despite *Enter the Dragon* being a major box office success—the top-grossing martial arts film at the time—critics like the *Chicago Tribune*'s Gene Siskel were so sick of sitting through these violent, crowd-pleasing exports that their reviews were filled with a shocking amount of venom that occasionally bordered on racism. Siskel's review was especially wrongheaded, though it provides some historical context about the Chicago movie theater scene.

Giving the film half of one star out of four, he called it "one of the most hateful films in years" and lamented that it was "doing slam-bang business and tonight will break the house record at the State Lake Theater with approximately $125,000 . . . a $50,000 gross at the State Lake is considered terrific business." Siskel explained that "the surest box office draw in the Loop has been the karate film" and that the audiences who frequented those theaters got off on the violence. He also blamed Lee's untimely death as another reason the unwashed masses flocked to see *Enter the Dragon*.

In his one-and-a-half-star review, the New York *Daily News'* Jerry Oster called it "the latest kung fu migraine" but did commend Lee's fighting skills. In the rare review that mentioned Kelly by name, the *Boston Globe* reported on "the silly little film produced by Warner Brothers, who should know better, and co-starring John Saxon and Jim Kelly, who also execute some fairly flamboyant Kung Fu moves, perhaps to compensate for their obtuse acting."

Critics be damned, *Enter the Dragon* grossed $25 million against an $850,000 budget in its initial run.

1974
1974

more to adore in '74

1974
1974

T his is the first year for which I have detailed memories. One I can recall vividly involved a scary-looking White man on CBS talking about something I didn't clearly understand, but it looked important. As this somber, exhausted, gravelly voiced guy read from a series of papers he was holding, I asked my mother who he was. I will forever associate Richard M. Nixon with her response: "A very, very bad man!"

If you were looking for a first-run movie to celebrate a very, very bad man's very, very good resignation (effective at noon on Friday, August 9, 1974), you had some interesting and rather appropriate weekend choices. Charles Bronson's violent vigilante fantasy, *Death Wish*, and Warren Beatty's paranoid thriller, *The Parallax View*, were happy to take your ticket money. *The Godfather Part II*, which would eventually win Best Picture at next year's Oscars, wasn't out for another four months, but if you wanted a Best Picture fix, that Newman-Redford movie by the producers of *Willie Dynamite* (*The Sting*) was still playing at your local bijou.

On the Black-hand side, visitors to the DeMille and other assorted urban theaters around the country could get an eyeful of Jim Kelly, Fred Williamson, and Jim Brown in the first of their three pairings together, *Three the Hard Way*. Militants and brothers down with the Cause could check out *The Mack* director Michael Campus's documentary-style biopic *The Education of Sonny Carson*.

Couples siding with the Coalition Against Blaxploitation that weekend had James Earl Jones and Diahann Carroll's Black romantic comedy, *Claudine*, to keep them warm. If they were in the New York City area, those same couples could really rev things up after that with some quality porn; Radley Metzger's bisexual "feast for the erotic gourmet" *Score* hawked its premiere with an ad on page 24 of the same *New York Times* whose headline that day screamed "NIXON RESIGNS." How better to ring in the Gerald Ford era?

Another vivid memory I have from 1974 is being bored out of my mind in various cars whose drivers (my aunt, my parents) were looking for gas. The 1973 OPEC oil embargo bled into 1974, with Nixon asking gas stations not to sell gas on Saturdays and Sundays as an act of preservation. On weekdays, I remember seeing the green flags tied outside, which meant that station had gas. The only fun part of this adventure was hearing the grown-ups in the front seat cursing blue streaks when those green flags were suddenly replaced with red "out of gas" ones. This usually occurred after we were stuck in a spiraling, long line for hours. Tougher economic times were ahead, especially for the city across the river from my hometown.

The Year of Our Lord 1974 was also the year I was introduced to Blaxploitation films! And Bruce Lee! My late aunt Brenda, one of those aforementioned cussin' adults at the gas station, took me and her two sons to see a double feature of *Black Belt Jones* and *Enter the Dragon*. I can still feel the excitement and tension that ran through my body as I watched all that action on the screen. This was probably the first time I saw an empowered Black character on the screen. Jim Kelly and his Afro looked a hundred feet tall to me.

A few weeks after that, one of my much older cousins took me to see a double feature of *Coffy* and *Foxy Brown*. Granted, these were not films little kids should be seeing—one of the admittedly valid arguments CORE and the NAACP had against Blaxploitation films— but to this day I can recall my female cousins "playing" Pam Grier in their make-believe games. Sure, there was violence in these films, but there was violence on our streets, too. We were more resilient than the grown-ups gave us credit.

Over in the music world: Stevie Wonder never wrote any music for a Blaxploitation movie, but the record that won him the 1974 Best R&B Song Grammy, "Living for the City," had a skit in the middle of it that sounded like a mini-Blaxploitation movie. Evoking the Second Great Migration, where Black folks came from the South to face struggles in the North, Wonder plays a guy fresh off the bus at Port Authority in New York City. Immediately, he's asked to hold something by a shady individual. Whatever it is gets him arrested, tried, and sent to jail. Wonder got a White studio worker to yell the song's still-jarring "GET IN THAT CELL, NIGGER!"

In sports, Muhammad Ali and Joe Frazier fought the second of their three big bouts in January, with Ali winning a unanimous decision that sent him to one of his most famous matches: the Rumble in the Jungle. Ali took on George Foreman, who currently held the belt, and used his "rope-a-dope" technique on his opponent. That is, he let Foreman pummel him for seven rounds, and when he was punched out, Ali KO'ed him in the eighth round. The Greatest was the heavyweight champ once again.

More Black people were on TV in 1974, starting with *Good Times*, the Chicago-based sitcom created by Eric Monte and the guy who played Lionel Jefferson from *All in the Family*, Mike Evans. Evans loaned his full name to a character, and *Good Times* made history in more than one way. It was a spin-off of *Maude*, which itself was a spin-off of *All in the Family*, thereby making it an unprecedented spin-off of a spin-off. It also was the first sitcom to have a two-parent Black household—at least for its first two seasons.

Along with *Good Times*, Black viewers could see our brethren on *Get Christie Love!*, *Tenafly*, and the *Shaft* TV show. Since VCRs were not in households back then, if you missed a program, you'd have to wait for the rerun in the summer, if you were lucky. The likelihood of people staying at home so they could catch an episode of their favorite show increased, though not enough to make a dent in the movie market.

Regardless, there were still a good number of Blaxploitation flicks to distract people from corrupt presidents, gas troubles, and their cities hurtling toward bankruptcy. There were horror movies, action movies, and the occasional drama like *Together Brothers* (which was also playing the weekend Nixon canned himself). Plus, the most famous Black actor in studio system–era Hollywood was fixing to intentionally make a fool of himself on the big screen for the first time, killing his Noble Negro status for good.

CHAPTER 19

BLACK BELTS, HARD WAYS, AND WOOF TICKETS

Enter the Dragon opened the door to Kelly's film career. "When I got back from Hong Kong," Kelly said, "I was immediately signed to a three-movie deal with Warner Brothers." The studio reteamed him with producers Weintraub and Heller and director Robert Clouse for *Black Belt Jones*, his first lead role. The film's Black writer, Oscar Williams, had just written and directed a Billy Dee Williams movie called *The Final Comedown*. That one was about Black revolutionaries; *Black Belt Jones* featured the exploits of a CIA agent avenging the death of Papa Byrd, a beloved dojo owner and community figurehead.

Byrd is played by Scatman Crothers in a cameo. Mere months before he'd voice Hanna-Barbera's incompetent kung-fu pooch, Hong Kong Phooey, Crothers portrayed a guy who was once as badass as Black Belt Jones. Unfortunately, Papa Byrd presided over a karate school located on a plot of land worth a lot of money. Equally unfortunate was the jarring, lopsided conk the normally bald Crothers sported on his head. It's so distracting that one can't focus on his acting.

The Mafia goons who want the land literally scare Byrd to death, but it's all for naught: the true owner of the dojo is Byrd's progeny, Sydney. After several hoods repeatedly assume Papa Byrd has a son, Sydney shows up to disabuse them of that notion. "Sydney's a broad!" says one of the bad guys on the receiving end of the ass kicking she dispenses on a gang of dudes. Apparently, Sydney was once the prize pupil of the dojo she now owns.

Gloria Hendry plays Sydney, and—thank you, Black Jesus—she finally gets a Blaxploitation-era role worthy of her talent! She's smart, quick with a comeback, dressed to the nines, and gets several exciting fight scenes that she trained for before filming started. Even her relationship with the protagonist is presented in a refreshing light; she's the playful aggressor in their physical tussle of a seduction scene. "I know what I've got," she tells Jones. "And if you want it, you'll have to take it."

In the *Charlotte News*, Hendry described *Black Belt Jones* as "entertaining and should make you laugh." It's clear from the outset that *Black Belt Jones* is intentionally funny, even as it delivers the nonstop action fans crave. Sydney and Jones spend the bulk of the second half taking down the entire Mafia with fists and feet. Bad guy bodies are sent flying every which way, usually smashing through windows as they land. (The breakaway glass budget on this movie must have been legendary.) Essentially bloodless, the fighting scenes play like slapstick employed in service to the vengeful protagonists. There's even an extended battle in a car wash with most of the participants covered in enough soap bubbles to full a suds party. "I guess you could call it clean violence," Hendry said of the film's action. That still didn't stop the MPAA from slapping *Black Belt Jones* with an R rating.

Kelly's choreography gets showcased by director Clouse and his editor, Michael Kahn. Unlike *Trouble Man*, Kahn's editing is less chaotic and more in tune with the overall product. There are a few sequences here that hint at what was to come once Kahn hooked up with Steven Spielberg. *Black Belt Jones* is no *Raiders of the Lost Ark*, but the origins of that film's comic pacing are evident. The overall light touch and Kelly's undeniable chemistry make *Black Belt Jones* one of the more entertaining films in both Blaxploitation and the martial arts genre.

Black Belt Jones was one of the first releases of 1974, opening in mid-January. Unsurprisingly, most critics were immune to a movie with karate in it, and a few were particularly mean to Hendry. "Jones is assisted by a comely female karate expert who insults the masculinity of any man who won't fight her," wrote Mimi Avins in a vicious *St. Louis Post-Dispatch* pan. Avins also preferred to see "an orgy of consenting chickens." William A. Henry III's *Boston Globe* pan confusingly stated the film was full of "racist and sexist violence" and seemed particularly upset that Hendry's character was an action hero. "The needless crushing of a white man's leg makes the heroine smile," he wrote. Henry also complained that "a self-sufficient woman must have a mannish name." Showing true ignorance, he ended by stating Kelly's championship-level fighting skills were "an approximation of karate."

At least the *Philadelphia Daily News* liked it—and was nice to Hendry, too.

Joe Baltake reviewed it when it opened at the Milgram. He compared Hendry's character to someone Ann Sheridan would have played (Sheridan was certainly tough enough to crush a White guy's leg in a flick if she had to), and called *Black Belt Jones* "a delightful send-up of those Cagney-Bogart Depression movies, replete with soul brother jive and chop-socky action for good measure."

Like most Blaxploitation films that turned a profit at the box office—this one did over $1 million—*Black Belt Jones* inspired a sequel of sorts. Oscar Williams and Jim Kelly reteamed for the PG-rated *Hot Potato*, which Williams wrote and directed in 1976. Kelly reprises his role as Black Belt Jones, and the film was given an international flair by virtue of being shot in Thailand. But the less said about this one, the better. An intriguing plot involving doppelgängers and kidnapping is derailed by the antics of George Memmoli as Jones's slovenly sidekick.

Nicknamed the White Rhino because of his size and his onscreen gluttony, Memmoli's antics reduce the amount of running time Black Belt Jones gets to fight. It almost feels like the actor was forced on the movie, though Kelly was the bigger draw. Additionally, it's clear Warners didn't want to pony up much money to get this made—the production values are atrocious, and there's a lot of voice-over to reduce scenes of characters talking to each other on camera. *Hot Potato* was a sad end for Black Belt Jones.

"Didn't you once cause quite a stir by challenging heavyweight boxing champion Muhammad Ali to a fight?" *Black Belt* magazine asked Jim Kelly in an interview. It was even more unbelievable than that! On December 16, 1973, UPI reported that the stars of the upcoming feature *Three the Hard Way*—Jim Brown, Fred Williamson, and Kelly—had challenged Ali, George Forman, and Joe Frazier to a fight. This wasn't a publicity stunt for the still-shooting movie, nor was it a staged event for charity. This appeared to be a good, old-fashioned street challenge, woof tickets being sold to three boxing champions by two former football players and a karate expert.

And what woof tickets they sold! "I just think that we're as tough as those three dudes," said Brown, who was being interviewed alongside Williamson and Kelly. "All [the boxers] do is talk about fighting in the ring. But how tough are they out of it?" Perhaps they'd forgotten that Ali came from Kelly's tough hometown of Louisville, Foreman grew up in Houston's Fifth Ward, and Frazier was a South Carolina sharecropper's kid who moved to Philly when he was fifteen.

Brown offered to fight Ali, because in the 1960s, the two sparred in practice. "He wasn't as strong as I am," he revealed. Kelly would fight Joe Frazier. "Fred's got the hardest assignment with Foreman," said Brown. "But I have no doubt we can handle 'em."

The fight never happened.

Three the Hard Way did happen, however, becoming the first of three films the trio would make together. Directed by Gordon Parks Jr. and written by Eric Bercovici and Jerrold L. Ludwig, it told the story of a racist plan to put some kind of plague in the water that kills only Black people. There's some mention of sickle cell anemia to keep things legit. It's up to the heroes to stop this racist group whose leader looks a lot like Howard Cosell. "It took God seven days to make the earth," says the head baddie. "It'll take us three days to cleanse it." The plot sounds crazy enough, but even more shocking is that the film was shot by veteran cinematographer Lucien Ballard.

In his five-decade career, Ballard worked with some of the greatest directors. Josef von Sternberg used him as a camera operator on 1930's *Morocco*, and he got his first cinematography credit working with von Sternberg on *Crime and Punishment*. Ballard also worked with Henry Hathaway (whose last film was a Blaxploitation quickie called *Super Dude*), Sam Peckinpah, Stanley Kubrick, and Budd Boetticher. Except for Kubrick, these directors used him multiple times. *Three the Hard Way* was Parks Jr.'s second collaboration with Ballard, after 1974's *Thomasine and Bushrod*, Max Julien's intriguing take on *Bonnie and Clyde*.

Like Gordon Willis, he was hated by the cinematography branch of the Oscars. Ballard was nominated only once, for a Joan Crawford film called *The Caretakers*. He shot 130 films in his career, mostly made in the days when there were two chances to be nominated (black & white and color), yet the Academy repeatedly snubbed him. This despite his invention of the Obie, a light he created to hide the facial scars his then wife, Merle Oberon, received in a car accident, and his work with legend Gregg Toland on how best to shoot Jane Russell's cleavage in Howard Hughes's *The Outlaw*.

Three the Hard Way was a fixture on New York City independent channels during the mid-1970s. On TV, it looked like hot garbage and was edited down to a PG-rated version. Comparatively, on the big screen, Ballard's widescreen compositions and his ability to light different shades of Black skin correctly made the film look better than its budget suggested. Some of it is still too dark to be effective, but the old master still has an impressive trick or two up his sleeve.

That plot about putting Black death in the water supplies of Los Angeles, Washington, D.C., and Detroit is merely an excuse for Kelly, Washington, and Brown to shoot, stab, and karate-chop hundreds of people. Record producer Jimmy Lait (Brown) is in LA producing the soul group who provide the film's soundtrack, the Impressions. An old friend who was being experimented on by White supremacists escapes from the compound where he was imprisoned. The guy seems delusional, so Jimmy doesn't believe him. Then his friend is murdered and Jimmy's main squeeze, Wendy (Sheila Frazier), is kidnapped.

After he barely avoids being killed, Lait heads to Chicago to see his friend, Jagger Daniels (Williamson). The villains try to kill him, too. Sensing that three is a magic number, at least where heroes are concerned, the duo head to New York City to recruit Mister Keyes (Kelly), a *sabom* who runs a tae kwon do studio. Mister is not an honorific, it's literally Keyes's first name.

Keyes is introduced in Kelly's most famous scene, the one every fan fondly remembers. After crooked cops plant cocaine in the red velvet interior of his car, an angry Mister asks, "Gonna set me up?" Then he dispenses a ridiculous and exciting slow-motion ass kicking on numerous cops, none of whom are quick enough to shoot him. The trio is now complete.

To get some nudity into the picture, Jagger also calls in three dominatrices, one Black, one White, and one Asian, to interrogate a witness. *Three the Hard Way* is too afraid to show their methods, but whatever they are, they're fatal. Mister asks for their phone number.

After much violence, the racist evil plan is foiled and *Three the Hard Way* ends on a freeze frame of an exploding Cadillac, as if the filmmakers suddenly ran out of money. That wouldn't be a surprise, considering that Allied Artists, the studio that made the film, was once a Poverty Row studio called Monogram back in the days of film noir. The budget was so low that Brown did his own dangerous stunts, the most impressive of which involved using a gun that never needed to be reloaded.

When *Three the Hard Way* opened at the DeMille in New York City on June 26, 1974, it was universally panned. Donald Mayerson of *Cue* magazine said, "The plot . . . is simply awful." The *Calgary Herald* called it a "comic strip gone berserk" where "several white enemies catch on fire and burn picturesquely to death." Williamson brushed off the criticism: "Most of my fans are kids in the ghetto areas and they relate to the characters I play." Those kids weren't writing reviews, but they were buying tickets. *Three the Hard Way* opened in eighth place, on its way to making $3 million at the box office, a million-dollar return on its $2 million budget.

Exploring the Wild World of Genre Filmmaking with Producer Jeff Schechtman

In the '70s, Jeff Schechtman was the assistant to producer Fred Weintraub, with whom he made several films before branching out as a producer in his own right. These include four films with Jim Kelly and five with director Robert Clouse. He worked with Sam Arkoff at AIP and Roger Corman at New World Pictures. He provided a very useful account of being on the set of some Blaxploitation classics and his own theory on why the Blaxploitation era ended.

I started by bringing up the fact that Blaxploitation lives on in today's movies, whether it's acknowledged or not. I also brought up the recent series of remakes of films like *Shaft*.

Blaxploitation hasn't gone away, at least not in theme or attitude. You see a Black guy on the screen doing something that's "cool," and chances are the trope that defined it as cool came from Blaxploitation. And the remakes of some of these films, like the two *Shafts*, they're done by Black directors, John Singleton and Tim Story. I wonder why they were remade. Perhaps they, like me, wanted to revisit these films out of a sense of nostalgia.

One of the things that's interesting about the remakes by Singleton and others is that there are Black directors remaking them. But back in those days, whether it was Jonathan Kaplan or Bob Clouse, these were White guys making Black exploitation movies.

Yeah, but in the case of Kaplan's *Truck Turner* or Clouse's *Black Belt Jones*—they were written by a Black guy. Oscar Williams was Black, right?

Yeah, Oscar Williams was the exception.

Well, you also had Gordon Parks, Ossie Davis, Melvin, and Hugh Robertson directing and writing movies. But you're right, it was primarily White filmmakers. So, I wanted to ask you about the other people behind the camera, like folks doing technical jobs—was it an integrated crew on the films you worked on?

It was, and you know, it really didn't matter. You had White producers and Black producers, White technicians and Black ones. I don't think people cared. They were there to do the job, and I don't think there were the interpersonal issues you might have today.

It was a different time. I mean, you had titles with words in them that would get bleeped today. And granted, some of these movies were offensive, but they weren't making Merchant Ivory movies. These were exploitation movies.

And they were up front about that. You knew what you were in for when you went to these films.

I'm trying to pinpoint when Blaxploitation ended and why it did. I have a cut-off point for this book for when it ended, and I have some theories as to why it ended. Number one is money, but number two is, toward the end, there were all these films that were trying to be respectable dramas. Things like *Amazing Grace* and *A Hero Ain't Nothin' but a Sandwich*. When you have Rudy Ray Moore lecturing you about the evils of drugs in *Disco Godfather*, the party's over. When they tried to make Blaxploitation movies respectable, people didn't want to go see them anymore. What do you think?

Well, I think that's part of it. The other part, as I remember it, is that television picked up a lot of the slack. Suddenly, you had much more integrated television. You had more Black characters on cop shows and on action shows. The respectability dramas were happening almost in reaction to

Blaxploitation. But more integrated casts on TV brought more Black characters people wanted to see into these action shows.

And television was free. I've also read theories that say blockbusters like *Star Wars* and *Jaws* were responsible for Blaxploitation's demise. As if Black people suddenly "discovered" White movies when they had been going to them long before Blaxploitation.

Exactly. It would be interesting to look at the demographics. You'd probably see that before Blaxploitation, Black people went to see White films and especially action movies in a larger percentage than their overall demographic.

There's that line in *Dolemite Is My Name* where Eddie Murphy says, "This movie has no titties, no funny, and no kung fu," and it made me laugh because, as kids, that's what we wanted to see. I took up martial arts because of Bruce Lee and Jim Kelly in *Enter the Dragon*. I'd rather see Jim Kelly kick somebody's ass than some Black guy getting arrested on *Baretta*.

Black people liking action movies was a given, but then when the kung fu movies came along, it was a surprise to Warner Bros. and the producers the degree to which there was a Black audience for *Enter the Dragon*. It was like a wake-up call. That's what inspired Fred Weintraub and Paul Heller to do *Truck Turner*, to do *Black Belt Jones*.

I found an interview Fred did in the *Cincinnati Post* around August 1973. He said he'd been trying to get a martial arts movie made for several years and that people were laughing at him because he wanted to put an Asian man's name above the title. But Bruce Lee had been acting since 1946, and he was known to Americans as Kato on *The Green Hornet*. I was wondering if you had any insight into why people didn't take Fred seriously.

No matter what people thought, there was no doubt in Bruce's mind that he was a movie star who deserved top billing. I remember the first time I met him in Fred's office in Burbank. The first thing Bruce does is take off his shirt and tell you to feel his stomach. Even before *Enter the Dragon* was made, his ego was gigantic!

So you got to meet Bruce? That's awesome! Since you worked on three movies he was in, what was Jim Kelly like?

He was a pretty gentle guy. He was 90—no, 80 percent reliable. Oscar was really good with him. [Williams directed him in *Hot Potato*.] Jim was just really easygoing.

A lot of Blaxploitation movies, and certainly several of the movies you worked on, were made in Asia. *Hot Potato*, for example, was shot in Thailand. Was that more for budgetary reasons?

It was definitely cheaper. And also, after *Enter the Dragon*, there was an arrangement with Raymond Chow [Golden Harvest's CEO] and his studio. So, it was definitely less expensive.

Did you go over there?

I went a few times. The longest time I spent was on a movie we're not discussing, *Golden Needles*.

Which I just found and watched right before talking to you! You can't buy it. It's on YouTube!

I haven't thought about it in a long time!

And Jim Kelly shows up for a few minutes in that. He has a mustache! I think it's the only time he has one in a movie.

That was a tough one to make. It was a little more ambitious.

And it has Ann Sothern tarted up like Mae West! I was like WHAT?!

[Laughs.]

Michael Kahn edited *Golden Needles* and the films we're talking about: *Black Belt Jones, Truck Turner*. He also edited *Trouble Man* and *The Spook Who Sat by the Door*. I'm fascinated by people who got their start in Blaxploitation. Did you have any interaction with him?

Oh, a lot. We lost touch but we were good friends for a while. I think his original arrangement with Fred came from the George C. Scott movie Fred produced.

The Savage Is Loose?

No, before that. *Rage*. And remember, this is before Spielberg.

Was *Close Encounters* his first movie with Spielberg?

I think so. I remember him being in Alabama a long time when they shot that.

And he never looked back!

[Laughs.] I remember asking him why he never wanted to direct. Even Spielberg asked him. I think it's a personality type mismatch.

You never directed anything. You stayed a producer. Ever wanted to?

NO!

Let's talk about the directors you worked with on these Blaxploitation films. Jonathan Kaplan, who directed *Truck Turner*, and Robert Clouse, who you worked with five times. Did they have different styles of directing?

I'm sure you know this, but there was a large age difference between them. I think their styles were more of a generational difference than an age one, though. Jonathan was much younger, hipper. It always surprised me he never went on to do more.

Yeah, his output was kind of sporadic and it's been a while since he directed anything. So, Bob was much older and, based on his movies, he had a thing for breakaway glass.

He was the most unexpected kind of director for the material. I wish I knew the why Freddy chose him to direct *Enter the Dragon*. And Bob was a really mild, quiet guy. Lived up in Santa Barbara. He internalized a lot of things. I think I saw him get outwardly mad less than ten times on all our movies. And Bob had a hearing problem, so the joke was, if he were mad at you, he'd turn off his hearing aids and that's how you knew.

After your films with Weintraub and Heller, you became a producer. You stayed in the . . . I'll call it the exploitation market.

Oh yeah, all my films were genre pictures.

I wanted to ask you about Joe Dante, who did the story for Pam Grier and Margaret Markov's *Black Mama White Mama*. You produced his *Piranha* movie. What was he like as a director?

He has a great sense of humor, never took himself too seriously. He'd never forget that we were making a movie about plastic fish!

You worked with Roger Corman and Sam Arkoff, both of whom made movies I'm covering in this book. They both seem like a similar type of pitchman. Were they alike?

Roger had better relationships with filmmakers than he did with other producers. People got along with him. I found him kind of aloof, whereas Arkoff and Arkoff's son were a whole different personality type.

I wonder if that was because Arkoff was a producer outright, while Corman produced but was also a director. It's a different kind of control.

There's something to that. And Roger had good instincts, obviously. But no one was going to accuse him of being P. T. Barnum. He was not a showman, whereas the Arkoffs were big, blustery personalities.

You know, with every type of exploitation movie, Black or White, there's probably a cycle you can track. Some movie kicks it off, some movie is the big crescendo, and then the genre just goes away.

CHAPTER 20

FOXY BROWN, FOXIER FELLINI

While *Black Belt Jones* was kicking around in theaters in January 1974, Pam Grier was also back on the screen. *The Arena*, her follow-up to *Scream, Blacula, Scream*, opened the same weekend and gave audiences a completely different type of fight picture. Reteamed with her *Black Mama White Mama* co-star, Margaret Markov, and their producer, Roger Corman, Grier played Mamawi, a Nubian woman. She's part of a crew of unlucky female slaves of the Roman Empire who are forced into gladiatorial battle. "We previously had worked together," wrote Grier of Markov in her book, *Foxy*, "and we had developed a wonderful friendship." It showed on the screen, even though they're initially antagonists.

As far as sword-and-sandals epics go, *The Arena* is quite entertaining and has a professional sheen that hides its low budget. The heroic group of women include Lucretia Love's Diedre and Maria Pia Conte's tragic Lucinia, who shares an odd yet tender love story with a male slave named Septimus (Pietro Ceccarelli). The evil Romans who order the battles are mocked with either cowardly acts or politically incorrect depictions. The most memorable of this batch is Priscium (Silvio Laurenzi), an extremely gay stereotype whose bitchiness and shade are played for laughs. The women are constantly under the threat of sexual assault, so whenever he shows up, they say, "Oh, it's just Priscium," with a mixture of scorn and relief.

Edited by future *Gremlins* director Joe Dante (who also co-wrote the story for *Black Mama White Mama*) and shot by genre movie legend Joe D'Amato, *The Arena* was full of brutal fight sequences featuring swords, shields, and (in Grier's case) a triton! The film was basically one of those Philippines-based women's prison movies, but this time, it was shot in Rome at Cinecittà Studios. "I was also going to Italy, a dream of mine," wrote Grier, "to act and do stunt horseback riding."

That last bit of information was important to the anecdote she details in *Foxy*. Both she and Markov always did their own stunts, due to the lack of stuntwomen as tall as Markov or Black like Grier. In fact, many stunts were still being done by White men regardless of the race or gender of the character. Viewers could see that it was clearly Grier and Markov engaging in fisticuffs, wielding weapons, and jumping from heights. Their tussle in *Black Mama White Mama* was an enjoyable display of their skills; this time, they briefly go at it with real weapons, not stage props.

Additionally, Grier's experience growing up in Colorado gave her insight into riding and caring for horses. For one scene, she was to ride a horse named Donatello. The horse appeared wild, but Grier knew how to handle him. Unfortunately, no one else on the set knew anything about horses, nor did they trust her advice. The marketing tour for *Coffy*, which had just come out at the time of filming *The Arena*, was to begin once Grier returned from Italy. It almost didn't happen.

Director Steve Carver was in a hurry to film Donatello's scene. Grier convinced him to let her earn the horse's confidence over lunch, because if he acted up, the other horses would follow suit. Someone on the set got the wild, dangerous idea to "assist" her by slapping Donatello's flank. Since horses "are flight animals," according to Grier, the horse took off with her on it. Several other horses followed, as she predicted. She held on for dear life as she was taken on a wild ride through Cinecittà Studios. At one point, as if in a silent film or screwball comedy, Donatello crashed through the backdrop on another movie's set.

Grier's description of the chaos is priceless: "The director's jaw dropped as he watched this nearly naked black woman with an afro, wrapped in a leopard skin, riding a black stallion with a group of wild horses following behind. He gasped, 'Oh Il mio Dio, my fantasy has come true.' It was Federico Fellini."

Thick, beautiful women like Pam Grier were Fellini's thing, so it's not hard to envision this scenario playing out in one of the director's film phantasmagoria. "You must live in Rome," he told her. "You must do movies here. Broaden your horizons." They cooked for one another—Fellini taught her a red sauce recipe and she taught him how to fry chicken—and kept in contact for years afterward. But they never made a movie together, yet another opportunity to be lamented. Just imagine Fellini's *Foxy Brown*. Alas, viewers had to settle for Jack Hill's version.

Foxy Brown was Pam Grier's third collaboration with Jack Hill, the director who once said she had "that something special only she has. She has *it*." As her movies showed up to this point, she could use "it" to beat the asses of anyone who challenged her. In 1974, she would have one of her most eventful years. She met John Lennon and was indirectly involved in a brawl that got him removed from a bar. In the melee, Grier lost several fingernails.

In April, she and Victoria Principal were chosen by the Academy of Motion Picture Arts and Sciences to be "Oscar Guardians," aka the pretty ladies who hand the Oscars to the winners once they reach the podium. What happened at that ceremony became the stuff of Oscar legend. Grier remembered: "I was standing in the wings and saw this flash—I have great peripheral vision. It was a nude body on the run. I said 'Oh, my God.' I had been watching Elizabeth Taylor [who was about to present Best Picture]. When the streaker went across the stage, she just started laughing."

After Beatles brawls and bare Academy Awards ass, *Foxy Brown* must have felt like the least eventful thing to happen to her.

Foxy Brown was supposed to be a sequel, a continuation of Nurse Coffy's exploits. "Nobody had an idea that *Coffy* would be such a big hit," Hill said. "So nobody gave any thought to a sequel." When AIP demanded one, Hill wrote a screenplay called *Burn, Coffy, Burn*. At the last minute, however, the studio reneged on the sequel idea and changes needed to be hurriedly made. This explains why Foxy Brown doesn't seem to have a job. "We were all upset," Hill recalled. "Oddly enough, *Foxy Brown* has acquired a cult following and is even more popular than *Coffy*."

While *Coffy* may have been the better film, *Foxy Brown* was the more influential. Rapper Inga DeCarlo Fung Marchand made Foxy Brown her moniker. Quentin Tarantino cribbed the film's violation scene, and its resulting scene of revenge, for Uma Thurman's Bride character in *Kill Bill: Vol. I*. (Hill's version is far nastier.) Additionally, when he adapted Elmore Leonard's *Rum Punch* into his best movie, QT not only cast Grier, but he changed Leonard's main character from Jackie Burke to Jackie *Brown*.

Spike Lee mocked *Foxy Brown* in his second-worst film, 1996's *Girl 6* (which QT appears in, believe it or not) by having Theresa Randle fantasize about becoming the character. Even Beyoncé paid tribute to Foxy (and Tamara Dobson), playing a character called Foxxy Cleopatra in the 2002 film *Austin Powers in Goldmember*.

Like its predecessor, *Foxy Brown* had a $500,000 budget. That was the maximum budget for all of AIP's "Black pictures." However, because of *Coffy*'s success, both Grier and her director cost more money this time around, so there was less money for everything else. "Even so, I brought the film in a day early," said Hill, "and because of that, [I] became a hero at the studio."

If viewers thought *Coffy* was rough going in the violence department, *Foxy Brown* was going to surpass those expectations. About this upgrade, Hill told Josiah Howard, "I hated the studio system so much that . . . by only going over the top could I get my own sinister kind of revenge." In hindsight, Hill regretted his decision. There are more violent films than this one, but *Foxy Brown* remains the only Blaxploitation film to run afoul of Great Britain's Video Nasties law. In 1982, the VHS version was seized subject to an Obscene Publications Act Section 3 seizure order.

The opening credits sequence of *Foxy Brown* is a love letter to its star. As *The Mack*'s composer Willie Hutch sings, "Hey, hey, hey, Foxy!" Grier winks at the camera before breaking into a dance routine choreographed by Anita Mann. As she boogies with Hutch's theme song, she also models five fantastic '70s outfits by costume designer Ruthie West, a preview of her wardrobe changes. The audience is also treated to Foxy dancing in a black bra and panties, with Grier's ample cleavage suddenly appearing onscreen in jarring fashion.

The plot hits the ground running. Foxy's ne'er-do-well brother, Link, played by the ubiquitous Blaxploitation star Antonio Fargas, is in trouble. There are several men in the area who want to do him harm. He phones his sister to ask her to come to a local hot dog stand to pick him up. Foxy shows up in her car and runs the men down while Link jumps in the car through her sunroof. Turns out Link owes twenty grand to shady heroin dealers Steve (Peter Brown) and his horny-as-hell girlfriend, Katherine (Kathryn Loder). Foxy threatens him but allows him to stay at her house until the heat's off.

Trouble with Steve and Katherine runs in the family. Foxy's main squeeze, Dalton (Terry Carter), turned a dime on their dealers, but the criminals were set free on a technicality. As a result, Dalton has to undergo facial reconstruction surgery so he can enter the Witness Protection Program. When Foxy visits him in the hospital, she awakens him with oral sex—and that's before she sees his new face. "I might not like it," she tells him. The rest of him is the same, he retorts.

Link figures out that the new man in Foxy's life is really Dalton, snitches on him, and Steve sends hit men to rub him out. An angry Foxy scares pertinent info out of Link—turns out Katherine runs a "fashion model agency" that's really a stable of women who sleep with judges in exchange for their dropping charges against her dealers. Foxy goes undercover as a sex worker, just like Coffy did. Also just like Coffy, Foxy gets into a fight with lesbians.

Between those events, she and another sex worker, Claudia (Juanita Brown) humiliate a White judge ("I know what to do with it, I just can't find it!" Foxy says of his manhood). As a result, he throws the book at Steve's drug dealers. This makes Katherine very, very irate. Foxy helps Claudia escape the henchmen sent to kill them, but Foxy gets caught, pumped full of heroin, and sent to "the farm," a torture shack run by unsavory-looking rapists.

Nobody gets their head blown clean off like in *Coffy*, but people still die in various gruesome ways. A villain is decapitated by guest star Sid Haig's airplane propeller. Foxy sets fire to the man who sexually assaulted her. And since Katherine can't get enough of Steve's love rocket (almost every scene they share has her demanding sex), Foxy brings it back to her—minus Steve. Loder makes for an excellent villain, and her satisfying reunion with Grier (after *The Big Doll House*) allows the latter to issue the coldest line in her Blaxploitation career. When Katherine demands Foxy kill her, as she has nothing to live for now that Steve's been neutered, Foxy replies, "Death is too good for you. Bitch, I want you to *suffer!*"

The critics apparently thought Foxy wanted them to suffer, too. When *Foxy Brown* opened at the Cinerama in Times Square on April 5, 1974, the *New York Times* was far from kind. "Miss Grier is obviously durable, but is fast becoming a bore," wrote A. H. Weiler. Ann Guarino in the New York *Daily News* unintentionally made it sound like a must-see, calling it "a rotten, trashy exploitation film that panders to the lowest tastes." Gene Siskel in the *Chicago Tribune* must have been blind the day he missed the three topless scenes in *Foxy Brown*, because he wrote, "Because Grier is a star, she doesn't have to show her nipples."

Meanwhile, historian Donald Bogle, interviewed in the *Philadelphia Inquirer* about the state of Black films and the female characters in them, said, "They are such far-fetched fantasies that I really don't know whether they are that directly connected to the matriarchal thing. Distorted as [films like *Foxy Brown*] are, you do get some glimpses of the independent, liberated black woman. The sad thing is she is not in a realistic situation that most black women can connect to."

Like *Coffy*, *Foxy Brown* made money—$2 million to be exact. Not bad against the $500,000 budget and in a month where *The Conversation*, *The Great Gatsby*, and Steven Spielberg's movie debut, *The Sugarland Express*, were also in theaters. Interestingly enough, Gordon Parks's *The Super Cops*, a "true story about the cops called Batman and Robin," as the tagline reads, also opened the same week as *Foxy Brown*. It was the Whitest film Parks made (though he still has his usual cameo and Sheila Frazier has a part). It was also the best-reviewed movie of his career.

Though Pam Grier and Isaac Hayes wouldn't appear in a movie in the Blaxploitation era, AIP got the bright idea to pair them in a double bill. *Foxy Brown* often played with *Truck Turner*, the Jonathan Kaplan film where Hayes finally gets to play the lead. Ike's Truck Turner is a skip tracer out to bring back a pimp named Gator (Paul Harris) for jumping bail. Ike provides the muscle and the film's score. He's stiff enough as an actor to prove Gordon Parks made the right decision to cast Richard Roundtree instead of him as Shaft, but Truck Turner isn't meant to be suave. When his cat pisses on his shirt, Turner calls him a nasty son of a bitch and knocks him off the dresser.

Though the film is plenty violent, its R-rating can be blamed on two words: Nichelle Nichols. That's right, Lieutenant Uhura from *Star Trek: The Original Series* is in a Blaxploitation movie and she's using words that would have made the NBC censor beam himself up. Every other word out of her mouth is "bitch," and she's just getting warmed up.

Nichols plays Dorinda, the lady pimp who oversees Gator's stable of sex workers. In a film with big guys like Isaac Hayes and Yaphet Kotto, the scariest person in it is Dorinda. She chews out Kotto's character, Blue, every chance she gets, and her hatred for Truck Turner is so strong she could probably kill him with her bare hands. Nichols joins Shelley Winters and Kathryn Loder in the Blaxploitation Bad Girls Hall of Fame with this scenery-chewing, massively entertaining performance. And the language! There isn't enough soap to wash out Dorinda's mouth, and that's the way it should be! Oscar Williams's script makes her say lines like, "Those two bitches that left better learn to sell pussy in Iceland because if I ever see them again I'm gonna cut their fucking throats" and "I haven't had to sell my pussy since I was fifteen and found out I could sell other bitches' instead. Don't you fuck with me, Blue."

Any movie with this much cussin', an editing job by Michael Kahn, and a hit man named after director Joe Dante can't be all bad. Director Kaplan's next gig, the excellent 1975 Hicksploitation film *White Line Fever*, came about because the producer of that film thought *Truck Turner* was an actual trucker movie. Kaplan took the job and stayed mum.

CHAPTER 21

POSSESSION IS NINE-TENTHS OF THE LAWSUIT

When *The Exorcist* opened on December 26, 1973, box office success was a given. Based on the best-selling novel by William Peter Blatty, who would win the Academy Award for adapting his book, this was the tale of a Georgetown-area mother whose daughter, Regan, started to exhibit signs she may be possessed by a demon named Pazuzu. People familiar with the story lined up outside theaters, as did any newbies brave enough to face it. Scandalous stories about viewers puking or passing out from fear spread like wildfire. There were even rumors of miscarriages and heart attacks. Warners would take the grosses any way they could get them!

"If *The Exorcist* had cost under a million or been made abroad, it would almost certainly be an X film," wrote critic Pauline Kael. It cost $11 million, so *The Exorcist* received a controversial R rating from the MPAA. This also contributed to the box office as well, because it meant that, with a parent or guardian, children under seventeen could get in to see a movie they obviously should not have been seeing. One of those children was the author; this was the first film he recalls seeing in the theater. He was a clueless lad of four, and unlike those fainting adults, he *thought it was hilarious*.

An equally inappropriate reaction came from the Catholic censor board, the National Legion of Decency. They may have been a thorn in Warners' side back when they condemned *Baby Doll* in 1956, causing the film to be pulled, but they passed *The Exorcist* despite it having a preteen masturbating with a crucifix and growling, "Let Jesus fuck you!" Could it be because the holy men who pulled Pazuzu out of Linda Blair's character were Jesuit priests, a testament to the

Catholic Church being the One True Church? After all, the Legion of Decency condemned the far less disturbing pagan horror movie *The Wicker Man* the same year.

Hits often beget sequels. They always beget copycats. Being the number one movie of 1973, *The Exorcist* was the beneficiary of both. There was its own disastrous sequel, *Exorcist II: The Heretic*, four years later, which was widely derided by critics, audiences, and the original film's director, William Friedkin. It still turned a minor profit. On the copycat side, there was 1974's Italian film *Chi Sei?*, wherein Juliet Mills was impregnated by Satan. Having the Devil as her "baby daddy" caused her to become possessed and puke up what one critic called "pistachio ice cream vomit." Film Ventures International, the ultimately doomed studio headed by Edward L. Montoro, outbid American International Pictures and bought the film. They released it in America in 1975 as *Beyond the Door.*

AIP decided to buy its own *Exorcist* knock-off anyway, and that's how Blaxploitation got 1974's *Abby.*

Originally titled *Possess My Soul*, *Abby* was a production of Mid-America Pictures, the company founded by then twenty-six-year-old Louisville, Kentucky, native William Girdler. Headquartered in Louisville (along with a small office in Hollywood), Mid-America specialized in low-budget movies—their films before *Abby* were horror films called *Asylum of Satan* and *Three on a Meathook*. The latter film attracted the attention of Sam Arkoff (and with that title, how could it not?), who eventually released *Abby* on Christmas Day 1974.

Girdler modeled his own studio after Arkoff's AIP, telling the *Courier-Journal* that Arkoff "knows probably as well as anyone on this Earth" what would make money. Girdler swore he wouldn't make a movie unless he knew it would make money. He also worked as quickly as the Arkoff's and Roger Corman's studios did; *Abby* was shot in six weeks.

Abby's $600,000 budget couldn't tolerate Girdler's original choice for the lead, a woman who demanded a masseuse and other perks unheard of on a low-budget film. So Carol Speed was cast as the eponymous preacher's wife. Born on March 14, 1945, in Bakersfield, California, Speed was raised in San Jose. She was originally known as a singer, performing in a group with two of her cousins. In Santa Clara County, where San Jose is located, she held the distinction of being the first Black woman to win high school homecoming queen, during her senior year in 1963. Speed also won a scholarship to the American Conservatory Theater in San Francisco.

By the time Girdler cast her, Speed was a known commodity in Blaxploitation. She was in *The Big Bird Cage*, played Goldie's girlfriend in *The Mack*, and was also the main squeeze of *Black Samson*. Fans of the NBC sitcom *Sanford and Son* remember her as the woman who jilted Lamont Sanford. NBC also used her in the pilot for the Black detective show *Tenafly* and in a recurring role on their soap opera, *Days of Our Lives*. In 1980, after she was no longer in demand as an actress, she wrote a book called *Inside Black Hollywood*.

As far as her acting, Speed considered *Abby* to be her favorite performance. She likened it to Joanne Woodward's Oscar-winning debut in 1957's *The Three Faces of Eve*. In that film, Woodward played a woman with three personalities. A psychological study based on a true story, Eve's personalities included her main personality, Eve White, and a wild, sexual, and nearly murderous woman named Eve Black. Black knew all about White's exploits, using that information to inform her actions and confuse those who knew her. But White had no idea about Black's existence. There are similarities, to be sure, though they seem purely coincidental.

"*Abby* gave me the opportunity to play three different characters," Speed said. "An educated Baptist minister's wife, a liberated sex-craving woman, and an egotistical demon." Those last two were a package deal: it wasn't until that demon got in Abby that she became super horny. Before that, she was the quiet, slightly goofy wife of Reverend Emmett Williams (Terry Carter). Her brother Detective Cass Potter (Austin Stoker) is a big shot with the police department, a job that will come in handy when Abby's body is suddenly inhabited by a Yoruba spirit of mischief named Eshu. As in *The Exorcist*, the voice of the demon is provided by someone else; in this case, the profane growls are courtesy of voice actor Bob Holt, who played Homer Zuckerman, owner of Wilbur the Pig, in the animated version of *Charlotte's Web*.

Giving the viewer a quick lesson on Yoruba customs is Emmett's father, Bishop Garnet Williams, played by Blacula himself, William Marshall. A scholar on African tribes, it was Marshall who incorporated this information into the script, as well as provided details for the climactic exorcism. However, he was disappointed in the final outcome, expressing that his suggestions for more Afrocentric details were ignored. What remains is choice, however, as Bishop Garnet is a far more soulful and funky exorcist than those Jesuits over in Georgetown. He was also inadvertently responsible for releasing Eshu while on an excursion to Africa.

Since Abby is an adult, Girdler and his screenwriter Gordon Cornell Layne make her possession a far more sexual and murderous manifestation than Linda Blair could portray at her age. Suddenly, Abby wants to bang everybody but her husband. When the good reverend tries to get some nookie by quoting biblical verses from Song of Solomon, Abby kicks him in the nuts and insults his manhood. During her marital counseling sessions, her solution to a couple's problems is to tell the wife she's going to "fuck the shit out of your husband!"

Eshu also gives Abby superpowers. She beats the crap out of several people, including her brother. Her mother's friend has a heart attack after being terrified by Abby's demonic temper tantrum. And, after singing a solo in the church choir (a gospel song written by Speed entitled "Is Your Soul a Witness"), she attempts to ravage the nerdy funeral director, Russell (Elliott Moffitt). Later, she literally screws the poor guy to death in the funeral home's limousine, an act accompanied by so much fake smoke it appears that Abby's nether regions are made out of dry ice.

As he did with his prior films, Girdler made *Abby* a local production. Most of it was shot in real locations, though its biggest set piece took place in a club built in an old warehouse in Louisville. Occurring before the finale, this scene provides the scenario for Eshu the demon to use Abby's body for carousing. She appears in a stunning white outfit no preacher's wife would dare model in public, picking and choosing her men before zeroing in on her fatal rendezvous with Russell. She also opens a can of whup-ass on anybody who stands in her way.

The climactic exorcism has Bishop Williams bypassing the blond hippie Jesus of the Catholic Church in favor of African rituals. It turns out that Abby is possessed not by Eshu, but by a cheap imitation posing as Eshu. It's only fitting for a Blaxploitation character to have the store-brand version of evil and not the good-label stuff. Fake Eshu is sucked into what looks like a precursor to the traps used by the Ghostbusters. Abby and her man live happily ever after despite her screwing around, killing several folks, and causing more property damage than humanly possible.

Audiences were ready for a Black take on *The Exorcist*, especially one with the misleading tagline "The Devil is her lover now!" Not even the critics could convince them to stick to the original. "Mercifully, Abby will have no memory of [her] horrid experience," wrote the New York *Daily News*' Jerry Oster. "I wish I could say the same thing." *Time* magazine stated that "the budget of this movie would appear to be approximately half the price of a ticket." Girdler fought back, saying, "I got more on the screen for the money spent on 'Abby' than Billy Friedkin got on the screen for the money spent on *The Exorcist*."

Despite entering a market saturated with blockbuster films like *The Towering Inferno*, *Earthquake*, *Airport 1975*, *The Man with the Golden Gun*, and *Freebie and the Bean* (which also opened on Christmas Day), *Abby* ultimately made $9 million at the box office. Had it been a flop, Warners never would have noticed the film's similarities to its top moneymaker. They thought *Abby* was similar enough to warrant a copyright infringement lawsuit. Truth be told, *Beyond the Door*, the retitled Italian film, was a bigger hit (making $15 million) and an even bigger rip-off, with its 360-degree head-turning effects and green vomit. Don't worry, Warners sued the makers of that film, too.

It appeared that Film Ventures got the better deal once they settled in 1979. *Beyond the Door* remained readily available and even got an early VHS release. AIP also settled with Warners, but the terms of that agreement remain vague. Regardless of the stipulations, *Abby* vanished from public view for decades. Though a DVD was eventually pressed, it was based off a lackluster 16mm print of the film. One of the rumors that circulated over the years was that Warners confiscated all the prints of *Abby*, making it virtually impossible to be reissued.

Despite *Abby* occasionally using camera angles that mimicked similar ones in *The Exorcist*, it was different enough that Sam Arkoff could have mounted a decent case. After all, the Devil held the copyright on possession, not Warners. That argument might not have held up in court, but it sounds like one a showman like Arkoff would have made. Even Speed questioned AIP's decision, though she'd had no idea the case existed until she started writing her own book.

"Sam Arkoff didn't care because he had already made a ton of money off of *Abby*," she speculated. "I believe Linda Blair and *The Exorcist* people wanted to be the leader of the possession films. *Abby* was fierce competition."

As for Speed's director, Bill Girdler, he gave Blaxploitation audiences the weakest of the Pam Grier AIP tetralogy, 1975's *Sheba, Baby*, before embarking on the biggest hit of his career. Over at Film Ventures, Girdler made a film that was a rip-off of an even more successful horror film: 1976's *Jaws* knockoff, *Grizzly* made $39 million at the box office. Its plot beats were so similar that critics called it "Paws." Universal would take its revenge on Film Ventures later—their 1980 Italian shark movie remake of *Jaws*, *Great White*, would get the studio sued into bankruptcy. It's even harder to find a print of that movie than it is to get one's hands on *Abby*.

CHAPTER 22

THE COSBY-POITIER TRILOGY I: BECAUSE I'M FROM OFF THE CORNERS

Let's address the elephant in the room. This chapter has the first of several mentions of films starring Bill Cosby in this book. He is a comedian who changed the landscape of stand-up comedy, hired or gave starts to numerous Black people, created a well-loved '70s cartoon and even more beloved '80s sitcom, and was once one of the author's childhood heroes. Cosby was also convicted in 2018 of aggravated indecent assault and served three years in prison before Pennsylvania's Supreme Court vacated his sentence. Civil cases against Cosby remain ongoing at the time of this writing.

For decades, there have been stories about Cosby allegedly drugging and raping women. In W. Kamau Bell's 2022 documentary *We Need to Talk About Cosby*, he interviews several women who tell harrowing stories about their alleged nonconsensual experiences with the comedian. It is impossible to discuss his films without acknowledging this information. Any positive commentary about his performances does not imply that the author disavows Cosby's troubled history, but it is difficult to tell the whole history of Blaxploitation without mentioning his movies with Sidney Poitier.

Before 1974, Sidney Poitier was not known for comedy. In the Hollywood of Poitier's heyday, comedy plus Negro equaled cooning. Poitier was held to a higher ideal, noble beyond any reasonable request. He could be charismatic and charming, but outright funny he could not be. Until, that is, Poitier took control of his own career and started directing and producing his films.

"When I first went to Hollywood, I and the shoeshine boy were the only blacks on the lot," he told the *Chicago Tribune*. "Now I see black secretaries . . .

and often blacks in the front office. That's very refreshing." That integration took the heat off Poitier and opened up more choices. "I don't have to fulfill everyone's dreams anymore," he said of this newfound freedom. "I'm not the only Black actor working in films, and I can pursue other directions."

In 1969, with Paul Newman, Steve McQueen, and Babs Streisand, Poitier created a production company called First Artists. This allowed him to direct the kinds of movies he wanted to headline. Under his production deal, he received 10 percent of the gross and one-third of the profits. After tackling a Western (*Buck and the Preacher*) and a bittersweet romance (*A Warm December*), Poitier was ready to direct his first comedy. It would become the first in a trilogy of films starring him and Bill Cosby.

Poitier intended to direct, but not star in, a film written by Newark, New Jersey, playwright Richard Wesley, a Drama Desk Award–winning writer. Wesley's 1971 play, *Black Terror*, won awards and acclaim. It told the story of a Black revolution and was a straight drama. The play was so popular it was taken on tour to Italy in 1972. However, the screenplay Wesley was pitching was about redemption, not revolution, and it was a comedy with characters whose unapologetically Black nicknames are masterpieces of moniker creation: *Uptown Saturday Night* introduced audiences to Leggy Peggy, Silky Slim, Madame Zenobia, Little Seymour Pettigrew, and Geechie Dan Beauford. That last guy is a Don Corleone parody played by Sidney's BFF, Harry Belafonte.

"It's time black people have some fun at their own expense," explained Poitier. "They don't always have to be angry or hostile. We made an effort to make the situation familiar. The characters are right out of Black life." Indeed, Black audiences like the one the author saw this film with back in 1975 were happy to see recognizable features like playing the dozens, side hustles, church picnics, and "hitting the number" depicted in comedic fashion on the big screen.

Attached to Wesley's story of two men trying to retrieve a stolen wallet containing a $50,000 lottery ticket were Richard Pryor and Redd Foxx. Bill Cosby blew away the executives during his tryout for the small part of a shifty private eye named Sharp Eye Washington. In fact, Cosby's audition for this part became the stuff of legend. But Warner Bros. didn't believe Foxx or Pryor were appropriately sized box office draws, despite their popular stand-up histories and their work in *Sanford and Son* and *Lady Sings the Blues*, respectively. Out went Redd and Rich, in came Sidney and Bill.

Heads should briefly bow in silent mourning for the movie that *Uptown*

Saturday Night would have been with its original casting. It's not certain which of the two lead characters they would have played, but in either role, Richard Pryor and Redd Foxx would have been Black movie dynamite. Viewers would instead have to wait fifteen years to see them together in the dismal Eddie Murphy vehicle *Harlem Nights*.

Still, the film benefits from the fine work by its two leads and all the supporting cast. Cosby picks Poitier's pocket and walks off with the picture, but Sidney purposely telegraphs where his wallet is. Their offscreen friendship translates to their onscreen characters, and things really start to cook when they're joined by Belafonte.

Uptown Saturday Night tells the story of Steve Jackson (Poitier) and Wardell Franklin (Cosby), two blue-collar guys who decide to live above their stations for one night. Cabdriver Wardell and factory worker Steve are working multiple jobs and, as *Uptown Saturday Night* opens, Wardell convinces Steve to go to Madame Zenobia's, a legal club with an illegal gambling ring behind a red door. This ritzy club is members-only, so Wardell types a fake letter on some stationery he stole from his wife's law office employer. The letter says he and Steve are important African diamond merchants and contains a forged signature for legitimacy. "Who is that guy?" asks Steve, referring to the fake name. "I don't know," says Wardell, "and I hope he doesn't show up here tonight."

Their evening proves financially fruitful. Wardell cleans up at a craps table where Leggy Peggy (Paula Kelly) is burning down the House with her hot dice. His fists are full of won money when Madame Zenobia's is hit by a group of masked robbers. Their faces are obscured, but any fan of Blaxploitation will immediately recognize their leader. Justifying the theft of everyone's jewelry, purses, and wallets, he says, "Never have so few owed so much to so many." Winston Churchill would not have been upset to be misquoted by the sexy voice of Calvin Lockhart.

Getting robbed after lying to their wives about their whereabouts is bad enough, but luck makes things worse. The newspaper prints the lottery numbers, and Steve's ticket hits for fifty grand. "Fifty thousand dollars," he and his wife, Sarah (Rosalind Cash), sing in unison. Then, Steve remembers his wallet is now the property of whomever hit Madame Zenobia's. So he enlists Wardell to help him find the culprits. Newbies in crime, their first few interviews don't go so well. In a scene played for laughs but is understandably cringe-inducing today, Wardell is roughed up by the cops in a scene of mistaken identity.

Seeking a professional leads them to Sharp Eye Washington, Private Eye. Sharp Eye is now portrayed by Richard Pryor, who still wound up in this movie after losing the lead. Pryor is onscreen less than five minutes, and in every second, he owns *Uptown Saturday Night*. Acting skittish and looking as bootleg as the cardboard sign on his door, Sharp Eye Washington can barely hide his con. He takes Steve's $50 and leaves before they can tell him what the job is. Going down the fire escape, Sharp Eye is met by the 5-0, who promptly arrest him.

Next is to visit to a local politician. Congressman Lincoln is a pandering, corrupt politician who is secretly hiding how ghetto he really is. It's perfect casting for Woodbury, New Jersey, native Roscoe Lee Browne. The always eloquent Browne had a smooth, unmistakable voice that was built equally for Shakespeare and signifying. Once, when a director commented that he "sounded White," Browne replied, "That's because we had a White maid." He excelled at this kind of bougie Negro role, so it made sense that he would chastise Steve for visiting "that den of iniquity" run by Madame Zenobia (Lee Chamberlin).

It also made sense that, in the middle of his stern lecture about the evils of illegal gambling, the viewer would discover the congressman is married to Leggy Peggy. Hell, he introduced her to Zenobia's den! Peggy's street vernacular makes Lincoln cringe, but she gives Steve and Wardell some advice. "Look up Little Seymour Pettigrew," she says before warning them that Little Seymour is a bad, bad man. He is indeed bad, a short package of fury embodied by Harold Nicholas, one half of the greatest tap-dancing duo to ever do a routine, the Nicholas Brothers.

The woof tickets Bill Cosby sells in the Little Seymour bar sequence are what audiences paid to see when they attended *Uptown Saturday Night*. "If the dude mess with me, I'ma knock him out," Wardell tells everyone within earshot. "You know why? 'Cuz I'm from OFF THE CORNERS!!" Steve gets in on it, playing the dozens and calling Little Seymour a "corny little runt." Poitier clearly enjoys the chance to finally cut loose after all the stoic roles that made him a legend. All that work leads to the discovery that Little Seymour lives up to his diminutive title, but he's accompanied by a very large bodyguard named Big Percy.

Immediately, the heroes start backpedaling, trying to clean up the mess they've made. Wesley said that, in the script, the scene was to have his heroes turn and run from the bar. This entire scene is improvised by the actors, including Cosby, who is funnier than he has ever been onscreen in this one moment.

"You see," he begins, before launching into this incredibly convoluted excuse about hospitals, the war, grandmothers, mental disorders, and doctor's cards. It doesn't matter. Little Seymour beats their asses in a sped-up sequence that highlights Nicholas's physicality. Even after crashing through the bar, he hops back up for more ass beating.

"What did he hit me with?" Steve asks Wardell during their recuperation at Steve's house. "His hands or his feet?" "Both!" says Wardell. "At the SAAAME time!"

Next, the guys try Leggy Peggy's other suggestion, Geechie Dan Beauford. As he did in *Buck and the Preacher*, Belafonte uglies himself up to the point of unrecognizability. Stuffing his face with cotton and adding a Southern swagger to his voice, Belafonte slurps down a raw egg, followed by a handful of pills and a snort from a Vicks inhaler. "Whatchu suckas want?" he asks.

Those suckas want to know if Geechie Dan knocked over Zenobia's. Dan says he didn't. "Sucka, if you don't get outta here, they're going to be pickin' yo' head up from across the street!" he threatens. Before anyone can leave, the bar is ambushed and shot up in spectacular fashion. Director Poitier makes the violence as exciting as any Blaxploitation movie's more violent shoot-outs.

Everyone escapes injury, but Dan thinks he's been set up. "Silky Slim did this?" he asks them later, interrogating them in an abandoned area. To get out, Steve admits Silky Slim set him up. (He has no idea who Silky Slim is.) "Put these dogs to sleep," Geechie Dan tells his henchmen.

As Steve and Wardell hilariously fight for their lives (what joy to see Poitier doing slapstick), Calvin Lockhart's Silky Slim shows up. When he utters his previous Churchill line, the guys know they have their man. Steve and Wardell use their fake lawyer letter, which was taken during the robbery, as a ruse to get Geechie Dan to partner with Silky Slim over a fictitious $300,000 worth of diamonds hidden in a law office. Slim brings all the loot he stole from Zenobia's, including the desired wallet, to Steve's church in a suitcase.

Uptown Saturday Night climaxes at a church picnic, and the film asks just how far viewers would go to retrieve $50,000. There's a happy ending and a rousing reprise of "How I Got Over" by an uncredited choir. Though they're singing about a different kind of getting over, it's a fitting way to end a film that shows how to get one over on the mob.

When *Uptown Saturday Night* had its world premiere on June 15, 1974, at 8:30 p.m. at Times Square's Criterion Theater, it was an immediate critical and commercial hit. The *New York Times'* Vincent Canby called it "a cheerful jape that has the effect of liberating all of us from our hangups." WABC's Kevin Landers told his television audience that "it is rather like a Marx Brothers style version of *The Godfather*." Even grumpy Ann Guarino at the New York *Daily News* dug it, giving the film three and a half out of four stars.

The film had international appeal as well. In September 1974, *Uptown Saturday Night* won Best Picture at the first-ever Black Film Festival in Kingston, Jamaica. Its fellow nominees were the 1973 concert film *Save the Children*, 1973's *The Spook Who Sat by the Door*, 1974's *Thomasine and Bushrod* and *Claudine*, and a television movie from that same year, *The Autobiography of Miss Jane Pittman*. Leggy Peggy herself, Paula Kelly, accepted the award along with her co-star, Rosalind Cash. Poitier lost the director award to *Save the Children*'s Stan Lathan.

When *Uptown Saturday Night* opened at the Chicago Theater in Chicago, Gene Siskel's positive review in the *Tribune* summed up the movie's allure for audiences: "Poitier grabs our attention by letting us see him as a regular guy. That's what the audience wants from Poitier right now." They also wanted a sequel, as the $4 million box office indicated. Eventually, they'd get two.

CHAPTER 23

WEREWOLF BREAKS AND ZOMBIE HIT MEN

This film is a detective story, in which you are the detective. The question is not "Who is the murderer?"—but "Who is the werewolf?"

—ANNOUNCER AT THE BEGINNING OF *THE BEAST MUST DIE*

After conquering vampires with the *Blacula* series (and, just to be inclusive, *Ganja & Hess*) and spoofing Frankenstein with 1973's *Blackenstein*, Blaxploitation next turned its monster movie gaze to that lover of the full moon, the werewolf. *The Beast Must Die* is a 1974 horror mystery in the vein of *The Hound of the Baskervilles*, and to be clear, it exists on the outskirts of Blaxploitation. However, it contains the first instance of a Black werewolf in a movie, and no, that revelation does not spoil the whodunit, or rather *"whoISit?"* Nor does it detract from the film's essential gimmick of asking the audience to solve the mystery in real time.

Amicus Productions, a British competitor of Hammer Studios, specialized in portmanteau movies, that is, anthologies where two or more tales are stitched together by a wraparound story or segment. They were the studio that first brought the EC Comics–based *Tales from the Crypt* and *Vault of Horror* to the screen in the early 1970s. Before that, they produced such delectable titles as *Dr. Terror's House of Horror*, *Torture Garden*, and *The House That Dripped Blood*. The latter two were written by frequent contributor and *Psycho* novelist Robert Bloch.

When not doing anthologies, Amicus did straight horror films, often with a gimmick. *The Beast Must Die* has a particularly amusing one: the Werewolf Break. Sixteen minutes in, Calvin Lockhart informs the guests who have come to his English mansion that one of them is a werewolf. After an hour of clues and drama, the film pauses. A clock appears on the screen for thirty seconds as a montage of the suspects runs behind it. One of the suspects, Paul Foote (Tom Chadbon) has actually eaten human flesh and is proud of the endeavor. He's too easy a choice. Or is he?

Screenwriter Michael Winder adapted *The Beast Must Die* from James Blish's short story "There Shall Be No Darkness." He and director Paul Annett open the film on Tom Newcliffe (Lockhart) running through some woods, chased by a helicopter as if he were a fugitive. There are microphones and cameras everywhere in this wilderness, and there's also someone in a room watching the footage and telling some gunmen on the ground where they can find and shoot their quarry. Eventually, the gunmen shoot Newcliffe as he is exiting the woods and entering an estate full of people having tea on the lawn.

Turns out this is an exercise, orchestrated by Newcliffe, to test the security around, and inside, his estate. The installation of alarms, mics, and video cameras is so extreme that it can record a human footstep a hundred feet away. A huge control room monitors every nook and cranny of the house and its grounds. If any guest tries to escape, Newcliffe will know and can immediately stop them. When the designer of the system, Pavel (Anton Diffring), asks why all this is necessary, Newcliffe points out that he can afford it. He also briefly discusses his upbringing in the Caribbean, a trait he shares with the actor playing him.

It might have been odd for American audiences to see Lockhart in England, but the actor had a history of working there before he became famous stateside. Born in Nassau, Bahamas, in 1934, Bert McClossey Cooper was the youngest of eight children. After spending time as an adult in Queens, driving a cab and doing manual labor, the newly rechristened Lockhart made his Broadway debut in 1960 in *The Cool World*, a show that lasted only two performances. He later started his own theater company and did performances in West Germany and England. While in England, he did plenty of British television and appeared in a small role in the Peter Lawford–Sammy Davis Jr. buddy movie *Salt and Pepper*.

After appearing in British director Michael Sarne's 1968 interracial romance, *Joanna*, he went back to America to star in *Halls of Anger*, his first lead role. After that, he was cast in a small role in Sarne's next movie. Unfortunately, that film was the infamous Raquel Welch–Mae West disaster *Myra Breckinridge*. This was 20th Century–Fox's second X-rated 1970 film (after *Beyond the Valley of the Dolls*) and a well-known hot mess of a film shoot.

The Beast Must Die sent Lockhart back to England, specifically the famous Shepperton Studios where it was shot. Sporting a mustache and leaning into a more distinctly English accent, he made quite a striking, regal figure, which was perfect, as Newcliffe is a rich hunter and a Black man who must command and terrify a group of White people. Those White folks include *The Rocky Horror Picture Show*'s narrator, Charles Gray, and the future star of *The Cook, The Thief, His Wife & Her Lover*, Michael Gambon. Also cast as his usual monster expert is Hammer and Amicus legend Peter Cushing, who is a suspect simply because he's been the bad guy in some of those movies.

Newcliffe drives these people crazy with werewolf tests like putting a silver bullet in their mouths and making them grab goblets made of silver. His wife, Caroline (Marlene Clark), tries to maintain order before she, too, becomes a suspect. Having Clark play the love interest of a rich recluse living in a sprawling mansion gives *The Beast Must Die* a coincidental tie with *Ganja & Hess*, though that film was far more avant-garde and strange.

It's not known how many people guessed correctly in theaters during the Werewolf Break. It doesn't really matter—as many times as the author has seen this film, he still can't remember who the real werewolf is. However, Marlene Clark does make history as the film's red herring; she's the first person to turn into a werewolf, though it's because she's been bitten by the actual culprit. Lockhart would have made history as the second Black werewolf, cursed after he's been bitten, but he shoots himself before he can turn. Like *Blacula* before him, he goes out on his own terms.

Black zombies were nothing new by 1974. Think of all those racist studio system Hollywood horror movies taking place in "darkest Africa." What was new about *Sugar Hill* was that these zombies were helping the Black hero seek her revenge. Marki Bey plays Diana Hill, nicknamed "Sugar" by her club-owning boyfriend, Langston (Larry D. Johnson). Sugar is independent and has her own career as a fashion photographer. She is also madly in love with, and supportive of, her man. Their relationship seems perfect, so it's obviously doomed.

Sugar Hill pulls an early bait-and-switch on the audience during its opening credits. After the American International Pictures logo appears onscreen, the viewer is plunged into a voodoo ritual. People dance, fall into trances, and roll around on the ground. It plays like a stereotype-filled fever dream accompanied by an underrated gem of a theme song, the Originals' "Supernatural Voodoo Woman." Though it doesn't get spoken of in any conversations on Blaxploitation songs, Dino Fekaris and Nick Zesses's theme is impossible to get out of one's head. As for the ritual, it turns out to be just a performance, staged for audiences at Langston's Club Haiti nightclub.

Club Haiti is a successful business, and the Mafia wants it. The kingpin, played by Robert "Count Yorga" Quarry, sends his henchman, a pimp named Fabulous (Charles P. Robinson), to convince Langston to sell. When he stands up to the men who came to muscle him out of his business, they beat him to death in the parking lot. Sugar finds his body and vows revenge. Initially, she seeks the help of her former flame, homicide detective Valentine (Richard Lawson). Knowing that justice may never be served by conventional means, Sugar decides to play the supernatural ace up her sleeve.

Sugar retreats to a home in the bayou and summons the voodoo priestess Mama Maitresse. Since *Sugar Hill* was made the year before she got her most famous role as Mother Jefferson on the hit sitcom *The Jeffersons*, viewers in 1974 would not have been jarred to see Zara Cully as Mama. With her shocking white hair and the demented glee that takes over her face when bad things are happening, Cully gives an excellent performance in this small but pivotal role. Anyone who knew her history would not find this surprising.

Though used as a booze-infused comic foil for Isabel Sanford's Weezy Jefferson, Cully was actually one of the most versatile Black artists of her time. Born in 1892 to an artistic family of musicians (she's eighty-two in *Sugar Hill!*), this preacher's kid graduated from the Worcester School of Speech and Music before embarking on a long career writing, producing, and directing plays on the stage. By the time she gained her widest audience, she'd had over fifty years of experience in the arts.

Like Roscoe Lee Browne, whom she co-starred with in her movie debut, *The Liberation of L.B. Jones*, Cully had a distinctive voice and a precise manner of speaking. She was widely hailed for her elocution skills, which she puts to great use as Mama Maitresse. Critic Linda Gross said Cully was "a black yenta type who looks like she would rather find Marki a husband than a practicing voodoo priestess." Actually, Mama Maitresse *does* summon a man for Sugar, the voodoo spirit Baron Samedi (Don Pedro Colley).

Last seen tormenting folks in *Live and Let Die*, Baron Samedi is now working for Sugar to help her exact revenge on the men who killed Langston, and the racist White woman who is Morgan's moll. It's a nasty revenge, too. Despite the PG rating, viewers get all the ritualistic goods. Voodoo dolls, slit throats, people hacked to pieces by impressive-looking zombie hit men and hit women with creepy-looking silver eyes (the ladies give a really lethal massage to Fabulous). One unfortunate baddie gets eaten by pigs. "I hope they like White trash," quips Sugar as the guy is torn to shreds. The tagline isn't "She's fascinatin' but assassinatin'!" for nothing.

Bey gives one of the better Blaxploitation performances in this, her only film of this type. She's vengeful, but she also shows a softer side around Valentine. One can buy both sides of her personality while marveling at the outfits she wears. Her white-and-red suit, like Goldie's similarly colored coat in *The Mack*, became iconic. She wears it during the murders, standing out like an avenging angel among all those cobweb-covered zombies.

Colley, a Blaxploitation staple, is superb as Samedi. Geoffrey Holder may have had Samedi's dancing part down pat, but Colley feels more like the real deal in the spirit's trademark hat, eye makeup, earring, and gold teeth. He has a ball tormenting victims like a precursor to Freddy Krueger, and since Samedi is so entrenched in voodoo lore, his prey knows who he is on first sight.

Like Bey, this was director Paul Maslansky's only Blaxploitation film. In fact, it was the only film he directed. He does a good job here, but based on his career, he enjoyed producing films more than helming them. If his name sounds familiar, it's because he produced all seven of the *Police Academy* movies. He also produced Hicksploitation classics like the far less infamous Peter Fonda horror hybrid from 1975, *Race with the Devil*.

In March of 1974, AIP dumped *Sugar Hill* in theaters as a drive-in double feature with *Scream, Blacula, Scream*. Coincidentally, that film also had Richard Lawson getting involved with voodoo. At least in that movie he's investigating it, not being enslaved by it. He also has a much better Afro here, because Sugar Hill wouldn't date a guy whose coif wasn't tight.

It's too bad the talented and striking Marki Bey didn't make many movies. After her debut in Hal Ashby's *The Landlord*, she made three films before ending her career in cinema with studio system director Henry Hathaway's last film, the Blaxploitation action quickie *Super Dude*. After a decade-long stint doing TV appearances, Bey retired from the profession and opened a mystery cruise business with her husband. A Werewolf Break would not be out of place on one of those boats.

make Yours
a Happy Home

Claudine was originally conceived as a vehicle for Diana Sands, the actress who originated the role of Beneatha in the 1959 Broadway production of *A Raisin in the Sun*. Ossie Davis was behind the camera at the time of its announcement in August 1973. In what would have been his film debut, Laurence Fishburne was cast as the second of her three sons. Unfortunately, the onset of cancer prohibited Sands from playing the part; she would die just a few weeks later, on September 21. Just before bowing out of the production, however, Sands suggested Diahann Carroll take the titular role alongside co-lead James Earl Jones.

Despite her nurse role on the groundbreaking sitcom *Julia* and her 1950s roles in *Carmen Jones* and *Porgy and Bess*, Carroll didn't seem like the obvious choice. This was a performer known for glamour and glitz. She was the first Black woman to win a Best Actress Tony in 1962 for Richard Rodgers's musical *No Strings*. Her appearances on *Johnny Carson* and other variety shows were fashionable affairs. Hell, she was so convincing as a glamour icon that she was able to live her dream of being "the first Black bitch on television" when she played Dominique Deveraux (what a name!), the rich nemesis of Joan Collins's Alexis Carrington on the '80s nighttime soap *Dynasty*.

Claudine has no such glamour within its frames. This is the bittersweet story of a welfare mother with six kids who finds love with a smelly old garbageman. When Carroll got the role, Davis had left the project and was replaced by Mercury Theater alumnus John Berry. The children were also recast, meaning that Fishburne would have to wait another year for his debut, in 1975's tearjerker *Cornbread, Earl and Me*. Another Laurence, or rather,

Lawrence, made his debut instead: Lawrence Hilton-Jacobs played Claudine's oldest son, Charles.

Now, it must be said that *Claudine is not a Blaxploitation movie!* Instead, it stood out in the sea of Blaxploitation the film found itself released into on April 22, 1974. It's one of the best examples of counterprogramming the era had to offer, and the kind of working-class comedy that was never offered to Black people. It is the author's favorite romantic comedy of all time, a movie that so changed his perspective on movies that its inclusion in this book was mandatory.

Claudine's script was by husband-and-wife screenwriters Tina and Lester Pine. Their prior work included episodes of *I Spy* and the 1969 Arthur Hiller film *Popi*. Hiller's film shared a plot similarity with *Claudine* in that it was about one parent (Arkin's titular widower) raising kids in the 'hood. It also featured a similar climactic sequence of the family running from law enforcement. The difference is that *Popi* had an absurd, situation comedy plot that was as believable as Alan Arkin playing a Puerto Rican. (He'd play a Mexican even less convincingly in *Freebie and the Bean*, released eight months after *Claudine* came out.)

Diana Sands must have seen something in Carroll to make her suggest her for *Claudine*, and her instincts were impeccable. Glynn Turman, who, as a child actor, starred opposite her in the Broadway production of *A Raisin in the Sun* (he was too old to do the movie version), said that Sands was one of the most intelligent actors he ever worked with in terms of knowing her craft. She would have brought that skill to the character of Claudine for sure. Once again, a moment of silence for what could have been.

Stripped of her glamour, Diahann Carroll is totally convincing as a cleaning woman. Yet Sands's spirit haunts every frame of *Claudine*, manifesting itself in Carroll's performance. It's in the way Claudine looks at those she loves, the comic timing of a well-timed putdown of a fool she won't suffer gladly, and the complete uninhibitedness of the performance. It feels and looks lived in, something that Sands knew how to convey. Carroll's outstanding work earned her a much-deserved, but surprising, Oscar nomination for Best Actress. The story goes that multiple showings on the pay cable network the Z Channel contributed to Academy voter visibility, which led to the nomination.

Carroll's Best Actress Oscar nod was the fourth for a Black woman. Her director, a White man, also worked with the first Black actress to receive one,

Dorothy Dandridge. In the *Chicago Reader*, film critic and historian Jonathan Rosenbaum wrote about why John Berry was a good choice for this film: "I'm not sure I would call Berry a great director, but he was sometimes an exceptionally good one, especially when he dealt with working class characters . . . and sometimes when he worked with black actors, whom he enjoyed directing."

Back in his Mercury Theater days, Berry was the stage manager on Orson Welles's theatrical production of Richard Wright's *Native Son* with the great Black actor Canada Lee, who played Bigger Thomas. The play ran for 114 performances. Like Lee, and fellow Mercury Theater colleague Abraham Polonsky, Berry was blacklisted and called to appear before the House Un-American Activities Committee. Lee died before he could appear; Berry went into exile and made films in France. *Claudine* was the first American movie he made after returning to the United States.

Some critics didn't buy Carroll as a Harlem charwoman on the dole, presumably because the mostly White writers couldn't fathom that there was beauty to be found in the 'hood. Their disbelief revealed they hadn't done their research. "I grew up on 153rd Street just a few blocks from where we shot *Claudine*," Carroll told the *Pensacola News Journal*.

The *Pensacola News Journal* noted that since Carroll left Harlem, "she hasn't done too badly." However, while she lived there, she won a Metropolitan Opera audition at age ten, then went to the High School of Music and Art before studying sociology at NYU. The article's depiction of her as being down to earth was reflected in other interviews. In the *Boston Globe*, Carroll told the story of her wig flying off during a performance. When her hairdresser begged her not to go back on after this fiasco, she told him that nobody out there believed that was her real hair!

Claudine's premise could easily have traveled the low road, but, through character development and a good story, it elevates the film above expectations. This could have been a sassy, caricatured movie about a woman on welfare and her bad-ass kids. But the filmmakers find the drama underneath it and treat it with respect. Claudine is on welfare, but she's also working as a domestic. As the film opens, she's taking an MTA bus to her job. Accompanying her every day is her group of fellow domestics. They joke about Claudine's lack of a sex life and their employers' lack of common sense.

The workday has one bright spot: a visit from Rupert (James Earl Jones). Rupert, or Roop, as he calls himself, is the local garbageman. He's quite fresh, makes comments about how fine Claudine looks. When Claudine declines his request for a date, Roop suddenly asks, "Are you on the welfare?" At first, Claudine is offended, but she chases down his truck and changes her mind about going out with him. Keep in mind that the American welfare system prevented its recipients from working *and* from having a man. Her involvement with Roop will cause all sorts of bureaucratic problems.

Claudine's home life is frenetic, to say the least. Her eldest son, Charles (Lawrence Hilton-Jacobs), has joined a Black movement targeted by the police. Her second eldest, Charlene (Tamu), is completely confused by her burgeoning womanhood. Claudine can see Charlene's future and doesn't like that it mirrors her past. Charlene's boyfriend, Teddy—or rather, Abdullah, as he's now known after his "Muslim conversion"—has been teaching her "how to socialize and hold her liquor." When Charlene comes home drunk, Claudine pokes her in the stomach and asks, "Is Abdullah teaching you about biology?" Unfortunately, he is. When Charlene yells for her mother to "not come home pregnant" as Claudine goes on a date with Roop, the quip is clearly foreshadowing the inevitable.

As the eldest, Charles is cynical about his mother's relationships. When Roop picks up Claudine for her date, Charles looks at him with a been-there-done-that disdain. Other men have dated his mother, and the result is always the same: they leave before any serious commitment occurs. Sometimes, they leave kids behind when they go. The lack of a father figure, and the multiple marriages and relationships that promise, then revoke, the possibility of a permanent dad, have a far greater effect on Claudine's four youngest children.

Long before 2006's *Little Miss Sunshine*, *Claudine* dealt with a kid who just stops talking and writes things down. In this case, it's Claudine's youngest son. Roop has a bittersweet conversation with him. "What do you want to be when you grow up?" he asks. "Invisible," the kid replies as he hides under Claudine's table. Curtis Mayfield, who provided the score, wrote one of his most heartbreaking songs, "To Be Invisible," for this character. Anyone who has experienced the trauma often associated with being Black and poor will find a kindred spirit here.

The scenes where a welfare worker visits Claudine are funny and frustrating. She has to hide items like her television set and most of appliances, lest the government deduct them from her check for not declaring them on her forms. She also has to hide her man. In one scene, Claudine puts both in the closet, where they are discovered by the snooping government agent. Now exposed as the boyfriend, Roop has to go to the welfare office and "declare himself" if he wants to continue his relationship with Claudine.

Claudine sounds like a brutal downer, but it is not. It is a blatantly romantic comedy populated with people one doesn't see in this type of picture. When Roop arrives for his first date with Claudine, he shows up in his convertible with his hat and his "evening attire." He may be a garbageman during the day, but he doesn't have to look like one at night. When Claudine's bathroom gets taken up by her kids, Roop offers her the use of his facilities. He promises her a fancy dinner. "It's still gonna wind up being chicken," Charlene correctly predicts.

Claudine and Roop begin their romance, and it feels genuine in both its triumphs and its problems. Carroll and Jones have excellent chemistry together, and Jones has that twinkle of mischief in his eye and that devilish grin. He's not leading man handsome, but it's easy to fall in love with him in this picture. The screenplay grants them a dignity that fed audiences starved for the kind of romance they had in their 'hood.

Curtis Mayfield's best post–*Super Fly* score plays like a Greek chorus under this film. Gladys Knight and the Pips sing it, and the title of this chapter comes from the song that plays over the final scene in the film. In that sequence, Roop and Claudine get married. During their wedding, Charles barges in, on the run from the police. Thanks to his protest rally, the entire family winds up being arrested. The closing credits play over them riding off, and then being released by the cops. The family that gets arrested together stays together, and in a Black movie, a two-parent family is a wonderful thing that wasn't shown very often.

As far as counterprogramming goes, *Claudine* is by far the best example. It made a nice $3 million at the box office on a $1.1 million budget, which should have told Hollywood that Black romantic comedies were something audiences wanted to see. Yet despite that Oscar nod, multiple Golden Globe nominations, and favorable reviews (the newspaper ads were covered with glowing quotes), movies like *Claudine* remained unproduced by Hollywood.

Vincent Canby's review in the *New York Times* may have provided the reason why: "[*Claudine*] is also the first major film about black life to consider the hopes, struggles, defeats and frustrations of blacks who aren't either supercops, supermusicians, superstuds, superpimps or superpushers." Blaxploitation was still way too lucrative to give up just yet.

A Millennial's Take on Blaxploitation Movies

Robert Daniels, a colleague from my days at RogerEbert.com, sat with me to offer his thoughts on Blaxploitation films from the perspective of the generation that followed their release. A native of Chicago and a fine critic in his own right, Daniels provided insight on how a Black person of his generation encountered and evaluated these films. He also discusses what the Chicago movie theater scene was like several years after the 1970s.

To what generation would you say you belong?

I'm a Millennial. Though sometimes I don't feel it. My father was born in 1941 and had me pretty late in life. So my tastes and views on the world really reflect his views. For that reason, I've always felt out of step with my generation.

When did you first discover Blaxploitation films? And where?

The first Blaxploitation film I ever watched was Gordon Parks Jr.'s *Super Fly*, when I was ten years old. We watched it at home. It was on some television station that I can't for the life of me remember. But I was far too young for it. That sex scene in the bathtub, which was basically porn, warped my brain. [Laughs.] It was one of many films that my dad showed me before my time. I also remember watching *Car Wash*, which isn't nearly as explicit, but whose politics, which went over my head at the time, are as pressing now as they were then.

Did your parents have any soundtracks from these films while you were growing up?

We definitely had the *Shaft* soundtrack. And the *Super Fly* one, too. My dad was a big Curtis Mayfield fan. My dad had a small gospel and R&B record label during the early 1970s that was based in Chicago. And so he always viewed Mayfield, who also hailed from the Chicago gospel scene, as well as the later R&B and funk scene, as a contemporary. I'm pretty sure the opening riff to the title track of *Super Fly* is embedded in my DNA.

Were you influenced/inspired by any of the heroes of Blaxploitation films when you were younger?

By the time I was a teenager, in the early aughts, Blaxploitation was having a resurgence. The newer *Shaft* [directed by John Singleton] starring Samuel L. Jackson recently dropped. [Malcolm D. Lee and John Ridley's Blaxploitation homage/parody] *Undercover Brother* was a major comedic influence for me that served as a gateway to get into Richard Pryor's comedy specials, and later, his film work with Sidney Poitier.

What were movie theaters like in your neighborhood? Were there any old movie palaces that were now theaters frequented by Black and brown people?

By the time I was at a moviegoing age, most of the big movie houses on the West Side of Chicago either had been demolished or were retrofitted for other purposes. So for us to go to a theater, we had to take a couple buses. That's a sad fact of the 2000s. Most of the neighborhood theaters for Black people were gone, except a few on the South Side of the city.

Do you think the Blaxploitation era caused irreparable damage to the images of Black people onscreen, as the NAACP and CORE seemed to think?

As Blaxploitation became commodified by White folks searching for a quick buck, it certainly produced images of Black people that were as gross as any mammy from the 1940s. *The Black Gestapo* comes to mind. But overall, I'd say no. The best Blaxploitation films—*Shaft*, *Super Fly*, *Cotton Comes to Harlem*, *Foxy Brown*, *Coffy*, and so on—were subversive political statements that showed African-Americans as a capable and fearless people, and as sex symbols, a notable change from the sexless characters of classic Hollywood. If anything, these big and showy extrapolations of Black life set the stage for the stripped-down interiority of the [student film movement] LA Rebellion and the later politicized Black films of the 1990s. You don't get there without these films.

Do you have a favorite Blaxploitation film?

John Berry's *Claudine*. I watched it when I was twelve years old and immediately developed a crush on Diahann Carroll. (I know I was one of the many imaginary suitors.) More immediate, however, was this being the first time I saw a family onscreen that reminded me of mine. We were similarly on welfare and needed the fullness of every benefit it offered. Much like Rupert [James Earl Jones], we were also held back by my dad's child support payments from a previous marriage. They greatly limited the kind of life we could have. It's a story that still hits close to home; I always cry at the ending because it's so hopeful and shows the resiliency many Black families face as we reach for a kind of uplift, even while we're systematically held back. And Carroll is so amazing in what's probably the best performance of her career. How she didn't immediately become the biggest star on the planet after *Claudine* speaks to how even Blaxploitation couldn't overcome Hollywood's racism.

A favorite Blaxploitation song?

Funnily enough, I heard "Freddie's Dead" long before I ever watched *Super Fly*. I don't know where exactly, but it was always omnipresent. I had no idea what the song was about: I just liked Mayfield rhyming "dead" and "said." Later on, when I really listened to the song, I was blown away by how much of the message I missed: it's a cinematic tune with sweeping subplots that serve its overall character study while maintaining a coherent political message. I also love Mayfield's silky voice, which somehow communicated heartbreak and an unlikely toughness at once.

Lastly, if you have seen it, what was your opinion of *Sweet Sweetback's Baadasssss Song*?

I totally understand the cinematic importance of *Sweet Sweetback's Baadasssss Song*, but it's not my favorite Van Peebles: I much prefer *Watermelon Man* and *The Story of a Three-Day Pass*. Van Peebles did many things well—acting, initially, was not one of them, and you can feel it here. So that always keeps the film at a distance for me. Having said that, its sexual politics are tremendous and forward-thinking: to go from the sexless African-Americans of classic Hollywood to a hero who uses his sexual prowess as a power move is still revolutionary, if not more so, today, on a cinematic landscape that has mostly reverted back to puritanical sexless heroes. This man literally fucks his way to freedom. And I can't be mad.

1975

1975

eaten alive in '75

1975

1975

In 1975, a lot of the people involved with Watergate went to jail.

But who cares about that shit?! This year was all about the two J's: *The Jeffersons* and *Jaws*.

On January 11, Archie Bunker's Queens neighbors, the ones from the race he called "the coloreds," said goodbye to America's favorite bigot. The next week, George and Louise "Weezy" Jefferson and their son, Lionel, moved on up to a deluxe apartment on the East Side of Manhattan. With its Black-as-hell theme song co-written and sung by Willona from *Good Times* herself, *The Jeffersons* was quickly a hit, ranking number four in the ratings its first season. In its eleven-season run, the show rose as high as number three.

The story behind the decision to move George and Weezy into prosperity (instead of the more typical choice of Archie) was told by Norman Lear in his autobiography. He wrote that three Black Panthers barged into his office at CBS to complain about another show he'd created, *Good Times*. "Every time you see a black man on the tube he is dirt poor, wears shit clothes, can't afford nothing," they told Lear. "That's bullshit."

Ever the troublemaker, Lear took their complaint to his associate, Al Burton, who liked the idea of finally having some truly bougie Negroes on television. Lear developed *The Jeffersons* after the pilot was created by Nicholl, Ross, West (the credit for Don Nicholl, Michael Ross, and Bernie West). *The Jeffersons* became the second-longest-running Black series on television and the first to feature an interracial married couple as main characters, played by Franklin Cover and Lenny Kravitz's mom (and tormenter of Diahann Carroll in *Claudine*), Roxie Roker.

Now, here's something you may not know. *Good Times* co-creator Eric Monte met Norman Lear through his fellow *Good Times* creator Mike Evans. Evans played Lionel on *All in the Family* and on *The Jeffersons* in seasons one, six, and seven. During the first season of

All in the Family, Evans asked Monte to write a script centered around the only Jefferson seen on the show at the time, Lionel. Lear was looking for scripts, and Evans put his and Monte's names on the result and submitted it. That script introduced Weezy Jefferson and her then unseen husband, George, to the show.

So, in addition to creating the Evans family on *Good Times*, Eric Monte created the two main characters on *The Jeffersons*! Monte would make his contribution to Blaxploitation in 1975 by writing *Cooley High*, basing it off his own Chicago high school experiences. That movie, in turn, would later spawn another sitcom with primarily Black characters, *What's Happening!!*

For those keeping track, we now have three major sitcoms focusing primarily on Black characters: NBC's *Sanford and Son*, *The Jeffersons*, and their CBS network mate *Good Times*. These were all hit shows, which meant Black people had more to watch on the free medium known as television. There's no proof at this moment whether that had much of an effect on their moviegoing habits. But even if it did, something was about to get *everybody's* asses to the cinema.

In 1974, Richard Zanuck and David Brown, aka the producers of *Willie Dynamite*, optioned the rights for a Peter Benchley novel about a killer white shark. They selected Steven Spielberg, who had just directed his film debut, *The Sugarland Express*, to direct it. Named *Jaws*, the book was a huge hit thanks to clever marketing. When Benchley and Carl Gottlieb adapted it, they focused on the main conflict between the shark and the three men on a boat named *Orca* who try to bring it down.

There are many stories about how the mechanical shark, nicknamed Bruce, did not work in the salty ocean water off Martha's Vineyard, where the film was shot. They all end with the malfunctioning shark being a blessing in disguise. By keeping it offscreen for most of the film, audiences would be less distracted by how fake it looked. Editor Verna Fields deservedly won an Oscar for her masterful command of the film's footage. Bruce the Shark's absence was hidden by the film using other visual representations of him and by that famous Oscar-winning score by composer John Williams.

"Why don't the people get out of the water?" I remember asking my cousin while we watched *Jaws* at the Hudson Mall Twin in Jersey City. "Can't they hear the music?!" Obviously not, but a lot of people heard the clarion call of a major league hit. Thanks to a successful marketing campaign and Universal releasing it in a then unprecedented 450 theaters in June 1975, *Jaws* drew enormous box office. Black audiences went to see it, and not just because we knew the shark ate only White people. It was a genuinely terrifying motion picture that had great word of mouth.

The soundtrack was a hit, repeat business was brisk, and there were parodies of *Jaws* all over television, the most famous being a *Saturday Night Live* skit featuring Chevy Chase as the "Land Shark." (Chase would also figure in 1975's infamous Richard Pryor word-association *SNL* skit, written by Mr. Paul Mooney.)

There was even a *Jaws* board game for kids, even though the poster for the film warned parents that Bruce's starring role "may be too intense for younger viewers." The object was to fish items out of a shark's mouth. If the mouth closed, the player lost the game. One of the items to remove was a spare tire. Another was a human foot. That '70s-era PG rating was something else, let me tell you.

As far as Blaxploitation was concerned, Fred Williamson came into his directorial own this year. In addition to *Cooley High*, another film that would later influence John Singleton's *Boyz n the Hood* came out. Laurence Fishburne's debut, *Cornbread, Earl and Me*, would lend some of its visuals and its ideas to Singleton. The writer-director was only two years older than me, so I wonder if he, too, saw that double feature of *Cornbread, Earl and Me* and *Cooley High* that I saw. One of the saddest afternoons I ever spent in a grindhouse.

Fishburne, who played Furious Styles in *Boyz*, said that *Cornbread* "was the original *Boyz n the Hood*." I tend to lean more toward *Cooley High* as being its primary influence. Either way, they were "more respectable" films that showed us Blaxploitation could be bittersweet.

CHAPTER 25

Pam, Pam, and more Pam

Fans of Pam Grier hit the jackpot in 1975. Not only did she complete her AIP tetralogy with *Friday Foster* and *Sheba, Baby*, she also starred opposite Fred Williamson and Thalmus Rasulala in AIP's *Bucktown*. Grier also had her own plans to "cross over"—that is, to make a movie that appealed to Black and White audiences alike. In a September 1975 *Philadelphia Daily News* article entitled "Who Will Be The No. 1 Black Actress," she told the reporter: "I'm doing a picture now, about a Roller Derby girl, 'Silky and the Outlaws.' I'm having a fight with the producers—who are white—about it. They want to aim for the black audience. I want to aim for both."

Silky and the Outlaws never got made. Yet another movie worth pausing for a moment to mourn.

When *Sheba, Baby* was playing at the Roosevelt back in March, she told Bruce Vilanch in the *Chicago Tribune* that "Superchick is dead. I'm finished with being 'the black Wonder Woman.'" This wasn't exactly true—she had yet to shoot *Friday Foster*—but she expanded on what she meant: "I think it's over. I think the black movie is coming of age. A picture like 'Claudine,' a picture like [Cicely Tyson's Emmy-winning 1974 TV movie, *The Autobiography of Miss Jane Pittman*], those are representative of a new consciousness. My old movies were fun, but I definitely believe there is something else to be said, and I'm ready to say it."

Grier also told Vilanch she wanted to write and direct and that she had two scripts her production company was trying to produce. One of them was a prison romance drama about two inmates who pass love notes to one another in the prison laundry. She hoped the other pen pal would be played by Billy Dee

Williams if she could "convince Motown to let him be in the thing." Of course, that movie never got made, either. Billy Dee was too busy playing Berry Gordy's doppelgänger in *Mahogany*.

(It might as well be stated that, as of this writing, Grier has yet to direct anything, and her only writing gig was a story credit for an episode of *Linc's*, a cable show she appeared on in 2000.)

Folks wondering what it would be like if "superchick" were indeed dead needed to look no further than Grier's second 1975 release, *Bucktown*. In one of her most violent pictures, Grier has not one action scene. She is basically the damsel in distress, a woman who needs Fred Williamson to swoop down and save her. Director Arthur Marks told Josiah Howard he thought "she did an excellent job." To Howard, Marks recounted the story of what he said when he cast her: "You're going to play a waitress, a girl who works in a bar, who falls in love with a guy from Philadelphia and it's going to be a love story. You won't be shooting anyone or any of that stuff; your job is to provide a solid base as to why he wants to stay in this small town."

Borrrrrring!!! Though she gives a good performance, Grier is miscast here. She would be better served by a role like this in a straight drama, as *Greased Lightning* would later prove. A filmmaker can't put Pam Grier in a brutal action movie and have her be docile. Someone like Arthur Marks should have known that, as he was no stranger to Blaxploitation movies. He'd make five of them, starting with the little-seen *Detroit 9000* in 1973.

Before his tenure in Blaxploitation, Marks had a long career in television as the producer of the *Perry Mason* TV series. Between 1958 and 1966, he also directed seventy-six episodes of Raymond Burr's most famous show. Before that, he was an assistant director on Orson Welles's 1947 Rita Hayworth vehicle, *The Lady from Shanghai*. Marks had his own stable of crew members in the 1970s, including Oscar-nominated screenwriter Orville Hampton, editor George Folsey Jr., and actors Yaphet Kotto, Tierre Turner, and the ubiquitous Blaxploitation star Thalmus Rasulala.

Bucktown tells an interesting story about how power corrupts. Williamson's Duke Johnson returns to a small Kansas town to attend the funeral of his late brother. The brother ran a nightclub in town, and he died under suspicious circumstances. When Duke reopens the club, he gets trouble from the racist cops, who demand the same kickbacks his brother provided. Knowing he'll need backup, he reaches out to his friend Roy (Rasulala). Roy enters Bucktown with his own brand of muscle led by Tony King. Predictably, they clean up the town. Not so predictably, they do it before the film is half over.

This was writer Bob Ellison's sole screenplay (he was better known for writing on sitcoms like *The Mary Tyler Moore Show*). He does something unusual in *Bucktown*: he suddenly makes the heroes the villains. Once Roy realizes the town is ripe for lining his pockets with corruption, he decides to stay and milk his good fortune. Now, Duke has to clean up the town by himself, making enemies of the same guys he called upon for help.

Pam Grier is in there somewhere, as Aretha the love interest. While it's exciting to see Williamson kicking ass, one can't help but feel deprived that one of the best ass kickers in Blaxploitation has been benched in favor of a "normal" role. Thankfully, 1975 had two other movies for Pam Grier to do her thing. One of those movies was the last film in the AIP tetralogy, *Sheba, Baby*.

"Unfortunately, *Sheba, Baby* is by far the worst of the group," wrote Gene Siskel in his review, and while he's technically correct that this is the least of the films in Grier's AIP tetralogy, his one-star rating is far too low. The first of her three 1975 films to be released, *Sheba, Baby* teams her with the director of *Abby*, William Girdler. Girdler brings Grier's Sheba Shayne to his hometown of Louisville after her father, Andy (Rudy Challenger), is brutally beaten by thugs trying to put the squeeze on his loan agency. The film's theme song, sung by Buddah Records' Barbara Mason, tells the viewer "she's kickin' ass and takin' names." Superchick ain't dead yet!

Shayne is a Chicago-based private eye, so her investigative skills kick in as soon as her plane touches down in Louisville. She's wearing one of Grier's best ensembles, an off-white pantsuit with a matching large-brimmed hat, pearls, and a blue-and-white polka-dot shirt. Girdler's love of his lead actress is evident; at times his camera almost caresses her. Every outfit she wears—and *Sheba, Baby* is a fashion show—is given maximum onscreen attention.

Girdler's love for his hometown is also evident as usual, with shots of the airport and other locations prominently featured. Papa Shayne's loan agency is even given a real address, 649 West Main Street, smack-dab in the middle of downtown and seven miles from Girdler's own office.

Andy is a tough, stubborn man. It's easy to see where his daughter gets her tenacity. She tells him she knows he thinks being a private dick is a man's job, but "I'm not gonna sit on the sidelines because I'm a woman." Soon after her arrival, it's revealed that the guy shaking down Shayne Loan Company is Pilot, played by none other than Dolemite's nemesis, D'Urville Martin. Pilot's surrounded by a multicultural group of doting women as he calls Papa Shayne to tell him his car has been wired to explode. Sheba barely escapes after she starts the car. Now she's mad!

Her former colleagues at the police department won't help (Sheba was once a cop), and her former flame, Brick (Austin Stoker), thinks she's unfit to fight Pilot and his crew. *Sheba, Baby* shows the audience otherwise; when Shayne Loan is attacked and shot up by hired assassins, Sheba responds with her own big-ass gun, shooting one guy in the eye and another through the heart. Unfortunately, her father is killed in the melee. Now she's *really* mad.

Despite its violent content, *Sheba, Baby* has the most humor of the four films for which Grier is most famous. Martin's Pilot is a cartoonish buffoon, and there's a hilarious, very politically incorrect questioning scene between Sheba and a pimp named Walker (Christopher Joy). Walker's Barry White–inspired UltraPerm suffers a great indignity and dies a painful death when Sheba runs its owner's face through an automated car wash. Blaxploitation's requisite catfight ends with a slapstick pie to the face.

Even the most graphic of scenes is kinder and gentler by comparison with, say, *Coffy*. For example, Pilot suffers the same fate as that film's King George, but his demise is on water, not land. Bullet wounds erupt with blood, but there's so much of it that the carnage becomes comical. The film's true villain, a White guy named Shark, barely roughs up Sheba once she's caught on his yacht. Viewers get to see Grier bloodlessly harpoon him while speeding through the Ohio River on a boat.

Sheba, Baby ends on a bittersweet, romantic note that evokes memories of Grier's last scene in Quentin Tarantino's *Jackie Brown*. That's almost as surprising as the film's MPAA rating: this is the rare Pam Grier movie to be rated PG. It's the old '70s-era PG, however, so she still appears topless. The more lenient rating would have allowed more people to see this film, but Grier's R-rated fare made more money.

The children who weren't naughty awoke on Christmas morning to find Pam Grier's *Friday Foster* in their local bijous. (All the kids who *were* naughty got Fred

Williamson's *Adios Amigo* in their theaters!) Grier's second film with director Arthur Marks was based on a long-running comic strip character created by White writer Jim Lawrence and an animator in Spain named Jorge Longarón. This made Grier the first Black person to play a comics hero, though she was a long way from Marvel or DC.

Friday Foster was a former-model-turned-fashion-photographer. Her strip ran from January 1970 to February 1974 in the *Chicago Tribune* and its affiliates. Foster wasn't the first Black lead in a comic—Black cartoonist Jackie Ormes's Cotton Club dancer Torchy Brown preceded her by thirty-three years—but she was the first one to get her own movie. In the newspaper, Longarón's drawings resembled actress Regina Hall, not Pam Grier, so if anyone gets the bright idea to reboot the character, they know who to cast. It's doubtful that imagined film would have a catchier tagline than *Friday Foster*: "Wham! Bam! Here Comes Pam!"

Once again, Marks worked from a screenplay by Orville Hampton, much of which takes place in the high-flying world of fashion models and the dueling designers who provide clothes for them. There's a mystery of sorts, involving something or someone called "Black Widow" and, since Friday Foster is in this world, Grier gets numerous costume changes. She also gets to bed several men, from the "Black Howard Hughes" Blake Tarr (Thalmus Rasulala) to Paul Benjamin's Senator Hart. Waiting for her in the clean world is Colt Hawkins (Yaphet Kotto), a private investigator whose help she enlists when things get heavy.

On New Year's Eve, Friday gets a call from her boss, Monk Riley (Kotto's henchman from *Live and Let Die*, Julius Harris). He wants her to cover Tarr's unexpected airport arrival. Actually, his arrival *was* expected . . . by some assassins led by Apollo Creed himself, Carl Weathers. Weathers's Yarbro leads the first of many violent altercations that earn *Friday Foster* its R rating. A nearly silent assassin, Yarbro will be responsible for a fair percentage of this film's impressive body count. For now, Tarr gets wounded by gunfire, and Friday gets some soon-to-be-incriminating photos.

Next, Friday attends Madame Rena's fashion show to see her friend Clorils (Rosalind Miles) model. Madame Rena is played by Eartha Kitt, whose dialogue is peppered with her trademark growls and some shocking homophobia. Hearing Kitt hiss the word "faggot" to describe her competitor, Ford Malotte (Godfrey Cambridge), is jarring even for 1975. Equally jarring is Cambridge's performance—it's all mincing and eye-popping gay stereotypes as he holds court in his nightclub. His business dealings are as shady as his one-liners.

As a result, Yarbro kills Malotte by gruesomely crushing him in a phone booth with a truck, but not before he murders Clorils. Marks's idea to have this doomed woman attempt to model her outfit with an enormous knife stuck in her back is unintentionally hilarious, proving that Madame Rena is such a tyrant her models would rather catwalk while skewered with cutlery than incur her wrath. After Clorils collapses, she whispers "black widow" to Friday before expiring.

Friday Foster is no Coffy (both in terms of the character and the movie). Friday's vengeance at Clorils's death is tempered by her desire to solve the mystery of the Black Widow, so she's nowhere near as violence-prone as her Pam Grier predecessors. At least Marks gives Grier some action scenes this time. While chasing various baddies, she steals a hearse and a truck. She also gets to shoot one person. But *Friday Foster* is more concerned with giving its star the full beauty treatment.

"We got her everything she wanted," Marks explained in an interview. "Good clothes, expert makeup, perfect hairstyles—the whole glamorizing treatment. She had a ball." Though her outfits in *Coffy* and *Foxy Brown* were often striking, she wound up battered, bruised, and not looking her best in later scenes. Here, Friday Foster looks dynamite from first frame to last. Whether she's flirting with Scatman Crothers's corrupt preacher Reverend Noble Franklin or telling flashy pimp Ted "Love Boat" Lange she'll never be one of his hos, Grier's look is flawless.

As for what Black Widow turns out to be: it's not even worth mentioning, except to say it has something to do with Jim Backus planning to eliminate important Black leaders. That's right, the guy who played Mister Magoo in cartoons and Thurston Howell III on *Gilligan's Island* is *Friday Foster*'s Mr. Big. No matter. The film sends audiences out of the theater walking on air after their beloved Pam solves the crime and winks at the camera.

For the most part, the critics spared *Friday Foster* by giving it mediocre ratings or damning it with faint praise. "When the razzle dazzle is over, you'll feel you wasted your time," wrote Ann Guarino in the New York *Daily News*. The *Philadelphia Daily News*' Joe Baltake, who saw the film at the Milgram (where many Blaxploitation films played), wrote that the film was "essentially more black-vien [*sic*] 'Super Fly' stuff—except that it's lighter, livelier and less contemptable."

However, some critics enjoyed the film. John Crittenden in the Bergen, New Jersey, *Record* wrote it was "several cuts above the blaxploitation pictures of the recent past . . . It's attitudes are bourgeois." Kevin Thomas in the *Los Angeles Times* called it "a lively Black action picture" and said Grier was "the closest thing to a female superstar these days aside from Barbra Streisand." However, he and several other critics wished and hoped for something different for Pam Grier. Thomas ended his review saying, "Let's hope the serious opportunities she has so well-earned are soon forthcoming."

CHAPTER 26

THE COSBY-POITIER TRILOGY II:
BIGGIE SMALLS IS DA ILLEST

After the success of *Uptown Saturday Night* in 1974, director and star Sidney Poitier did what his audience wanted by commissioning a sequel of sorts. Screenwriter Richard Wesley returned to craft a new adventure for Poitier and his co-star, Bill Cosby. The result, *Let's Do It Again*, followed the rules of the sequel: it was bigger, louder, sillier, and raunchier. The stakes were higher, and the plot required a leap of faith that was almost too large to support one's suspension of belief. The film was full of action, comedy, and Cosby doing what he does best: trying to improvise his way out of a jam.

Poitier directed several of the same actors from *Uptown*, including Lee Chamberlin and Calvin Lockhart, who played that film's villainous thief, Silky Slim. In this film, Lockhart was once again the beneficiary of one of the best "Black" names that Wesley pulled out of his hat. Several rappers got their names from Blaxploitation movie titles (Foxy Brown, for example). Brooklyn native Christopher Wallace dug deeper into the "movie crates" and christened himself after Lockhart's comic criminal, Biggie Smalls.

For the soundtrack, Warners got the guy who turned *Super Fly* into a top-selling album, Curtis Mayfield. As he did for his superior Gladys Knight song score for *Claudine*, Mayfield crafted his music around one artist: the raspy-voiced goddess Mavis Staples and her family group, the Staple Singers. The former gospel group had been singing "the devil's music" for the past few years on the Stax label, but they had never done something as overtly randy as *Let's Do It Again*'s title song. Church ladies were mad as hell about this. Not only were these formerly pious, God-fearing folks singing about fuckin', they were singing about fuckin' *after they just got finished fuckin'*! If Mavis chanting, "Do it again! Do it again," didn't bring that point home, there was another song on the soundtrack album called "After Sex." It was nearly seven minutes long, filled with an arousing groove and the Staples' sensuous "oohing" as its only lyrics.

As with *Super Fly*, the pre-release of the soundtrack helped with the film's box office. Specifically, Mayfield's Curtom label put out a 45 of "Let's Do It Again" (the B-side was "After Sex") and it sold like gangbusters. The song eventually went to number one on the *Billboard* chart just after Christmas. It also topped the *Billboard* Soul Chart twice. The Staples would never have a hit this big again, though Mayfield would later commission Mavis to sing the soundtrack for the third movie in this Cosby-Poitier trilogy, 1977's *A Piece of the Action*.

A little-known fact is that the film's title wasn't decided by Poitier or Wesley or even its distributor, Warner Bros. After speaking to a group of Los Angeles grammar school students about film and life in general, Poitier asked them to choose from a list of potential titles for his "sequel" to *Uptown Saturday Night*. *Let's Do It Again* was the runaway choice. True to his word, the director christened his film with the winning selection. One wonders what Curtis Mayfield would have done if those kids had chosen *Uptown Saturday Night Part 2*.

Producing through First Artists, the company he shared with Redford, McQueen, and Babs Streisand, Poitier began his two-month shoot on March 10, 1975, in Los Angeles. Angelenos will recognize locations like the Biltmore Hotel, the Ramada in Culver City, and the Olympic Auditorium (which is now a Korean church). Poitier also shot scenes in New Orleans and Atlanta, the latter serving as the hometown of Cosby's Billy Foster and Poitier's character, Clyde Williams.

If *Uptown Saturday Night* liberated Poitier through comedy, *Let's Do It Again* ensured he'd never go back to being stuffy Sidney again. He makes a damn fool of himself by spoofing Blaxploitation movie clothing. His character is also a bigger catalyst for trouble this time, hatching an incredible scheme to earn money for the lodge he and Billy belong to in Atlanta. Their means of obtaining the money involve cheating some bigtime hoods. Geechie Dan Beauford was an angel compared to the bad guys who populate *Let's Do It Again*.

Clyde's and Foster's significant others are introduced in a scene at the lodge. It's Foster's anniversary, and his gift to his wife, Beth (Denise Nicholas), is a trip to New Orleans. Clyde and his wife, Dee Dee (Lee Chamberlin), are along for the ride. Since female characters were not given enough screen time in *Uptown Saturday Night*, Richard Wesley decided to get the wives in as much trouble as their suspiciously acting husbands.

"They're up to something," Beth tells Dee Dee. Dee Dee concurs.

What their husbands are up to is fixing a fight to generate money to save their lodge. Lodge elder Ossie Davis tells them they have two weeks to come up with the money to break ground for a new lodge. They need $50,000, and the collection plate only has $18,000. The plan is for Clyde to use his army-learned hypnosis skills to hypnotize the underdog in a New Orleans prize fight, then bet on the underdog to win big. After the fight, Clyde will deprogram the underdog so that no one knows what transpired. Their marks are bookies Kansas City Mack and the aforementioned Biggie Smalls. The scenes where Foster and Clyde visit Mack and Smalls, respectively, are highlights of *Let's Do It Again*. Both Cosby and Poitier look absolutely ridiculous in their outfits. Cosby looks like a reject from Parliament Funkadelic (his outfit has short pants and weird sunglasses) and Mr. Tibbs looks like Willie Dynamite.

Since there were more Black folks on the TV screen, and more Black people watching them, Poitier wisely recruited two of the stars of the latest Black hit show, *Good Times*. John Amos, who played the show's patriarch, James Evans, was cast as Kansas City Mack, and Jimmie "J.J." Walker was cast as Bootney Farnsworth, the underdog in the soon-to-be-fixed fight. The physicality of these actors plays a major role in their parts. Amos, a six-foot-tall former athlete, gives Kansas City Mack a toughness that makes the viewer worry about the heroes.

Despite being taller than Amos, Jimmie Walker was cast for his weight. He was notoriously skinny, so *Let's Do It Again* mines some hilarious physical comedy out of his newfound, hypnosis-induced strength. Under Clyde's spell, Farnsworth runs faster than the Bionic Man, leaps into trees, and punches the heavy bag off its stand and through the wall. One look at the size of Farnsworth's competitor, 40th Street Black, reveals that his punch will knock Farnsworth all the way across town to 1st Street Black and Blue. The old Farnsworth, that is; this new model knocks his opponent out in the first round.

Both Kansas City Mack and Biggie Smalls smell a rat. Farnsworth's trainer tells Mack his boxer was in a trance, and that leads Mack back to Clyde. He forces Clyde to put the whammy on Farnsworth again for the rematch so that he can take Biggie Smalls for all he's worth and run him out of town. Through an insane amount of plot machinations, Foster and Clyde have to try to hypnotize 40th Street Black as well. Here's where the wives come in, with Nicholas and Chamberlin getting ample screen time to assist their husbands. Nicholas in particular is as funny as Cosby; in the climax she delivers a line so fall-down funny that it brought down the house at screenings.

Obviously, there's a happily ever after, and not just on the screen. *Let's Do It Again* made a lot of money at the box office: $12 million on a $700,000 budget. And the critics liked it, too. It got the best reviews of the trilogy, and deservingly so. Both Gene Siskel and his soon-to-be television partner Roger Ebert gave three-star reviews. *Variety* said it was "a funny, free-form farcical revue reminiscent in substance of classic Hal Roach comedy." Some of the jokes and physical comedy were old when Hal Roach was doing it, so that's a fitting description. Kevin Thomas of the *Los Angeles Times* thought Poitier's direction was "affectionate."

All that box office goodwill begat another sequel. The less said about *A Piece of the Action* the better, but it's an example of what ultimately happened to Blaxploitation. Instead of being a freewheeling comedy like its predecessors, or a straight-up action movie like the film's expertly directed opening scene mob heist, *A Piece of the Action* becomes a very preachy high school message movie.

The filmmakers—director Poitier and screenwriters Charles Blackwell and Timothy March—aim for a more dramatic feature with a message. They change the tone and add a bunch of teenagers to undercut the adults. Instead of getting in over their heads with wannabe criminal shenanigans, Cosby and Poitier are now expertly skilled master thieves who have never been caught. Instead of a group of colorful, memorable criminal types played by big-name actors like Harry Belafonte, audiences got one-note, cynical kids played by up-and-coming actors like Eric Laneuville and Ernest Thomas. The kids are looking for jobs, and Cosby and Poitier are forced to help them or risk going to jail when a retired cop (James Earl Jones) blackmails them with evidence of their crimes.

The "help the kids" plot does not play nicely with the "rob the mob" plot. This was clearly a one-or-the-other proposition. *A Piece of the Action* never once attempts to stitch these mismatched elements together in a convincing fashion. Elegant Black safecrackers were something new in 1977, yet this movie doesn't do enough with the two leads when they're in that mode. Conversely, by that year, a dozen preachy, generation-gap, smart-ass ghetto kids movies had come and gone.

Once *A Piece of the Action* realizes it's been spending too much time with these broke-ass kids, it introduces another blackmail plot into the mix. This one involves the old reliable "one last heist" cliché. This drags out the film well past the two-hour mark, exhausting the viewer and removing any last remnants of goodwill.

Sidney Poitier retired from acting after this movie, only to resurface eleven years later with a great role in Roger Spottiswoode's wilderness actioner *Shoot to Kill*. In 1980, he directed *Stir Crazy*, which is (adjusted for inflation) still the highest-grossing comedy directed by a Black person. He would also reunite with Cosby, though only from behind the camera, for the nadir of both their careers, *Ghost Dad*. As far as their famed trilogy goes, *A Piece of the Action* is their *Godfather III*, a movie everyone knows exists, but nobody wants to remember that it does.

CHAPTER 27

COOLEY HIGH HARMONY

Michael Schultz is one of the most important Black directors, and he should be more well-known than he is. He directed Al Pacino in *Does a Tiger Wear a Necktie?*, the play that won Pacino the 1969 Best Actor Tony. He helmed the respective movie debuts of Sam Jackson and Denzel Washington. He is also one of the few directors who knew how to use Richard Pryor properly in films, casting him in *Car Wash* and the raucous *Which Way Is Up?*, a gleefully nasty remake of Lina Wertmüller's *The Seduction of Mimi*. In that film, Pryor played three oversexed roles, including an old man, his son, and the preacher who sleeps with the son's wife. Pryor's preacher gets one of the best sight gags in all of cinema: After being run over by a tour bus, his coffin's dimensions are hysterically flat.

Schultz was one of the first Black directors to direct television shows and movies that were not about Black people. His biggest fiasco, *Sgt. Pepper's Lonely Hearts Club Band*, was a movie about the Beatles in which no actual Beatles appear (unless Billy Preston qualifies). Schultz was given that film by Robert Stigwood after his schedule did not permit him to direct the film Stigwood originally offered him, the movie version of the musical *Grease*. He went on to direct films featuring rap artists the Fat Boys and Run-DMC, Kimberly Elise, Vanity, and Ralph Bellamy.

The movie that put Schultz on the map, however, was 1975's *Cooley High*. Based on the autobiographical stories Chicago native Eric Monte wrote down after co-creating the television show *Good Times*, Schultz helped shape those stories into the shooting script. "This guy, Eric Monte, is a really funny guy," said Schultz, "but this is not a movie yet." He told the producer at AIP, Steve Krantz, to get him a stenographer to take down the stories Monte told him, and he'd work on the throughline that the script would hang on. Schultz and his wife and casting director, Gloria, picked out the best stories. A month later, they were ready to film with a $900,000 budget ponied up by AIP. The two-month, on-location shoot took place in late 1974.

To play Preach, the Eric Monte stand-in, Gloria Schultz cast thirty-year old Glynn Turman. Turman had already made his Blaxploitation bona fides, appearing in several films by Black directors, including Gordon Parks Jr.'s *Thomasine and Bushrod* and Oscar Williams's adaptation of the stage play *Five on the Black Hand Side*. Before that, his biggest claim to fame was originating the role of Walter Lee and Ruth Younger's kid in the Broadway production of *A Raisin in the Sun*. Like Ralph Macchio in *The Karate Kid*, Turman did not look his age and credibly played a high school senior alongside the actual teenagers who made up some of *Cooley High*'s cast.

Preach was the nerdy kid, a poet and aspiring playwright who didn't want people to know he was sensitive. The rules of coming-of-age movies state that he needs a jock best friend as a counterpoint, so the script gave him Cochise, a basketball wizard who has the best chance of getting out of the Chicago Near-North Side neighborhood where the film takes place. Cochise is also the film's tragic figure, cut down in his prime and earning decades of audience tears.

Lawrence Hilton-Jacobs auditioned for the part, and he told the audience at the 2022 TCM Film Festival screening that Michael Schultz didn't technically ask him to read. Instead, they spoke for a time and, when Hilton-Jacobs exited Schultz's Times Square office, the director offered to walk him to the subway.

"I was walking with Schultz and we stopped in front of Forty-Sixth Street and Seventh Avenue," Hilton-Jacobs said. "I looked up and saw that *Claudine* was playing behind us. It was a sign."

(*Claudine* was playing at the DeMille, of course.)

For Preach's love interest, the rather bougie Brenda, Schultz cast new-comer Cynthia Davis. This was her first and only role. The two share a love of poetry, and she's the one person for whom Preach lets his guard down. However, the requisite third act breakup must occur, and it has to do with an ugly bet Cochise and Preach made about whether the latter could sleep with Brenda. While their love scene is realistic and skirts the PG rating, Brenda's postcoital discovery of Preach's intentions is rather jarring. For a film with so few women,

Cooley High uses them all in the same fashion—as lessons or points of conflict between men.

Many of the memorable vignettes that make up *Cooley High* involve Preach, Cochise, and his friends going to parties or sneaking out of school to go on adventures. Anyone who lived in the 'hood will recognize the characters and situations that arise, from random fights that broke out at house parties to embarrassing events that the crew will be talking about for decades. Of the latter, the funniest involves a monkey throwing shit on one of Preach's buddies at the zoo, resulting in his having to ride the El while chasing off any passengers who get near him.

And since this takes place in a school, there needs to be at least one teacher the kids can play off. For the role of Mr. Mason, Schultz wanted Garrett Morris. A few months before his big break on *Saturday Night Live* in 1975, Morris taught at PS 71 on Avenue A and Sixth Street of Manhattan's East Village. A Black teacher teaching Black and brown students in an urban environment was the exact role he was up for, yet Schultz had to fight AIP to cast him. "They were looking for a more Sidney Poitier type," Morris said.

"I haven't seen one Sidney type teaching a class yet," added Schultz.

Morris has one of the most memorable dialogue exchanges in the film. After chastising Preach for clowning around instead of doing his work, and pointing out that he has the potential to do anything, Mr. Mason asks, "What do you want? Don't you want something?" Preach breathlessly replies, "I wanna live forever!"

With its wall-to-wall soundtrack of oldies and its nostalgic setting, *Cooley High* was referred to "the Black *American Graffiti*." In the *New York Times*, Jack Slater wrote, "The movie is now being called 'a black "American Graffiti,"' but it has, in my view, far more vitality and more variety than 'Graffiti,' which profiled bored, despairing youth in small-town America of the early sixties. No one in 'Cooley High' is bored."

George Lucas's film took place two years earlier and had doo-wop in its speakers. Michael Schultz populated his film with Motown classics, opening it with the Supremes' "Baby Love" and closing it with an effective use of the Four Tops' "Reach Out (I'll Be There)." To the contemporary viewer, this multitude of Motown hits seems like it would have cost a swooping arm and a sequined leg. According to Schultz, it was a very cheap expense.

"No one valued Motown music but us," he said.

It's ironic that a lily-White piece of garbage like *The Big Chill* would be the movie to "reboot" Motown into the American consciousness. At least *The Blues Brothers*, a fantastic movie, put the old, nearly forgotten soul artists they adored in their movie and let them perform. Coincidentally, that Chicago classic also co-starred *Cooley High*'s Steven Williams.

Edwin G. Cooley Vocational High School was a real place, attended by Eric Monte and immortalized in the hearts of decades of viewers. Of the movies discussed in this book, it is one of the most influential. Its one original song, "It's So Hard to Say Goodbye to Yesterday," was covered by '90s New Jack Swing singing group Boyz II Men, who named their 1991 album *Cooleyhighharmony*. John Singleton's Oscar-nominated debut, *Boyz n the Hood*, hews so closely to some of its predecessor's beats that it feels like a remake of *Cooley High*. The meandering feeling and the loose structure of scenes of young Black men can be found in Spike Lee's work.

Cooley High was an enormous hit, touted as an example of a Blaxploitation-era film that some thought was more suitable for Black youth. It made $13 million and was one of AIP's biggest grossers. The critics liked it as well. Chicago's own Gene Siskel gave it three and a half out of four stars, writing, "*Cooley High* has been given the honor of a world premiere at the Chicago Theater, our town's biggest . . . People who attend will not feel ripped off."

So successful was the film that ABC commissioned a TV sitcom version. When that didn't work, the pilot was retooled but enough remnants of *Cooley High* remained for the producers to have to credit Monte at the end of every episode. That sitcom was called *What's Happening!!*, and it ran from 1976 to 1979.

In 2021, *Cooley High* was added to the National Film Registry.

After making *Cooley High*, Lawrence Hilton-Jacobs went to *Welcome Back, Kotter*'s sitcom version of Brooklyn to become one of high school teacher Mr. Kotter's Sweathogs alongside future star John "Vinnie Barbarino" Travolta. Hilton-Jacobs's character, Freddie "Boom-Boom" Washington, had his own catchphrase ("Hi, there!") and unique pronunciation of Gabe Kaplan's character's surname ("see here, Mister Kot-TERRR"). Garrett Morris went on to be underutilized by *Saturday Night Live* as the only Black Not Ready for Prime Time Player. Ingmar Bergman saw Glynn Turman and cast him in his disturbing English-language film, *The Serpent's Egg*. As for director Michael Schultz, his next film was his best, 1976's *Car Wash*.

CHAPTER 28

DOLEMITE IS HIS NAME

Alabama native Rudy Ray Moore trod more pathways to attempted stardom than Carter's had liver pills. He tried singing in a variety of styles, from R&B to country. He was a shake dancer. He read people's fortunes, preached in churches, and performed stand-up comedy at clubs that needed an emcee. But it wasn't until he was working in a record store in Los Angeles that he stumbled upon his claim to fame.

To hear the self-proclaimed "ghetto expressionist" tell it, a wino named Rico came into the store and performed storytelling raps for food. Rico's tales were about a bad motherfucker named Dolemite. Dolemite's verbal antics and sexual bragging kept the store's patrons in stitches. Moore decided to take Rico's stories, polish them up using his stand-up skills, and perform them in his act. So, he got Rico high on weed and recorded everything he knew about Dolemite. Then, dressed as the flyest pimp who ever wielded a cane, Rudy Ray Moore stepped onstage and told the audience, "Dolemite is my name, and fucking up motherfuckers is my game!"

The rest is history.

Moore recorded comedy albums in his living room, then sold them out of his car because they were too dirty for a "respectable" record company to press into vinyl. His first one, *Eat Out More Often*, was a major underground success. As chitlin circuit comedians like Redd Foxx would do, Moore talked about sex, and he did so as filthily as possible. He also practiced the old 'hood art of the dozens, or *signifyin'*, as many folks called it. This skill involved leveling a bevy of insults on a competitor who would, in return, insult back. The subjects of the dozens were usually people's mothers or some physical defect. "Ask yo' mama" (shortened to just "YO MAMA!") was a popular retort to a slight.

Playing the dozens may have been a low art, but people as distinguished as Maya Angelou played them. And it was this game that gave Dolemite his most famous routine. Called "The Signifyin' Monkey," it was an extremely profane verse set "way down in the jungle deep." A lion stepped on the titular character's feet, leading him to do what his name suggests. As a result, the lion would beat the monkey's ass every day. But the monkey got wise, as the poem goes, and set a trap for the lion. He tells him that an elephant has been talking shit about the lion's family. "He talked about your people 'til my hair turned gray!" said the monkey.

Being a badass, the lion wasn't going to stand for anybody talkin' 'bout his mama. So he ran up on the elephant, ready to fight, and the elephant whupped the lion like he owed him money. Weakened, the lion crawled back to where the monkey was. The monkey viciously signifies, knowing the lion is too beat up to react.

Unfortunately, the monkey falls out of his tree, practically landing in the lion's mouth. "That was the end of his bullshitting and signifying career!" bellows Dolemite with a flourish.

It's much funnier when Moore does it, as seen in his movie version of *Dolemite*. Shot in January 1974, Moore convinced actor D'Urville Martin to direct and appear in it as the villain, Willie Green. The plot involved the nightclub where Dolemite performed being taken over by Green. The club's owner, Queen Bee (Lady Reed), and her band of all-female kung fu experts, team up with Dolemite to exact revenge. Quintessential Blaxploitation plot and tropes, right?

Well, Moore didn't know how to do any form of martial arts, and it shows. Additionally, the movie was shot very cheaply—Moore paid for most of it out of his own pocket. That showed, too, despite having a pedigree behind the camera: the cinematographer was Nicholas Josef von Sternberg, son of the famous director Josef von Sternberg. The highlights of the film were Dolemite's raps. The movie's plot even stops for him to perform one of them for some adoring fans on the street.

No studio would touch *Dolemite*. So, Rudy Ray Moore four-walled it at the Grand Lake Theater in Detroit. Promoting it himself, on the radio and in person, he managed to sell out the theater. Securing a distributor, *Dolemite* started playing urban theaters in mid-1975. The reviews were brutal, but it was enough of a hit for Moore to make a sequel called *The Human Tornado* in 1976. In that film, he hired actual martial artists to choreograph and perform the fight scenes. His own skills were a lot better here, as well, though nobody was going to mistake Rudy Ray for Jim Kelly.

The Human Tornado also has a hilarious sex scene showing off Dolemite's incredible sexual prowess. His coupling with a White woman literally destroys the house they're screwing in. Before the scene happens, there's a parade of very attractive and very naked Black men rising out of a trunk and sliding down a slide toward the camera. It's meant to symbolize that Dolemite has the sex power of all these men, but it's impossible to believe that no one picked up on just how unapologetically homoerotic this is. Blaxploitation was not known for unabashed displays of naked male flesh absent any female flesh, nor was it known for jokey sex. In that regard, Moore was a bit of a pioneer. He also was not afraid to expose all of his pudgy dad bod onscreen, which made a lot of similar-bodied men feel seen.

In a shocking turn of events, Moore's next film was rated PG! Arthur Marks's *The Monkey Hu$tle* was a disjointed series of vignettes about theft and cons where young Kirk Calloway played Oliver Twist to Yaphet Kotto's Fagin. Moore shows up briefly as Goldie, a pimp who owes Kotto's Daddy Foxx a favor Foxx won't let him pay back. The movie isn't very good, but Kotto is exceptional in it.

Back in R-rated territory, Moore made his funniest—and most offensive— movie, *Petey Wheatstraw, the Devil's Son-in-Law*. A tale of revenge in which the murdered titular character makes a deal to marry the Devil's hideous daughter so he may return to earth and exact vengeance on his killers, *Petey Wheatstraw* made no attempt to be anything but a one-joke idea peppered with violence. It begins with Wheatstraw being born at age seven. A watermelon follows him out of the birth canal. He then curses out his father for "interrupting his sleep" while he was in utero. And that's the respectable part of the movie! Suffice it to say, it's Moore's masterpiece. *Dolemite* gets all the praise, and deservingly so, but *Petey Wheatstraw* is too jaw-droppingly lowbrow to dismiss.

By the time Moore was preaching an anti-drug message in the super weird *Disco Godfather* (and saying "put your weight on it" so many times the phrase gets its own onscreen credit), Blaxploitation was long dead. Moore made more albums and, when rap became popular, was credited as an influence by many, many hip-hop artists. The Godfather of Rap, he was called.

"Mandingo" is racist trash, obscene in its manipulation of human beings and feelings, and excruciating to sit through in an audience made up largely of children, as I did last Saturday afternoon. The film has an "R" rating, which didn't keep many kids out, since most came with their parents.

—ROGER EBERT

CHAPTER 29

DJANGO, CHAINED

In 2011, there was a new critical interest in the 1975 slave movie *Mandingo*. That interest did not come from old heads like Ebert, whose opinion of the film got even more negative over time. This attempt to maudit *Mandingo*, that is, to re-evaluate it as some kind of misunderstood classic, came from young, White male critics. One of these clearly clueless fools likened director Richard Fleischer's pulpy softcore sex soap opera to a Toni Morrison novel. Another declared it "better and more honest" than *Roots*. Well before that, in 1985, Jonathan Rosenbaum wrote, "Apart from this film and Charles Burnett's recent *Nightjohn*, it's doubtful whether many more insightful and penetrating movies about American slavery exist."

What malarkey! The blog sites ran brown with bullshit, and this author stepped in with his own list of reasons why *Mandingo* should be evaluated only for what it is: TRASH!

And it's good trash, too! Those expecting an honest look at slavery or anything remotely respectable need to stay far, far, far away from *Mandingo*. Not since *The Birth of a Nation* and *Gone with the Wind* has such a popular, downright racist, and disgusting book been given such a blockbuster transfer to the screen. Paramount Pictures spared no expense to adapt Kyle Onstott's 1957 novel, making them the first studio to produce a big-budget exploitation movie.

Producer Dino De Laurentiis must have been licking his chops for this deal. He'd get to lick them even more when *Mandingo*'s box office begat a sequel, *Drum*, which finally cast Pam Grier in a role she hadn't done before, an American slave. *Drum* was also based on a novel overseen but not written by Onstott. It was the last in a series of books about the fictional Falconhurst Plantation in Alabama. Onstott, a dog breeder, started chronicling Falconhurst when he was sixty-five years old. He said he wanted to write something that made him rich. *Mandingo* sold four and a half million copies and begat a 1961 Broadway play featuring actors Franchot Tone and Dennis Hopper that closed after eight performances.

Mandingo did have its Black defenders. It comes "highly recommended" in Josiah Howard's Blaxploitation book, and Black historian Donald Bogle says it's "a pulpy, lurid, antebellum potboiler that turns the fantasy world of a romanticized film like 'Gone with the Wind' inside out." But for the most part, the Black critics were even more outraged than White critics like Ebert or Vincent Canby, who likened the movie to pornography and wrote, "[It] make[s] you long for the most high-handed, narrow-minded film censorship."

For example, the *Pittsburgh Courier*'s Black journalist Althea Fonville called *Mandingo* "sickening" and the *Baltimore Afro-American* said, "It makes you want to vomit." Jacqueline Trescott in the *Washington Post* wrote, "The film is a racist and senseless exploration of human degradation in a whirl of slave auctions, hangings, whippings and fornication." This sounds too good for a certain exploitation-loving director to resist, and sure enough, Quentin Tarantino would merge the boxing sleaze of *Mandingo*, other Blaxploitation films, and Corbucci spaghetti Westerns to deliver *Django Unchained* to theaters.

Since *Mandingo* is about a boxing slave who makes plenty of cash for Massa Hammond (Perry King), Ken Norton was cast as Ganymede, Mede for short. Following in the footsteps of the numerous former-athletes-turned-Blaxploitation-icons, boxer Norton tried to stake his claim for Jim Brown glory. Unfortunately, he could not act, though props must be given for his keeping a straight face on the slave auction block while an old German lady shoves her hand down his loincloth and says, "This is what I lookin' for, *ja!*"

Fans of *The Jeffersons* probably had a hard time keeping a straight face when that show's Mr. Bentley, Paul Benedict, shows up to purchase slaves (after checking them for piles). He prevents the German woman from buying Mede as a sex slave. Her response tells viewers everything they need to know about *Mandingo*'s intentions. "You are no gentleman!" she exclaims. "Trying to take the nigger away from the poor German vidow voman!"

Falconhurst Plantation looks decrepit as hell, and there's a reason: there isn't a single scene in *Mandingo* where anybody does any work. Nobody picks a bale o' cotton, let alone jumps down and turns around before doing so. Everybody is either having interracial sex, doing Ultimate Fighting Championship–style bouts or giving ridiculous speeches about Black pride. Actor Ji-Tu Cumbuka brings a fiery Nat Turner vibe to his role as Cicero, but his dialogue isn't off the plantation, it's pure Blaxploitation! Before being lynched, he tells Hammond to kiss his ass. In an even more blatant audience pander, Cicero yells, "When I hang, you gonna know they HUNG A BLACK BRUVA!"

A scene between Cicero and Mede alludes to the fact that Mede will pick up where Cicero's militancy left off. Mede looks like he can kick some ass, which is why Hammond buys him. There's also a violent boxing match at a brothel, which Tarantino later lifted for *Django Unchained*, where Mede rips out his opponent's throat. One would think this foreshadowed a bloody revolt against Massa. *That* would have been the "anti–*Gone with the Wind*." However, when Mede finally rebels against the slave life, his rebellion is two words: "No mas-suh." Massa murders him with a pitchfork, a gun, and a cauldron of scalding-hot water. (In the book, he boils his bones down to soup. Perhaps Paramount didn't want to pay for that scene.)

Finally, an example where Black folks didn't win at the end! Well, almost.

Why did Hammond kill his prize Nigra? It's because his wife/cousin Blanche raped Mede as revenge for her husband taking a Black slave as his lover. Susan George is over-the-top ridiculous in this role. Deflowered by her brother, Blanche jumps at the chance to marry Hammond so she can get away from her family. Hammond is furious when he realizes after marriage that Blanche is no virgin. Surprisingly, this plot line is presented with minimal trashiness, and Hammond's refusal to touch Blanche is credible.

But Blanche is the key to Hammond's undoing, and as played by George, she's so absurdly rendered that her performance is hilarious. And she's no match for the "other woman," played by a larger, tougher Brenda Sykes. When George causes Sykes to fall down the stairs and miscarry Hammond's baby, George chews the scenery to bits. It's not harrowing at all, and George is the movie's one true camp attribute.

Blanche's seduction of Mede is the best example of *Mandingo*'s display of "shocking" sexuality in the false guise of revisionism. Until this scene, Maurice Jarre's score has an overly cheerful, out-of-place jauntiness. Once Blanche threatens Mede, Jarre's score emulates that of a horror movie. This is the only sex scene shown in its entirety, and the shot of the huge Norton laying between the legs of this small, "genteel" White woman was there for one reason only: to titillate the nasty motherfuckers who came to see this movie.

Though our "hero" is very much dead at the end, he is avenged by Hammond's "favorite nigger," Agamemnon (Richard Ward)! Early in the film, Hammond's daddy, Warren (James Mason), tells Hammond he should shoot Agamemnon because he's learned to read. But Hammond is one of dem new-fangled massas who tries to be fair where appropriate. He doesn't want to shoot Agamemnon, so he agrees to have him beaten instead. Hammond strings up Agamemnon, naked and upside down, and tells another slave to beat him, but not as badly as normal.

Agamemnon repays this favor by blowing Hammond's pa away with a rifle before escaping Falconhurst. Consider that a win on a technicality! Warren's death is the perfect fate for Mason, who should have been ashamed of himself for taking a role where his Southern accent is a crime and his main purpose is to put his bare feet on little Black kids because "slave bodies can draw out my rheumatiz'!"

"This is a film I felt soiled by, and if I'd been one of the kids in the audience, I'm sure I would have been terrified and grief stricken," wrote Roger Ebert. He couldn't have felt worse than those kids who had to spend endless takes under James Mason's funky-ass feet. Ken Norton got a better deal as well; he went back to boxing and won the heavyweight championship in 1978.

CHAPTER 30

BLAXPLOITATION RIDES THE RANGE

Buck and the Preacher opened the door for a slew of Westerns to ride through the Blaxploitation era. Oddly enough, most of them featured Fred Williamson, who later starred in several movies he produced and/or wrote and directed. His Po' Boy Productions was responsible for films like the 1975 Western *Adios Amigo* and that year's Mafia movie, the awesomely titled *Mean Johnny Barrows*.

Williamson's Westerns had a serious fetish for the word "nigger" in their titles. He had 1972's *The Legend of Nigger Charley*, which is a surprising yarn co-starring D'Urville Martin. Even back then, some papers were skittish about running ads with that word in the title, opting to call it *The Legend of Black Charley*, which is what it is called today. Williamson was amused by this. "I called it *Nigger Charley* because it was controversy," he said. "The word nigger in the '70s was hot. Controversy is what sells."

Man, did it keep selling! Like all successful features, *Charley* spawned a sequel in 1973, the hard-to-obtain *The Soul of Nigger Charley*. Williamson followed that up with *Boss Nigger*, a movie whose theme song is unforgettable (yes, the chorus is the title). When TCM ran *Boss Nigger* on its cable channel, the listing just said "Boss." Shocking titles notwithstanding, these were far from the worst movies in Blaxploitation.

Two Westerns worth mentioning are 1975's *Take a Hard Ride* and Gordon Parks Jr.'s 1974 film *Thomasine and Bushrod*. The latter is more a *Bonnie and Clyde* homage than a true Western, but it has several scenes on the frontier and in saloons, so it qualifies as one. There's a complicated plot that includes tensions and friendships between Blacks, Mexicans, and Native Americans, bounty hunting, and bank robbing. It's all rather riveting.

Max Julien stars as Bushrod, and he also wrote the screenplay, the best of his trilogy of Blaxploitation movies. He's joined by Vonetta McGee's Thomasine, his former and current flame. Thomasine's first scene, where she brings down a wanted man in an attempt to collect the bounty hunter fee for him, is a great introduction to her character. Bushrod has a similarly intriguing introduction.

When the duo finally meet in a saloon room (they both pull guns on each other before recognizing each other), McGee and Julien have the hottest chemistry of any two actors in this era. Though the movie's rated PG, their heat is a definite R.

Once again, Parks Jr. uses slow motion, but it's a lot more innocent than what he used it for in *Super Fly*. And though Julien and McGee are excellent, the film is stolen by Glynn Turman. He plays Jomo, a Rasta on the Range, an old friend who saves Bushrod from being ambushed when he's recognized as a bank robber. Turman's accent alone is worth watching this movie.

Of course, like *Bonnie and Clyde*, *Thomasine and Bushrod* ends with the characters' deaths.

As a producer of the film, Julien had a lot of pull. He and Parks Jr. reportedly clashed, and he also aired his grievances against some of the White guys in charge. Perhaps that's why the film is not so well-known today.

Take a Hard Ride reteams the *Three the Hard Way* cast of Jim Brown, Fred Williamson, and Jim Kelly. It contains what is easily Fred Williamson's best performance. The Black trio are joined by some old White studio system actors who did time in Poverty Row movies or film noir features.

Williamson plays Tyree, a snake-throwing con man with an agenda. First seen rigging a card game with a strategically placed snake, he puffs on cigars, flashes a million-dollar smile, wears his Western duds with finesse, and oozes charm and charisma. His light touch is matched by an unusually subdued Brown, who channels a more laconic, quiet hero on a mission. The duo makes an odd couple. "Do you ever shut up?" asks Brown. "Talking is how I know I'm alive," responds Williamson. The two are a little more antagonistic than usual, and they answer the question of who would win if Jim and Fred got into a fight. But the film doesn't piss off fans by making them enemies. As in many Westerns, the two join forces against a common enemy.

Spaghetti Western legend Lee Van Cleef, last seen with Brown in the Larry Cohen–John Guillermin 1970 film *El Condor*, is the villain du jour. His bounty hunter Kiefer gets the first scene in *Take a Hard Ride*. Kiefer is all about the Benjamins, shooting a reformed criminal for the $200 bounty still hanging over the criminal's head. "You don't shoot a well-liked man for two hundred dollars!" he is told. "He made his choice," says Kiefer, "and I made mine." Kiefer's second choice is to follow and kill Brown, but not for the reason the audience thinks.

Screen legends Dana Andrews and Barry Sullivan show up, both far older than the noir characters they made famous. Andrews sets the plot in motion by dropping dead; before he does, he asks his friend Pike (Brown) to deliver $86,000 in payroll money across the Mexican border to his wife and her fellow townspeople. Pike is a reformed criminal, not unlike the man Kiefer shot in the opening, and he's an honest man. The townsfolk in Pike's town are worse than a sewing circle, so news travels fast about a Black man on a horse carrying $86,000. He becomes real popular real fast.

"We're practically invisible," says Tyree to Pike. "Everybody's looking for one darky on a horse, now there's two. How they gonna know you now?" This is a good question, as the multitude of White folks who come gunning for Pike shoot the wrong Negro on more than one occasion. The film has a little fun with this. One of the unfortunate victims is *Super Fly*'s Charles McGregor. McGregor and Brown look as much alike as Justin Timberlake and Ethel Merman, yet he winds up getting shot anyway.

Kelly's mute Native American Kashtok joins Tyree and Pike when they come to the aid of a woman about to be gang-raped. The woman, Catherine (Catherine Spaak), has just seen her husband murdered by the same marauders Tyree and Pike dispatch to save her. Kashtok is a kung fu Native American, sort of a Black Billy Jack, who pummels and stabs several people before the credits roll. Before that, there are machine guns, enough dynamite to stock the entire Looney Tunes catalog, and the aforementioned Barry Sullivan as a corrupt sheriff named Kane.

Composing legend Jerry Goldsmith wraps this movie in a nice, Elmer Bernstein–style score. *Take a Hard Ride* is the best of the trio of films Brown, Kelly, and Williamson did in the Blaxploitation era. Their third film, 1976's *One Down, Two to Go*, teams them up with Richard "Shaft" Roundtree. Williamson is behind the camera and the script for that one. It's not very good.

CHAPTER 31

I'm Mahogany, and You're Nothing!

Rex Reed's review of *Mahogany* in the October 10, 1975, New York *Daily News* was a bit much even for him. No stranger to bitchy quips that often veered sharply into personal attacks, Reed was, to quote Charlie Murphy, "a habitual line stepper." More than once in his career, "Sexy Rexy" was called on the carpet for saying something, to put it kindly, racially suspect.

This is what he said about the film's director, Motown founder Berry Gordy, and its star, a diva named Diana Ross: "Berry Gordy, the Motown mogul who discovered Diana Ross, makes his directorial debut guiding her through her paces like a trained chimpanzee. It's as though he sat down one day, said 'Blacks have been ripped off long enough by honky visions of glamour on film and now with Diana we can do anything they can do better' and set out to prove it."

Ignore the offensive part where he compared Ross to a chimpanzee. Focus instead on the very amusing yet also offensive "honky visions of glamour" statement. The only reason why Berry Gordy was making his directorial debut was because he'd fired the very talented—and very White—British director Tony Richardson halfway through the shoot. According to the *Los Angeles Times*, Richardson was canned because "he was not sensitive to the black experience." So perhaps Rex Reed had a point about those glamorous visions!

Speaking of glamour, *Mahogany* tells the story of Tracy, a Chicago secretary who dreams of international fame as a fashion designer. Ross plays Tracy and, in a move that had never been done before (or since), the lead actress also serves as the film's costume designer. "In high school, I studied fashion and costume illustration," she explained. "I took the script home and realized it was about a fashion designer. I thought to myself, 'Gee, wouldn't it be something if I could design the clothes!'" Ross saw the idea as a form of Method acting. Berry Gordy thought she was bonkers, but she talked him into it.

With the help of her right-hand woman, Susan Gertsman, Ross drew and churned out fifty outfits. Several of these appear in the big, climactic fashion show, and they're inspired by Kabuki theater and Erte, a French designer. "Diana has creativity on the tips of her fingers," gushed Gertsman. The duo worked on the outfits from March to November of 1974. It took half the time to shoot the entire picture, including the sequences on location in Italy. *Mahogany* was a year behind schedule, though presumably not because of Ross.

Rob Cohen, the twenty-five-year-old Gordy hired to run the motion picture arm of Motown back in August 1973, after the label's success with *Lady Sings the Blues*, explained the studio's philosophy: "We aren't making 'Super Fly' or the story of violent high school kids in Detroit strung out on dope . . . We are making classy films with glamour and love that whites and blacks can identify with."

Seconding that, VP Mike Roshkind reeled off a litany of upcoming projects Motown raised $8 million to make, including a film by *The Sting* director, George Roy Hill, and a rock musical written by Stevie Wonder. He also told the *Los Angeles Times* that Motown planned to make a movie star out of Marvin Gaye. Sadly, none of that stuff happened. Massive grief for the loss of the Stevie musical, as it would have certainly been better than *Mahogany*.

Tracy's rise to fame in the fashion world is merely an excuse to reunite Ross with her *Lady Sings the Blues* co-star, Billy Dee Williams. "I'm just a character actor," he said when asked about being a matinee idol, "and that's where my head still is." Films like the underrated Sidney J. Furie film *Hit* and the excellent Motown-produced baseball yarn *The Bingo Long Traveling All-Stars & Motor Kings* proved Williams's acting assessment correct, yet all anyone remembers is his two pairings with Ross.

Their chemistry is admittedly off the chart, which made selling the shaky, rather sexist love story a lot easier. Williams plays Brian, a community activist who basically wants his girlfriend, Tracy, to toss her dreams so she can support his political aspirations. The world of fashion is cutthroat and full of White male predators who, for some reason, can't get it up whenever Ross tries to jump their bones. *Mahogany* posits that she'd be better off at home with brokeass Brian even after she becomes a raging fashion success in the last reel.

Before Tracy comes to her senses and crawls back to her man in Chicago, she becomes a model and falls under the mentorship of fashion photographer Sean, played by Norman Bates himself, Anthony Perkins. He christens her Mahogany because she's Black, and gets her modeling gigs. Being the main character in *Psycho*, it's only a matter of time before Sean goes batshit and, in a scene that must be seen to be believed, he takes pictures of her while driving like a maniac.

"Success is nothing without someone to share it with," Brian tells her during one of their massive arguments, which sounds like a rip-off of *Love Story*'s equally dopey "Love means never having to say you're sorry." Tracy responds with "I'm Mahogany . . . and you're NOTHING!"

Mahogany also has an Italian designer, played by French actor Jean-Pierre Aumont, who takes an interest in Mahogany's designs, turning her into the hottest thing in Europe. Eventually she gets that successful fashion show that showcases Ross's terrifying fashion outfits, yet she gives it all up to go back home. The film shows a Black heroine who makes it, regardless of the hardships, and ships her back home to be barefoot and pregnant behind some activist who'll probably lose his damn campaign. That's more infuriating than anything else that happens in *Mahogany*.

It didn't matter to audiences! What woman wouldn't want to come home to Billy Dee every night? When *Mahogany* opened at the Loews State on October 8, 1975, demand for it was so great that the theater started showing the film all night long two days later. Patrons could see Miss Ross pour hot candle wax on her boobies and hear her sing the hit song "Theme from *Mahogany* (Do You Know Where You're Going To?)" at 3:00 a.m. if they so desired!

Regarding that theme song: it took a major fight to get it Oscar consideration, but the Academy Awards nominated the song's writers Michael Masser and Gerry Goffin. Like Ross's performance in *Lady Sings the Blues*, it should have won the Oscar, but it did not. Ross did get a number one hit out of it, and she graciously sang it on the Oscars telecast. To this day, the song is a major moment in her concerts, and she often sings it while wearing the one outfit in *Mahogany* that looked great.

I Didn't Know Where
I Was Going To

Despite it being eleven years old at the time, "Theme from *Mahogany*" was the theme for my high school senior prom. Since I went stag because my date ditched me for her ex-boyfriend the night before the prom, I didn't have anyone to dance with when the DJ kicked it up. I had just turned sixteen and was still recovering from the botched eye surgery that cost me the vision in my left eye the year before. I wore a hideous '80s-era gray tuxedo with a red tie and cummerbund, and big sunglasses my mother loaned me because my eyes were still so sensitive to light. I left them at the prom venue and, to this day, she still hasn't forgiven me.

I did not want to go to the prom, but my mother not only made me go, she also made me pose for professional pictures, one of which is currently on display in her house so that it may torment me with bad memories every time I visit. Oddly enough, though I hate *Mahogany* and have thought it's an awful movie ever since I first saw it in 1976, I harbor no ill will toward its theme song. I sang along with Miss Ross all three times I saw her in concert. I listened to it on repeat as I wrote the chapter on the film. I think I love it.

Now, my mom's youngest sister graduated high school the year *Mahogany* came out, and she went on a first date to see it with the boy who'd become my uncle by marriage. They fell in love at this movie, and then they went back to see it twenty-three more times. No wonder the damn Loews State had to stay open all night. I've always wanted to ask them what they saw in this travesty, but I never got the courage to do so. Still, with the dearth of Black romances during the Blaxploitation era, *Mahogany* served a noble purpose in bringing people together. As usual, I was born too late to reap the benefits of anything wonderful.

My favorite experience of many on the Deuce was a double feature of *Car Wash*, which I'll get to in the next chapter, and *Willie Dynamite*. Double features never had any regard for ratings or appropriateness. These two were thrown together for the same reason *The Wiz* and *Which Way Is Up?*, an even less appropriate double bill I saw, were matched: they were all from Universal. That grungy ol' Universal logo of my youth, with its Earth spinning in what looks like clouds of dirt, was as much a symbol of my childhood as the AIP logo in the sky.

Going to the movies in Times Square was always an experience. The theater often smelled of popcorn, sticky candy on the floor, funk from various patrons, and something I could never place but I now realize was semen. Hopefully, that wasn't what made us stick to the floor, but you never know. As for Willie D on the Deuce, the audience hooted and hollered for his every costume change. "Yeah, Willie!" one wino yelled at the screen. *Car Wash* played almost as well, but I thought it was corny as hell. I've changed my mind on that one since I became an adult.

Which Way Is Up? scarred me for life, though. That was the day I learned about S&M. I was eight.

1976–1978

WHEN BLAXPLOITATION LEARNED ITS FATE

1976–1978

By 1976, it was clear that Blaxploitation was on its last legs. Dreadful, uber-violent movies like *The Candy Tangerine Man* and *Lady Cocoa* (both directed by Matt Cimber) were stinking up theaters. So, I decided to combine these last three years into one section. This time period ushered in several factors that contributed to the genre's demise, including the film that may have been the final nail in the coffin.

Additionally, three films that are considered Blaxploitation fan favorites and potential classics were released between 1976 and 1978. Oddly enough, they were all written by a White former costume designer named Joel Schumacher. Two of those films, *Car Wash* and *The Wiz*, starred Richard Pryor, who was very, very busy at this time. He co-hosted the 1977 Oscars, appeared in eight movies, and had a short-lived NBC variety show that introduced Robin Williams and Sandra Bernhard to TV audiences.

One of the shiny, new objects that kept folks at home was the miniseries. Though it officially started on American TV in 1974 with *QB VII*, 1976 was the year this multiepisode contraption became must-see TV. An adaptation of Irwin Shaw's 1969 novel, *Rich Man, Poor Man*, debuted on ABC and ran every Monday from February 1 to March 15, 1976. The show made a star out of actor Nick Nolte and inspired a sequel on ABC in September 1976.

The show that immortalized the miniseries format, and kept Black folks at home glued to their television screens, aired in January 1977. An adaptation of Alex Haley's 1976 novel about his enslaved ancestors, *Roots*, ran for eight consecutive nights starting on January 23. ABC programmed it that way because they were sure the show would flop in the ratings. Instead, it drew a record-breaking number of viewers; an estimated 140 million viewers tuned in, leaving theaters empty in the dead of winter.

Roots had a score by Quincy Jones and brought LeVar Burton, who played Haley's ancestor, Kunta Kinte, instant stardom. The cast included several actors who did time in Blaxploitation: John Amos, Cicely Tyson, Lou Gossett Jr., Thalmus Rasulala, Ji-Tu Cumbuka, Lawrence Hilton-Jacobs, Moses Gunn, and Richard Roundtree. *Willie Dynamite* director Gilbert Moses helmed one and a half episodes.

The miniseries also had the Blaxploitation penchant for casting nice guy White actors in bad guy roles. Enslaved characters were owned, abused, and traded by *The Brady Bunch*'s Mike Brady (Robert Reed) and Ed Asner, the gruff but lovable boss on *The Mary Tyler Moore Show*. Even Ralph Waite, the kind patriarch on *The Waltons*, was in on it! At least he played a villain in *Trouble Man*, so we knew he was not to be trusted.

Not wanting to be left out of the "keep 'em at home sweepstakes," CBS kicked off the era of prime-time soap operas on April 2, 1978. *Dallas* originated as a miniseries and eventually ran for fourteen seasons. The episode that resolved its famous "Who Shot J.R.?" cliffhanger drew ninety million viewers in 1981. In case you've forgotten, J.R.'s affair partner, Kristin Shepherd, did it.

Hollywood continued to bypass Blaxploitation in favor of blockbusters. Movies like 1976's Best Picture Oscar winner *Rocky*, which was inspired by the Muhammad Ali–Chuck Wepner fight, made a lot more money than the movie Ali himself starred in, 1977's *The Greatest*. The end of 1976 brought one of its biggest hits, a remake of *King Kong* that's memorable to me because I had my first cup of coffee just before seeing it on the Deuce. (Every addict remembers his first hit.)

And if you thought *Jaws* was a movie that got Black asses into seats despite the lack of Blackness on the screen, May 25, 1977, brought a little movie called *Star Wars* to the local bijou. Granted, Darth Vader was technically Black (he *was* voiced by James Earl Jones), but he was hidden behind all that hardware.

In December 1977, Norman Wexler, the guy who wrote the screenplay for *Mandingo*, created a White version of a Blaxploitation movie: It had a New York City–based antihero named Tony Manero (John Travolta), incredible fashions, brutality and profanity galore, and a song-filled score that sold millions of copies. Paramount called this massive hit *Saturday Night Fever*.

In addition to 1978 birthing Travolta's megahit musical, *Grease* (which was supposed to be directed by Michael Schultz), the year also brought us *Superman*, the first superhero movie to make gobs of dough at the box office. All of these films proved that Hollywood didn't need Afrocentric stories to draw Black people into the theater.

Meanwhile, in the real world, 1976's biggest event was the Bicentennial of the United States, a celebration of the 200th anniversary of the signing of the Declaration of Independence. The only remnants of that PR campaign are the bicentennial quarters that occasionally show up in your laundromat money today.

Apple and Oracle, two behemoth computer companies, started in 1977, as did the presidency of the one Democratic president in the Blaxploitation era, Jimmy Carter. This peanut farmer from Georgia, a man who once told a story about a rabbit attacking him in a boat, eventually became a great humanitarian in his post-presidential days.

But in the time period I'm talking about here, he was busy setting the stage for Ronald Reagan to win in 1980. Like Nixon, Reagan would have made a great version of "The Man" in a Blaxploitation movie. Also like Tricky Dick, Ronnie would usher in a new era of racism, religious zealotry in politics, and the government treating Black and poor people like shit whenever possible.

There was some good news, thankfully: The New York Yankees won back-to-back World Series in 1977 and 1978, thanks to home run hero Reggie Jackson and a murderers' row of players. Well, it made me happy!

CHAPTER 32

JOEL SCHUMACHER, VOICE OF BLACK AMERICA?!

In 1976, two of the most beloved Black movies of the era were released. One was *Sparkle*, a film about a girl group that looked a bit like the Supremes, and the other was *Car Wash*, a freewheeling comedy about a Los Angeles car wash. Both had Black characters for their leads, though *Car Wash* was a more integrated affair, with comedian George Carlin and Melanie Mayron hobnobbing with the likes of Bill Duke and Richard Pryor.

Sparkle was released by Warner Bros. in April and *Car Wash* by Universal in October. The directors of the films, Sam O'Steen and Michael Schultz, respectively, were well-known commodities. O'Steen was a well-regarded editor (he edited *Chinatown*, *Rosemary's Baby*, and *The Graduate*, among other major hits) who turned to directing. Schultz's last hit, *Cooley High*, made lots of money. What their films had in common was a name that wasn't well-known, unless one paid attention to costume and set designer credits.

Joel Schumacher is credited with writing both of these films, as well as 1978's much-maligned yet ultimately beloved movie version of the hit Broadway musical *The Wiz*. How did a White man with a degree from Parsons School of Design and a list of credits that includes the costumes for Woody Allen's *Sleeper* wind up somehow being the go-to guy for writing Black movies?

Well, to hear him tell it, as he did to the *Los Angeles Times* on June 2, 1976, "I just make up what I want to see, then I work with the director to find out what he wants to see." For *Sparkle*, he said, "I wanted to make a black *Gone with the Wind*, but that was not financeable at the time, so what we accomplished was far more modest."

Watching *Sparkle*, this comparison seems very odd. For starters, it's a musical of sorts about an aspiring girl group (shades of the Supremes), with songs by Curtis Mayfield. This is his second-best post–*Super Fly* soundtrack, and though his songs are sung by the film's stars on the screen, he once again focused on one singer on the album. In this case, it was Aretha Franklin. The album she recorded was a huge hit; *Sparkle* was not. None of this explained why first-time screenwriter Joel Schumacher had anything to do with this movie.

In a 2017 article for *The Daily Beast*, producer and story writer Howard Rosenman shed some light on how the pieces came together for *Sparkle*. He met Schumacher in 1971 and they both shared a love of Motown and soul songs. One night, Schumacher put red sequined dresses on some mannequins and inspiration struck. Rosenman said they would do a movie about a singing group, and it would be called *Sparkle*. He wrote a treatment for it, which he sold to the head of Robert Stigwood Organization (RSO) for $5,000. RSO got Oscar-nominated screenwriter Lonne Elder III to write a full screenplay for *Sparkle*.

As per Rosenman:

> Elder's draft came in, and it wasn't any good . . . I said to Joel: "The Lonnie [sic] Elder screenplay doesn't work. Unless you write the screenplay on spec, the project will die." Joel had never written a full-length screenplay before, but went ahead and wrote a 200-page version that became the basis for Sparkle. It was an epic and sweeping story of a black family.

So the scope explains the *Gone with the Wind* comparison. Schumacher was going to make his directorial debut with this behemoth, but this screenplay was too "epic" to be made. When Rosenman took it to then head of Warners, John Calley, he imposed a set of rules on the film before he'd let Warners pay to make it. Again, per Rosenman:

> But Calley said: "I read Joel's screenplay. It's really good. I'll make the movie under the following four conditions: 1. Cut the movie down to 110 pages. 2. Sam O'Steen has to direct it. 3. Curtis Mayfield has to write the music. 4. We'll make the movie for $1.2 million. Why don't you two take a walk around the studio? Come back and tell me your decision."

There's no explanation as to why O'Steen had to be the director. It was the only wild card in the deck. Rosenman and Schumacher agreed to Calley's demands. *Sparkle* got made with a cast of unknowns who were making their debuts. Schumacher and O'Steen were likewise making their debuts as screenwriter and director, respectively. Irene Cara, Lonette McKee, and Dwan Smith played the singing Williams sisters Sparkle, Sister, and Delores, respectively; the latter two were making their first film. Cara had done Gordon Parks Jr.'s *Aaron Loves Angela* the year before. Philip Michael Thomas, who played the male lead, had a résumé that dated back to actor Raymond St. Jacques's 1973 directorial debut, *Book of Numbers*.

Rosenman admitted that Curtis Mayfield was the real reason *Sparkle* was getting made. His prior soundtracks grossed over $1 million, according to his White record label partner, Marv Stuart. But, Stuart continued, Mayfield did not get the respect he deserved from Warner Bros. Records, Curtom's distributor. He felt Mayfield was getting screwed over because of a different kind of Black exploitation, that of Warners taking advantage of a Black musician. This is why Curtom's next soundtrack, for 1977's *Short Eyes* (which Mayfield also co-starred in), was produced under a different deal.

The success of his albums explains why Calley so strongly insisted on Mayfield. And as usual, the man delivered. "Look into Your Heart," the climactic song from the movie, is one of his best movie songs. And "Something He Can Feel" was a hit not just for Franklin but for the singing group En Vogue almost two decades later. In their video for the song, En Vogue went so far as to re-create the scene where Sister and the Sisters, the group led by McKee, sing the song in the movie.

Though *Sparkle* is a cult classic and a majorly beloved film among Black people old enough to have seen it first-run, it's still a very bad movie. The editing job is shockingly bad, an odd error considering its director was an Academy Award–nominated editor. Even worse, Bruce Surtees, the cinematographer, had no idea how to light or shoot Black skin. McKee, Cara, and Mary Alice are all light-skinned actors, but Surtees made them look like the ace of spades. Tony King, who plays the film's brutal villain, literally disappears from the screen because the lighting can't show his dark skin.

This is not just the author's opinion. Rosenman himself said, "The movie was too dark, and there were times when you couldn't even see the characters." He added, "It lent an elegaic quality to the film," which is as wrong as it is outrageous. If a cinematographer can't light Black skin, don't cast Black actors in the movie. Or can the cinematographer and try again.

Of the poor box office, Schumacher said, "I don't want to be negative, but Warner Bros. treated *Sparkle* like a small Black movie. They didn't treat it seriously enough." They got a hit album out of it, which appears to be all they wanted. Schumacher didn't think *Car Wash* would suffer the same fate over at Universal. "It's just a movie," he said, using no qualifying adjectives. He got that job after Universal's Ned Tanen read his script for *Sparkle*.

Car Wash is often referred to as a comedy, and it is, but just labeling it as such ignores the film's stunning, dramatic climax and its nods to old Hollywood musicals. Director Michael Schultz fills his masterpiece with wall-to-wall music, most of it written by former Motown legend and producer Norman Whitfield. His group, Rose Royce, is the conduit for Whitfield's compositions, including the handclap-filled titular song. The employees at the DeLuxe Car Wash in Los Angeles even dance to this song as they go about their daily business. Often, the soundtrack emanates from someone's car radio or an AM/FM box radio sitting in an office, the songs presented by real-life disc jockeys Jay Butler, J. J. Jackson, Rod McGrew, Sarina C. Grant, and Billy Bass.

Rose Royce's songs "Car Wash" and "I'm Going Down" were later remade by Christina Aguilera (for the movie *Shark Tale*) and Mary J. Blige, respectively. For his trouble, Whitfield won the 1977 Grammy for Best Soundtrack Album. Along with Isaac Hayes's win for *Shaft*, also a double-album soundtrack, *Car Wash* was the only other Blaxploitation soundtrack to win this award.

Perhaps the episodic nature of *Car Wash* is why it gets filed under "comedy." Schumacher's screenplay is a series of vignettes acted out by a diverse group of people and anchored by the shenanigans of one Theodore Chauncey Elcott—T.C. to his friends. Viewers follow T.C. on this day in his life, interweaving his plot thread with the travails of the customers waiting for service. T.C. wants to win a radio contest prize of concert tickets so he can woo back his ex-girlfriend, Mona.

Played by comedian Franklyn Ajaye, T.C. is a magnificent fashion plate, a preening peacock even in his dull orange car wash uniform. Books should be written about Ajaye's preternaturally perfect, mesmerizing Afro. Hyperbole does not do it justice; it is the most enviable coif in all of Blaxploitation (natural version, that is, as Glynn Turman's conked 'do in *J.D.'s Revenge* is the processed version). T.C.'s Afro enters the room before he does, and Ajaye's gentle treatment of it, patting it down as delicately as if it were too fragile to touch, reeks of a realism anyone who rocked a 'fro could easily identify.

The patrons of DeLuxe Car Wash and other tangential characters are as colorful and strange as the employees. Lorraine Gary, Mrs. Brody from *Jaws* and the real-life wife of MCA/Universal's CEO Sidney Sheinberg, has a cameo as "Hysterical Lady," a woman who gets barfed on by her kid. Schultz's wife, Gloria, played the role of a woman who kept hogging the car wash bathroom to change clothes. Counterculture icons George Carlin (as a cabdriver) and Professor Irwin Corey (as a suspected terrorist called "the pop bottle bomber") have memorable scenes. The bomber subplot runs through the film, culminating with the revelation that the wrongly accused Corey's bomb is actually a bottle of piss.

Richard Pryor shows up as "Daddy Rich," the first of two corrupt preachers he'd play for Michael Schultz. Daddy Rich and his bevy of singing beauties, played by the Pointer Sisters, stop by to collect donations from DeLuxe employees. The Pointers sing a rousing number called "You Gotta Believe" to loosen the change purses of their impromptu "congregation." That song, and Pryor's entire scene of dialogue, also appear on the soundtrack album.

On the employee side, there's Ivan Dixon as Lonnie, the take-no-bullshit ex-convict elder statesman who should technically be the boss at DeLuxe instead of its White owner, Mr. B. Dixon came out of acting retirement to play this part—he had specifically gone to directing only—and his performance is nothing short of superb. His character arc intersects with Bill Duke's angry young man, Duane. Actually, Duane now refers to himself as Abdullah, having converted to Islam as a Black Muslim. (Teddy, the guy who impregnates Diahann Carroll's daughter in *Claudine*, underwent a similar name change/conversion, also calling himself Abdullah.) Every time Lonnie refers to Duane by his gov'ment name, it pisses hm off more.

Garrett Morris returns to the Schultz stable as a fellow DeLuxe employee and he's joined by DeWayne Jessie, soon to be the lead of *Animal House*'s Otis Day and the Nights and the mute baseball player in *The Bingo Long Traveling All-Stars & Motor Kings*. There's also a guy who scares people while wearing a construction paper pig on his head. In a bold move, Joel Schumacher wrote a cross-dressing gay man named Lindy, who also washes cars at DeLuxe. Played without stereotype by a game Antonio Fargas, Lindy is one of the rare positively depicted homosexuals in Blaxploitation. A gay man himself, Schumacher gave Lindy a surprising amount of agency. When Duane, oops, Abdullah, criticizes him for dressing as a woman, Lindy retorts, "Honey, I am more man than you'll ever be and more woman than you'll ever get."

Manhood, or rather the concept of it, is the focus of that aforementioned dramatic climax. Fired by Mr. B., Abdullah returns to the car wash to rob it at gunpoint. He encounters Lonnie. The resulting scene is so powerful that it tilts *Car Wash* on its axis. Universal did not want this scene, and director Schultz had to fight to keep it in the movie, but it enriches the film while making the kind of statement lesser Blaxploitation "message" pictures only dreamed of making. In a 2020 interview with Matt Zoller Seitz's at *Vulture*, Bill Duke talked about that scene and about Dixon, the man who encouraged him to start a directing career of his own: "Ivan Dixon's a genius, as a director and an actor and a writer. I loved him. He passed much too soon. And I gotta say, in that scene, I wasn't really acting, because I was an angry young black man at that time. I had gone through what my character had gone through. It was a privilege to be able express those emotions through that character—it was a *privilege*—without overdoing it or anything and being able to speak for so many young black men who have no voice."

Like *Ganja & Hess* before it, *Car Wash* was welcomed at the Cannes Film Festival and was even nominated for the 1977 Palme D'Or. The film itself became a cult classic, though it was also a critical and commercial hit when it premiered in September 1976. It was liked by Gene Siskel and Roger Ebert, who were by then on their iconic movie review show. Vincent Canby called it "a cheerful, somewhat vulgar, very cleverly executed comedy." *Los Angeles Times* critic Charles Champlin called it "funny, sexy, jivey and jokey" and wrote, "The achievement of *Car Wash* is that it plays at more than one level."

In a 2011 interview, Schumacher said: "I know that in the African-American community, *Sparkle* and *Car Wash* and *The Wiz* are movies that a lot of people grew up with. I know that a lot of exploitation movies were made at the time for the African-American audience, and I'm very proud that people see *Sparkle* and *Car Wash* and *The Wiz* not in that category. That means a lot to me."

Joel Schumacher and Michael Schultz parted ways after *Car Wash*, but they should have stayed together. Schultz's next job was filming Richard Pryor's

1977 racetrack movie *Greased Lightning* for Warner Bros. Schumacher went on to adapt for the screen the movie Michael Schultz should have directed, 1978's *The Wiz*. Directed by Sidney Lumet, a man not known for making musicals, it was tragically misdirected and had an actor in the lead who was twenty years too old for the part.

The Wiz would have been Schultz's fourth collaboration with Richard Pryor had the stars aligned for him instead of Lumet. Through a stroke of luck, he got to direct a third feature with the comedian. An item in the August 28, 1976, *Pittsburgh Courier* reported that Melvin Van Peebles had been removed from the director's chair while on location in Madison, Georgia. This would be Van Peebles's last attempt to work for a major studio. The tale of real-life race car driver Wendell Scott seemed right up Van Peebles's alley, if only for its true-to-life ending where Scott gets screwed out of accepting the trophy he rightfully won.

Van Peebles's name did remain on the screenplay credits—he wrote the film with Lawrence DuKore, Leon Capetanos, and Kenneth Vose. Though it can't be credibly proven, there's one line in the film that sounds quintessentially like Van Peebles wrote it. After a young Scott executes a daring stunt move on his bicycle during a race with some White kids, their leader says, "That's one crazy nigger!"

Though he was fired, no tears need be shed for Melvin; in 1976, he had a book, *The True American: A Folk Fable*, arrive in stores in March. He also wrote *Just an Old Sweet Song*, a TV movie pilot starring Cicely Tyson and the father of her *Sounder* son, Robert Hooks. Van Peebles would adapt/write several scripts for television going forward.

When *Blazing Saddles* was being cast, Mel Brooks wanted Pryor, one of his co-writers, to play the lead. This wouldn't have worked, as Sheriff Rich would have scared those racist Rock Ridge residents to death as soon as he rode into town. Plus, with his well-known drug habit, Warners wouldn't insure Pryor for a film where the most active thing he'd be doing was riding a horse. Fast-forward three years later and Rich is still on drugs, but Warners allows him to drive a race car!

In fact, folks who were at the Macon International Speedway on September 18 and 19, 1976, could not only see Pryor drive, they could get roles as extras in *Greased Lightning*. Jay Merritt, whose article about observing a day of filming ran alongside that ad calling for extras at the Speedway, wrote, "The film has been Hollywoodized for art's sake . . . but the flavor of the era and the characters manage to shine through."

Pryor's *Blazing Saddles* replacement, Cleavon Little, was among a list of co-stars that included Richie Havens, Beau Bridges, and Pam Grier. Since this was a comedy-drama, Grier played Scott's wife and inspiration. It's a fully dramatic role, and unlike in *Bucktown*, it worked very well. She and Pryor had amazing chemistry, which explained why they fell in love on the set of this film and had a very tough courtship that Grier covered in her book, *Foxy*.

Greased Lightning opened in July 1977, a year after shooting began. It opened opposite another racing movie, *Race for Your Life, Charlie Brown*.

Pryor stuck with Schultz for his next movie, the extremely R-rated *Which Way Is Up?* The headline of David Dugas's review in the Arlington Heights, Illinois, newspaper *The Daily Herald* read, "*Which Way Is Up?* Is Crude, Racial [*sic*] and Sexist." He left out that the movie is one of the most tastelessly hilarious films of this or any other era. The first Black remake of a foreign movie (namely, Lina Wertmüller's equally crude and sexist *The Seduction of Mimi*) was a showcase for Pryor's uninhibited, raunchy humor. Given the Peter Sellers treatment of multiple roles, he excels at each. He's a father, a son, and a reverend whose name is actually Pryor's own middle names.

NBC may have been so terrified of Pryor's television show that they cancelled it before it finished its first season, but Schultz knew to let his star work without a net. Supported by Lonette McKee and Margaret Avery, Pryor went places most big-time celebrities wouldn't dare. In one scene, Avery, as his wife, decides to try sadomasochistic sex without first informing her husband. After whipping him senseless, she produces a large vibrator that, after putting it on Pryor's face, she proceeds to shove into his other end.

That's just one of the many violent slapstick scenes in the film. True to the work of its origin's director, *Which Way Is Up?* has plotlines and scenes that more than one critic called misogynistic. It's hard to argue against that, especially today. One's tolerance for the film will be based on whether the viewer thinks it goes too far in its comedy. Its downer ending, which is deserved, is a bit of a surprise. At least it sends Pryor bopping up the street to Stargard's funky theme song, written by Norman Whitfield.

A SiDE HUSTLE
The Top Ten Best Blaxploitation Songs

Soundtracks are just as important to Blaxploitation as the super fly clothes and the badass heroes. If these movies accomplished one thing, it was tying the people onscreen to the music playing behind it. Whether it's playing over the opening credits sequence or under a major action scene, a song can heighten the audience's joy and expectation.

As someone who loves lists, I couldn't get out of here without doing at least one. My criteria was to take only one song from a movie, no exceptions, and that song had to be the one heard in the movie. Personally, I think "Freddie's Dead" is the best cut on the *Super Fly* soundtrack, and it would have been in the top three absent my rule. But the song is an instrumental in the movie, so I had to disqualify it.

Runners-up: the entire *Claudine* soundtrack, Pam Grier's "Long Time Woman," *Coffy*'s "King George" and Isaac Hayes's masterpiece, "Soulsville."

Honorable mention: the trilogy of songs from *Car Wash*: "Car Wash," "I'm Going Down," and (my favorite) "I Wanna Get Next to You."

Herewith, the top ten Blaxploitation Songs:

10. *Sugar Hill*'s "Supernatural Voodoo Woman." The chorus is a major earworm. The vocals by the Originals are raw and scary, and the opening chords promise impending doom and danger. And it's used in the movie very well, playing over a bunch of writhing people who appear to be under an evil spell. The actors, camera movements, and church harmonies of the Originals add to the creepy atmosphere.

9. *The Mack*'s "Brothers Gonna Work It Out." Willie Hutch's song is a boisterous, joyful paean to everyone coming together to make the world

a better place. It plays over the end credits, reassuring us that Goldie, and we, are gonna be OK.

8. *Sparkle*'s "Something He Can Feel." "Look into Your Heart" is the best song on the *Sparkle* soundtrack, but the scene where Sister and the Sisters perform this is the scene you paid to see when you bought a ticket to this movie. Lonette McKee's lead vocal is gorgeous, and the choreography and backups by Dwan Smith and Irene Cara make this a quintessential girl group number. And they sing it better than Aretha does on the album!

7. *Foxy Brown*'s "Theme of *Foxy Brown*." Maybe it's Pam Grier dancing and modeling over the opening credits, but this was the first song I thought of when considering Grier's tetralogy. It's got such a driving, propulsive beat, and that "Hey, hey, hey FOXY!!" is one helluva opening.

6. *Shaft in Africa*'s "Are You Man Enough." When I did an impromptu Twitter poll, this placed quite high. Levi Stubbs's tough baritone really sells this song, and his fellow Four Tops back him up with conviction. The lyrics by Dennis Lambert and Brian Potter are exceptionally good, some of the best on this list.

5. *Trouble Man*'s "Trouble Man." If I were talking about the version on the soundtrack album, this would be number one. Both versions are lyrically 90 percent the same, and the music is the same irresistible jazzy shuffle with a prominent percussion section. Mr. T's theme song is one of Marvin Gaye's best compositions. My problem is the vocal on the movie version. The soundtrack's familiar, clear-as-a-bell falsetto is accompanied in the film's version by Gaye duetting with himself in a lower register. Low Gaye sounds disinterested, and I really, really dislike it. The fact this version still made the list is a testament to Gaye's songwriting prowess.

4. *Black Caesar*'s "Down and Out in New York City." "The Boss" is a damn good song, but James Brown sings the hell out of this. Those insistent horns backing him on the chorus send a chill up my spine. This is the true representation of Caesar—"The Boss" is his braggadocio disguise. "Down

and Out" is his soul laid bare. Who better to put soul down on a record than the Godfather of it?

3. *Willie Dynamite*'s "Willie D." This is my FAVORITE Blaxploitation song, hands down. Martha Reeves makes Roscoe Orman's hapless pimp cooler than the movie he's in does. J. J. Johnson's horn-heavy theme, with its girl group harmonies and catchy-as-the-common-cold chorus, has nestled its way into the deepest recesses of my heart, never to escape. Sing with me: "Will-AY! Ohhh! Will-AY D! WILL-AY D!"

2. *Super Fly*'s "Pusherman." Curtis Mayfield's smooth falsetto is a seductive invitation, running its game on all the defenseless Freddies on the corner now. This is pure game on a record, so confident in its delivery that you barely notice that bit of vulnerability Mayfield slips in near the end of the song. If you didn't believe in Youngblood Priest, after this song is played in the movie, you can no longer resist him.

1. *Shaft*'s "Theme from *Shaft*." Oh, come on. You knew this was number one. It won the Oscar. It's the coolest damn theme song in Blaxploitation history. There'd be no *Shaft* without this song. Willie Hall said Isaac Hayes gave him a metronome set to Richard Roundtree's walking pace so he could perfectly sync it on percussion. "I slept listening to that metronome," Hall said. It paid off.

CHAPTER 33

DON'T NOBODY BRING ME NO BAD NEWS

The Wiz is where Pryor, Joel Schumacher, and one potential reason for the death of Blaxploitation meet up. After PG- and R-rated films, Pryor worked in a G-rated movie for Sidney Lumet. In January 1977, as Pryor was filming *Which Way Is Up?*, it was reported that *The Wiz* had been cast as follows: Pryor as the Scarecrow, Bill Cosby as the Tin Man, and Ted Ross re-creating his Tony-winning Broadway role as the Lion.

In the role of Dorothy, who had once been played by eighteen-year-old Judy Garland for MGM and twelve-year-old Stephanie Mills for Broadway, Universal cast thirty-three-year-old Diana Ross. When they did that, the budget for the film quadrupled, and its original director, *Bingo Long*'s John Badham, quit the production. "I knew I was wrong for it," he simply said after that.

Let's get this out of the way now: Diana Ross was, is, and always will have been TOO DAMN OLD FOR THIS ROLE. Even Berry Gordy, the producer of *The Wiz*, told her so. And he never said no to Diana. But even he knew the score. Hell, even if she weren't thirty-three, she was still Diana Ross! Diva with a capital D, lead singer of the Supremes, an actress Oscar-nominated for playing a heroin addict. She was Mahogany back when you were nothing, remember?! Who the hell was going to buy that she was this meek Harlem schoolteacher who had "never been south of 125th Street?"

By the time September 1977 rolled around, the cast for *The Wiz* had been set. Eighteen-year-old Michael Jackson was making his movie debut as the Scarecrow, Pryor was now the Wiz, Nipsey Russell was the Tin Man, and Ted

Ross, the sole nonnegotiable element of this cast, was the Lion. Lumet and Ross, the two things that brought down *The Wiz*, were still there, too.

Miss Ross had some ammunition regarding all those folks who were saying she was too old before they saw the movie. In the September 25, 1977, *Los Angeles Times*, she went off! "Frank Baum never described Dorothy, her age or anything about her . . . It's the first time in my life someone has ever said to me, 'Don't you think you might be too old to do this?' It shocked me, because never have I thought that I was too old for anything . . . I said, 'Who you talkin' about? Me? I'm still a kid.' But then I had to look at myself, hard, maybe for the first time and say: 'This is supposed to be about a little girl, and you might not be able to do the part. And then I got very . . . defensive and I told myself, 'It's not about a little girl at all. It's about a human being.'"

Ross was trying to sell folks that bridge in Brooklyn she and Mike's scarecrow ease on down in the movie.

The one major element Joel Schumacher added, and it's a big one, is to make New York City a character in the film. On Broadway, Dorothy was still from Kansas. Here, she's in Harlem and the Emerald City was the World Trade Center's Twin Towers and outside area. The Wiz lived at the top. Different parts of New York would be where her cohorts were found. The Tin Man was on Coney Island; the Scarecrow was in a cornfield outside the Brooklyn Bridge; the Lion was exactly where you'd find a lion in Manhattan: in front of the New York Public Library. (Other sources credit these details to Sidney Lumet, so there's some dispute here.)

The yellow brick road itself looked like linoleum (it was marketed for home use after the film was released), and New York, real and rebuilt, was covered in it. Danger lurked in the subways in one of the most terrifying sequences ever put in a children's movie. When things needed to be re-created, they were done at Kaufman Astoria Studios, which had just reopened its doors to fiction moviemaking after over thirty years. *The Wiz* was their first production. And it was a costly one.

For such a big production, Lumet insisted on two months of rehearsal. While he worked with the actors, choreographer Louis Johnson worked on the dance moves and two hundred workers built Tony Walton's Oscar-nominated sets at Kaufman Astoria. *The Wiz* would be shot in thirty-two real New York City locations and twenty of Walton's own design. For the Emerald City sequence, 450 dancers were slated to perform on the plaza at the World Trade Center. The

City of New York was about to get a new mayor, Ed Koch, and his city would be paid $10 million by the producers, the cost of *The Wiz* being shot there.

No wonder this thing's budget was $30 million, ten times as much as MGM's 1939 original and $18 million over its original budget. Lumet noted in his book *Making Movies* that filming the Emerald City sequence on the plaza at the World Trade Center was protracted because of wind and scheduling. There were other glitches and setbacks, and as the budget ballooned, so did the worries in Hollywood.

The Wiz has its positives. Quincy Jones souped up the soundtrack, strengthening the arrangements. Sidney Lumet engineered the triumphant return of his mother-in-law—some legend named Lena Horne—to the silver screen. Her return is beyond transcendent, even if the Oscar-nominated costumes make her look ridiculous. She stands in the sky, basically, surrounded by gorgeous little Black children, and delivers a heart-stopping rendition of "Believe in Yourself."

Michael Jackson is spectacular—the best thing in the picture. His take on "You Can't Win," a song cut from the original musical, is a stunner, staged with dancing crows who mock him viciously. These crows are a subversive fuck-you to the racist-ass crows in Disney's *Dumbo*. Jackson's innocence really works, but to be honest, isn't Dorothy the one who's supposed to be innocent?

No amount of meek acting can make that work for Diana Ross, though she sings her heart out. Her version of "Home" is beautiful, and as she did with *Lady Sings the Blues*, she incorporated some of her songs from here into her concert repertoire. Her interactions with Jackson have a chemistry that sparks from their longtime friendship. When he's with her, one can almost buy Dorothy's reticence.

Nipsey Russell is fine as the Tin Man, though he tends to speak his songs rather than sing them. Meanwhile, belter Ted Ross, and his fellow Broadway holdover Mabel King, make the most of the roles they originated onstage. Ross's duet on "Be a Lion" with his fellow Ross is an emotional standout. King, as Evillene, the Wicked Witch of the West, makes a meal out of the movie's (and the musical's) best song, "Don't Nobody Bring Me No Bad News."

The bad news on the screen was the lackluster, wimpy performance by Richard Pryor. They made a garish giant Zardoz talking head for his flashy "scare them into doing my bidding" scene, and Pryor gamely talks smack from behind it. But when he's presented as a fraud and shown in his human form, he's given nothing to work with script-wise.

Even worse, somebody was about to bring Universal and Berry Gordy a lot of bad news. When *The Wiz* opened in October 1978, it was a box office failure compared to films like *Grease, Superman*, and *Animal House*, each of which earned more than $100 million. The flop designation was mostly due to the budget going over, as it turned $21 million in ticket sales against its $30 million price tag. Suddenly, the story was a familiar one: "Black people don't come out to see movies about Black people!" Hollywood overlooked all the other factors and, as usual, zeroed in on blaming everything but itself. Even with the four Oscar nods it received (Oswald Morris's cinematography, Quincy Jones's score adaptation, Tony Walton's sets and costumes), there was no respect for Lumet's folly.

Admittedly, *The Wiz* is far from a great movie, but it's also more than a cult classic. There is genuine love for the film all throughout Black America, even today. So rather than beat a dead horse with a litany of quotes from bad reviews, here's just one review from Al Auster in *Cineaste*. His comments shed some light on the differences between stage and film, and why that may have dissuaded some fans from seeing it or disappointed the fans who did. Remember, *The Wiz* had just left Broadway before filming began.

> The Broadway musical was a cheerful piece of miscegenation that blended Geoffrey Holder's charmingly decadent costumes, some easy on the ears music by Charlie Smalls, and allusions to black history from slavery to the northern migration. It also had some cute bits of social and cultural self-parody . . . All of this is bleached out in the film version . . . With so much social uplift as its major theme, it's no wonder that the Broadway musical's black culture got lost. From time to time, however, it does rear its head in songs like the spontaneous "Ease on Down the Road," the tinman's Fats Wallerish rendition of "Slide Some Oil to Me" and, most of all, in Lena (Glinda, Good Witch of the South) Horne's bluesy riff in the inspirational "Believe in Yourself." But the fact that we even notice the score is the most damning commentary on THE WIZ.

Regardless of how *The Wiz* flopped, Hollywood had spent big money on one Black movie, and its failure meant another one would be too costly to make. The party was over. The Blaxploitation era was dead.

EPILOGUE

So what killed Blaxploitation?

When I started researching this book, I had a theory in my head that I intended to follow. I believed that the quality of the films was to blame. Movies had become very cheap cash grabs (well, cheaper than usual) that either threw extreme violence on the screen for no reason or were preachy to the point of excess. When even Rudy Ray Moore is lecturing folks about the perils of drugs, the party is over. While there's a special place in my heart for Moore's psychedelic, almost Lynchian at times *Disco Godfather*, it's not as much fun as *Petey Wheatstraw* or even *Dolemite*.

Additionally, I thought that Hollywood had finally realized that Black people go to movies that don't have Black people in them, namely blockbusters like *Jaws*, which taught me that sharks don't like dark meat, and *Star Wars*, which taught me that James Earl Jones should be heard and not seen. So, they stopped making Blaxploitation films altogether. "Hollywood has an Achilles pocketbook," Melvin Van Peebles reminds us.

And yet, in doing research for this book, I am now convinced that my reasons weren't the only ones that could be blamed for the demise of Blaxploitation. Jeff Schechtman believed it was the addition of more Black faces on television, a free medium that didn't require anyone leaving the house. Certainly, shows like *The Jeffersons*, *Good Times*, and *Sanford and Son* were hits, and *Roots* was appointment TV, a ratings blockbuster so potent that its viewing numbers—51.1 percent of all American homes watched it—have never been repeated.

In his 2022 documentary *Is That Black Enough for You?!?*, Elvis Mitchell theorizes that the exorbitant price of *The Wiz* is the reason Hollywood said "*Basta!*" to Black movies. This was a theory I never gave much thought to, as there were still some stray Blaxploitation movies floating around post–Miss Ross vs. Oz. Jamaa Fanaka's *Penitentiary* (1979) was a major hit, spawning two sequels and inspiring a trailer with an announcer who said Fanaka's name in an unforgettably dramatic fashion.

When I interviewed Mitchell for the *Boston Globe* in 2022, I told him I disagreed with his assessment, stating that *The Wiz* was just an excuse. "We're saying the same thing," Mitchell replied. "*The Wiz* became, and I mean this, the noose upon which Black movies were hanged. It became the easy way of saying, 'Oh, this one failed. That's the end of it.' It was a pitiful excuse."

Black folks did pretty much disappear from movies for a while. Unless you were Richard Pryor, Eddie Murphy, or in an independent film like *Losing Ground*, Black faces were no longer a constant.

As an aside: Murphy and Pryor did appear in films one could consider Blaxploitation-adjacent. For example, Pryor's *The Toy* has all the makings of a Melvin Van Peebles satire (Black man is bought as a toy by a racist played by Jackie Gleason), and Murphy's Axel Foley from *Beverly Hills Cop* is the quintessential wiseass Blaxploitation detective.

Michael Schultz put Denzel Washington in *Carbon Copy*, a film where George Segal was his dad, but that made no money and, quite frankly, it deserved to be forgotten. Denzel wound up on television alongside Alfre Woodard on *St. Elsewhere*. A lot of Black folks were on TV by the early 1980s.

There have been a few attempts to reboot Blaxploitation. Fred Williamson reteamed with Jim Brown and Jim Kelly in 1982 for *One Down, Two to Go*, a film Williamson wrote and directed. Larry Cohen also tried his hand in 1996, putting Pam Grier, Williamson, Richard Roundtree, and Jim Brown in *Original Gangstas*. But by this time, Blaxploitation had been pretty much spoofed and mocked rather brilliantly by Robert Townsend's 1987 satire, *Hollywood Shuffle*, and by *Shuffle*'s co-screenwriter, Keenen Ivory Wayans, in 1988's *I'm Gonna Git You Sucka*. Wayans had the good sense to cast Brown, Isaac Hayes, Fred Williamson, Bernie Casey, and Antonio Fargas in spoofs of the Blaxploitation characters they played. Despite it being a loving tribute, this movie was so successful that one would think it was the final nail in the coffin.

But two years later, Curtis Mayfield and Ice-T teamed up for the soundtrack for 1990's *The Return of Superfly*.

One year after Cohen's *Original Gangstas*, Quentin Tarantino pulled Pam Grier back to the big screen with his 1997 masterpiece, *Jackie Brown*. With Elmore Leonard's help (he wrote the novel on which it's based), Tarantino fused his own style with some Blaxploitation tropes but gave Pam Grier the big romantic role *and* allowed her to have some action scenes. Fifteen years later, QT would once again go to the Blaxploitation well, merging it with Sergio Corbucci's violent spaghetti Western style for 2012's *Django Unchained*.

In the clean world, as we say, the Black New Wave was starting in 1986 with Spike Lee's *She's Gotta Have It*. Suddenly, Black folks were back on the screen, and not in exploitation movies. They were in the same neighborhoods as Blaxploitation movies, but they were living lives far removed from Foxy, Coffy, or Black Caesar. There was the first (and thus far only) epic film about a Black leader, Spike Lee's *Malcolm X* (1992). Julie Dash had *Daughters of the Dust* (1991). Matty Rich had *Straight Out of Brooklyn* (1991).

But there were glimmers of a possible return. John Singleton got two Oscar nods for his *Boyz n the Hood*, his homage to *Cooley High*. The Hughes Brothers took a more pessimistic view of the same topic with *Menace II Society*, an honorary Blaxploitation movie. Truth be told, if one wanted to feel nostalgic for the Blaxploitation era at this time, all one had to do was turn on the radio. Gangsta rap put those tropes to poetry and music, led by NWA; the newer version of Calvin Lockhart's namesake, Biggie Smalls; and a duo from the Bronx called Camp Lo, whose 1997 debut, *Uptown Saturday Night*, is dripping with Blaxploitation references.

Fast-forward to the 2000s and 2010s, and there are remakes of *Shaft* (two of 'em, both with Richard Roundtree returning in cameos) and *Super Fly*. But these seem to be aberrations; Black action heroes are side by side with White characters, integrated into blockbuster movies that are all based on comic books.

Still, there is a market for nostalgic looks back, as evidenced by streaming services like Brown Sugar and Elvis Mitchell's 2022 documentary. The fiftieth anniversary of *Super Fly* was marked, and there's an entire Turner Classic Movies podcast on Pam Grier, the guest of honor at their 2022 film festival. (I'm prominently featured in several episodes.) And again, so many movies incorporate tropes from Blaxploitation into their films, sometimes blatantly, and sometimes on the sly.

Blaxploitation hasn't completely gone away. Even if the reboots stop happening, its spirit will burn bright in the attitudes and appearances of anything that's meant to look cool. The swagger of Black heroes, the threads they wear, the music that accompanies them—there will always be a hint of Blaxploitation, if not a blatant hat tip.

Though there is room for different ways to show how we win at the end, nothing beats the films that first showed us how it was done.

ACKNOWLEDGMENTS

The origin of this book came about fifteen years ago when I took over a blog called *Big Media Vandalism*, under the guise of embarrassing its owner by writing one entry a day for the entire month of February. I called the series "Black History Mumf" and wrote about Black films that meant something to me. Despite having pneumonia at one point, I still turned out one entry a day.

The series was a hit. I would do it for five years. During the first few years, Jim Emerson discovered it and put my writing on the radar of Roger Ebert. That's how I got the contributing reviewer job at RogerEbert.com, a position I was honored to hold for eleven years.

The person who owned *Big Media Vandalism* was named Steven Boone. Without Boone's guidance, his humor, his camaraderie, and his support, I don't know if this book would exist. Thank you, my Ace Boone. A Black Power fist is raised in your honor.

Thanks to Abrams Press for taking a chance on a soul brother.

Special thanks are also in order to the folks who helped shape my reviews and essays over the past sixteen years. Take a bow, editors Ed Gonzalez, Keith Uhlich, Jim Emerson, Brian Tallerico, Nell Minow, Matt Fagerholm, Nick Allen, Alan Scherstuhl, Genevieve Koski, Chris Heller, and the dude who edited this book, Jamison Stoltz.

I cannot in good conscience leave off one other editor of my work over the years, Matt Zoller Seitz, who saw something in me and invited me to write for his new blog, *The House Next Door*. Let's give it up for a great writer, a great mentor, and my dear friend of eighteen years.

Thank you to my interview subjects Robert Daniels, Aisha Harris, Elvis Mitchell, and the exceptionally informative Jeff Schechtman. Your contributions were greatly appreciated. I owe Maya Cade of the Black Film Archive a fancy dinner for helping me find an obscure film and assisting me in my research on Bill Gunn's *Stop!*.

Shout-outs to Chaz Ebert, Dan Callahan, Steven Santos, Craig Simpson, Dennis Cozzalio, Bruce Lundy, and Simon Abrams.

Honorable mentions to the cats that won't cop out when there's danger all about: Cookie, Renko, Pokey, Juju, Chowder, Toast, Sturges, Patterson, Bing, Bobbie, and Frankie. These are *actual* cats, not figurative cats like John Shaft. Can ya dig it?

My mother, Miss Arlene—thank you for giving me my love of movies, for beating my ass and keeping me in line. Thank you, Lonnie, my pops, for taking me to some of the movies I discussed in this book.

Thank you to my university lit prof, Dr. Kathy Monahan; my high school creative writing teacher, Miss Ellen Gibney; and my English teacher, Mr. John Kilinski. My love of words increased under your tutelage.

Lastly, and I have indeed saved the best for last: Thank you infinity times infinity to Dr. Michał Oleszczyk, the biggest cheerleader and fan any writer could ever have. I owe to you far too many things to list here. Your love and support, not to mention your assistance whenever I needed a Pauline Kael quote, helped me get through the often tough job of writing this book. There are four things I'm sure of: taxes, death, trouble, and your friendship. It's an honor to dedicate this book to you and Boone.